Montessori Strategies for Children with Learning Differences

The MACAR Model (Montessori Applied to Children At Risk)

Joyce S. Pickering, SLP/CC, MA, CALT QI, LDT, HumD

With Special Contributions by

Sylvia O. Richardson, MD

Laure Ames, PhD

Amy Kelton, MEd

K. Michelle Lane-Barmapov, MHS

A division of Montessori Services
www.montessoriservices.com

"A Pediatrician Looks at Montessori for Neurologically Impaired Children"
is reprinted with permission from the American Montessori Society.
© American Montessori Society, www.amshq.org.
Originally published in *The American Montessori Society Bulletin*,
Vol. 4, No. 4, 1966. All rights reserved.

Chapter 8 (Montessori Applied to Autism Spectrum Disorder) © K. Michelle Lane-Barmapov;
all other text, charts, and images © 2019 Joyce S. Pickering.

All rights reserved. No part of this book may be used or reproduced in any
manner whatsoever without written permission except in the case of
brief quotations embedded in critical articles and reviews.

This book is presented solely for educational purposes. The content of this book
is not intended to be a substitute for professional medical or psychiatric advice.
For diagnosis or treatment of any medical or psychiatric problem,
please consult a professional. The publisher and authors are not responsible
for any specific damages from any treatment, action, application, or preparation,
to any person reading or following the information in this book.

ISBN # 978-0-939195-62-6 (Paperback Edition)

ISBN # 978-0-939195-63-3 (eBook Edition)

Library of Congress Control Number: 2019933532

First Paperback Printing 2019

A division of Montessori Services
www.montessoriservices.com

This book is dedicated to my teachers:

Etoile DuBard

Sylvia O. Richardson

June Ford Shelton

Charles Livingston Shedd

Celma and Desmond Perry

Robert G. Pickering

and to all the children who have taught me how they learn.

Table of Contents

Acknowledgments ix

Foreword x

Prologue xi

For the Reader xiv

Chapter 1 1

Montessori History & Philosophy: A Medical—Scientific Pedagogy

    Behaviorism and Constructivism: The Differences Between Montessori and Traditional Education 1

    Behaviorism and Constructivism: Testing and Assessment 2

    The Montessori Classroom Environment 3

    Maria Montessori: A History and Legacy 4

Chapter 2 9

The Montessori Method & Curriculum

    The Montessori Method and Curriculum 9

    The Montessori Teacher 11

    The Montessori Lesson and the Child's Work Cycle 11

    Practical Life Curriculum 13

    Sensorial Curriculum 18

    Oral Language Curriculum 23

    Written Language Curriculum 25

    Mathematics Curriculum 32

    Montessori Cultural Subjects: The Sciences, Geography & History 37

    Montessori Cultural Subjects: The Arts (Art, Music, Literature, Drama) 42

    Conclusion 43

Chapter 3 47

The First Plane of Development for "Typical" Children & Early Intervention for Children with Learning Differences & Varying Exceptionalities

    The Four Planes of Development and the Absorbent Mind 47

    The First Plane of Development in Relation to Cognitive Ability, Executive Functioning, and Emotional Quotient 49

What are "Deviated/Deficient" Children, Exceptionalities, Disorders,
    Learning Disabilities, and Learning Differences? 53
Learning Differences: Rate and Frequency of Occurrence 54
Children with Learning Differences at Various Ages and Stages 55
A Pioneering Article from The American Montessori Society
    Bulletin 1966 60

Chapter 4 67
The Montessori Method Combined with Inclusion Strategies for Children with Learning Differences & Varying Exceptionalities

The Montessori Method and Enhancements for Children
    with Varying Exceptionalities 69
Contrast of Typical Development and the Development of Children with
    Varying Exceptionalities; Montessori Strategies that Enhance
    Learning for Children with Varying Exceptionalities 77
Montessori Practical Life and Additional Supports
    for Early Childhood 82
Montessori Practical Life and Additional Supports for Elementary
    and Adolescents 82
Montessori Sensorial Curriculum and Additional Supports 84
Montessori Mathematics and Additional Supports 88
Conclusion 89

Chapter 5 91
Montessori Applied to Communication Disorders, Including Speech & Oral Language

Speech and Oral Language 92
Speech and Oral Language Development 93
Reasons for Speech-Language Delays 96
Characteristics and Frequency of Occurrence
    of Oral Language Disorders 97
The Three-Period Lesson and Language Learning 99
The Three-Period Lesson and Additional Therapeutic Strategies 103
Additional Vocabulary and Expression Support 105
Strategic Teaching and Partnership 106
Conclusion 107

Chapter 6 109
Montessori Applied to Written Language, Dyslexia & Related Disorders

- Dyslexia and Related Disorders 109
- Characteristics of Dyslexia 110
- Definition of Dyslexia 110
- Neurophysiology and Anatomy of Dyslexia 111
- Other Related Disorders 113
- Multisensory Structured Language (MSL) Learning and Sequences . . . 116
- Montessori and Handwriting Preparation 117
- MSL Strategies Combined with the Montessori Written Language Curriculum 120
- Multisensory Structured Language Therapy 125
- Additional MSL Approaches 129
- Conclusion 130

Chapter 7 133
Montessori Applied to ADHD & Delayed Attention Development

- Definition of Attention-Deficit/Hyperactivity Disorder 133
- ADHD: History and Characteristics 134
- Montessori, Movement, and Learning 135
- ADHD: Executive Function 137
- Coexisting Conditions 139
- ADHD Treatment 140
- Montessori, Inclusion, and Children with Attention-Deficits/Hyperactivity 141
- The Montessori Silence Game and Children with ADHD 144
- Conclusion 147

Chapter 8 151
Montessori Applied to Autism Spectrum Disorder

- Definition and Characteristics of Autism Spectrum Disorder (ASD) . . . 152
- Working with Children with Autism 153
- Early Indicators of Autism Spectrum Disorder (ASD) 154
- Brain Research 156
- Montessori Techniques Combined with Applied Behavior Analysis . . . 156
- Discrete Trial Teaching (DTT) 158
- Montessori, Autism, and Inclusion 161
- Conclusion 166

Chapter 9 173
Montessori Applied to Varying Intellectual Abilities, from Gifted to Disabled

- Intelligence and Processing 174
- Intelligence Assessment 174
- Definition of Gifted and Talented Children 175
- Characteristics and Signs of Gifted Children 175
- Montessori for the Gifted Child 176
- Intellectual Disabilities 178
- Language Training for Children with Intellectual Disabilities 179
- Tribute to Dr. Sylvia Richardson 182

Chapter 10 185
Assessment: Observation, Screening, Evaluation

- Why Do We Assess? 186
- Observation in the Classroom is of Critical Importance 187
- Types of Evaluations 191
- Screening Battery 191
- What a Thorough Evaluation Includes 193
- Explanation of Tests 194
- Information Provided in Evaluation Reports 201
- When a Child Needs More Support 203
- Conclusion 204

Becoming Leaders: About the Authors 207
Additional Contributors 213
Appendix I: Resources 215
Appendix II: Developmental Charts 216
References 221

Acknowledgments

I wish to acknowledge and thank the many people with whom I have worked over the years. Each came into my life at just the right time, each shared their expertise completely and unselfishly, and each gave me valued knowledge to help children.

I am especially grateful for my relationships with Maureen Martin, Anne Wheless, Alexia Alegria, Roberta Roberts, Margie Barry, Paige Geiger, Sister Anne Rita Mauck, and the entire staff of the Shelton School and Evaluation Center led by Suzanne Stell, Linda Kneese, Joy Martello, Letah Samuelson, Amy Kelton, Christine Davis, Sharon McEachern, Mellany Barnett, Sally Baird, and Jenny Cheatham.

Many thanks to my grandchildren, their friends, and all the other children in the photos.

A great experience for me was working with Dr. Leanne Tamm and Dr. Carroll Hughes on our research projects. Thank you for the collaboration.

I owe a particular debt of enormous gratitude to Theresa M. Ball who helped organize, format, and prepare this manuscript. She is unmatched in her skills. My deepest thanks to Joe Campbell, Jane Campbell, and the staff of Parent Child Press for countless hours of discussion, editing, and unwavering support for this book.

The greatest thank you is to my children, Howard, David, Charles, Jessica, and Leslie, and to my husband, Bob Pickering, for the years of patience with and understanding of the work I do.

And finally, thank you to all, for the many years of love and collaboration.

Foreword

As a credentialed Montessori early childhood educator, and as a parent and grandparent, I have had many opportunities to observe how children learn. While my experience, for the most part, has been with "typically" developing children, I have always believed in Montessori's philosophy of "following the child."

I have observed the language-learning benefits children receive while in a Montessori classroom. Dr. Maria Montessori's ingenious techniques and curriculum help guide children through oral language development to reading and writing. In a Montessori classroom, the majority of children joyfully begin to read and write at a young age.

I have also observed that some children do not take to reading and writing as others do. My younger son was one of these children. While he was in a lower elementary Montessori program, in partnership with his teacher, I offered him direct support and instruction in reading and writing every morning before school.

This book contains a wealth of information that Montessori teachers can use to address the needs of children with learning differences. At the same time, it can familiarize special education teachers with Montessori techniques they can use in their classrooms. In these pages, the authors' expert, technical knowledge of Montessori techniques, language development, and remediation shine through.

It is my hope that this book will help many children who have challenges learning to read and write, as well as children who struggle with ADHD, autism, and other learning differences. All children are deserving of education and the lifelong benefits it provides. It is my privilege to bring you this resource and the accumulated wisdom within these pages.

Jane Campbell
AMI Diploma (primary), 1972
Founder/President, Montessori Services

Prologue

From 1960 to 1966, while I worked as a speech-language pathologist in a small school district, I received training from Dr. Etoile DuBard, a pioneer in the field. I then implemented her methods in my speech-language remediation work with children with hearing impairment and severe oral language disorders. My remedial instruction proved to be so effective that the district allowed us to set up the first class in the state for young children with language disorders.

The success of that class inspired me to request funding to start another program for children with a specific reading disorder: dyslexia. The Department of Health Education and Welfare funded a three-year program, and I became the director of the Perceptual Development Center, which accomplished the assessment of thousands of children, instruction of hundreds in a pull-out program, and the operation of a full-time school. Dr. Sylvia Richardson was a consultant to our program.

Dr. Charles Shedd, a psychologist and researcher, was also a program consultant and created the therapeutic dyslexia remediation program we used in our study. One of the most important results of the study was the discovery that the earlier remediation begins, the more effective the results.

Sylvia Richardson and Joyce Pickering

In 1969, I was awarded another grant for an early intervention program for children ages 3 to 6. Dr. Richardson suggested that I contact Dr. June Shelton, who was using Montessori methods to remediate children with language learning disabilities. I met with her and was easily convinced that the Montessori method was right for my program. I began Montessori training with Dr. Shelton, and soon thereafter I started employing Montessori techniques in my early intervention program. In 1972, we published data from our study, and the Early Childhood Study Montessori Program was named one of the most promising programs funded by Title III that year.

In 1990, I became the Executive Director of the Shelton School and Evaluation Center, which June Shelton founded. At the time, the school had an enrollment of 170 children. I directed the school for 20 years, and in 2010, when the school was serving 700 children, I transitioned to the Shelton Outreach department with a focus on our Montessori Applied to Children At Risk (MACAR) teacher-training program. Shelton now has an enrollment of over 900 children and is the largest school in the world for children with dyslexia and other learning differences. MACAR training serves hundreds of teachers every year, and I continue to train teachers, consult at schools, and present at educational conferences.

Sylvia Richardson was my teacher and mentor. She guided me to our colleague, June Shelton, who generously shared her experience and trained me to implement Montessori methods with children who learn in a variety of unique ways. Sylvia, June, and I were all dedicated to early intervention for at-risk children. Over many years, we witnessed in our individual programs how children with learning differences struggle in preschool, and we also witnessed the incredible amelioration children can experience when teachers apply Montessori enhancements to their specific learning needs. We became convinced that language is the core of early childhood development. We understood that a Montessori program for young children could foster astonishing language development, helping children achieve their greatest potential.

For many years, Sylvia and I spoke of writing a book together on the subject of using Montessori strategies with children who learn differently. In 2011, we finally decided to begin this book and document the work we had accomplished. We began writing when Sylvia was 91 and just as sharp as she had ever been. We pored over many of Sylvia's beautifully written papers and mine, and we began to combine our knowledge into the pages before you today. In 2013, she told me to please finish the book; she would write the introduction as her last contribution to our magnum opus.

On October 24, 2014, Dr. Sylvia Richardson passed away at 94 years of age. I regret that she did not live to write the introduction and complete her edits, but I am grateful for all she taught me. I hope she would be pleased with this finished product.

Joyce S. Pickering
January 2019
Dallas, Texas

For the Reader

Montessori Strategies for Children with Learning Differences: The MACAR Model provides educators and administrators with the tools for applying the best practices of the Montessori method to work with young children with special needs. A primary purpose of this book is to give teachers the knowledge of language learning differences and other exceptionalities, and to provide the ways in which Montessori education and additional therapeutic supports can be applied to these differences.

How to Use this Book: Comments to Specific Audiences

This book may be useful for diverse groups of readers. Three primary categories of readers may be especially interested in this book:

- Montessori-trained educators
- General and special educators
- Parents and guardians of children with special needs who are considering a Montessori program

Chapter 1 summarizes the life and work of Dr. Maria Montessori and notes the effectiveness her educational method for all children. The philosophy of Montessori, Piaget, and other constructionists is explained.

Those who are not familiar with the Montessori educational method will be provided a background to understand the chapters that follow. The trained Montessorian will scan this chapter.

Chapter 2 offers a brief description of the Montessori integrated curriculum. The nine basic disciplines encompassed by the Montessori curriculum are described. These content areas and disciplines are interwoven with Montessori teaching strategies as introductory information for those not trained as Montessori educators.

This chapter will be scanned by Montessorians and read thoroughly by those not trained in the Montessori curriculum.

Chapter 3 describes Dr. Montessori's understanding of the Four Planes of Development, focuses on the first plane (from birth to age 6), and considers the development of children with language learning or attention differences. Definitions of learning differences, disabilities, disorders, and exceptionalities are clarified. The rate and frequency of learning differences and related disorders are presented. Signs of learning and attention differences are described at various ages and stages from early childhood to adulthood.

This chapter will be useful to trained Montessorians as well as special educators and parents.

Chapter 4 presents Montessori techniques from the training course, Montessori Applied to Children At Risk for Learning Differences (MACAR). These techniques enhance learning for students with learning differences and varying exceptionalities. Dr. Sylvia Richardson, a pediatrician, speech-language pathologist, and trained Montessorian, helped develop this course, which is taught at the Shelton School in Dallas, Texas. The course analyzes the aspects of the Montessori method that benefit children with learning differences and suggests additional therapeutic strategies that can be combined with the Montessori approach.

Chapter 5 describes how Montessori can be applied to communication disorders, including speech and language disorders. This chapter gives the definitions of communication disorders and the characteristics of each difference. It is vital for the teacher to recognize the early signs of these difficulties so they can begin a program of early intervention. It is also critical to understand the cause of these speech and language differences and their influence on learning.

Chapter 6 presents Montessori techniques applied to written language, dyslexia, and related disorders. The definitions and characteristics of dyslexia are highlighted and Montessori strategies and additional therapeutic techniques that can be combined are explained.

Chapter 7 highlights attention-deficit/hyperactivity disorder (ADHD) and co-existing conditions. Definition, characteristics, and techniques are included. The Montessori classroom environment can offer children with ADHD a structured and supportive learning space.

Chapter 8 presents how Montessori strategies can be applied to children on the autism spectrum. This chapter includes the definition of autism spectrum disorder and describes the characteristics seen in children who are on this spectrum. Combining the Montessori method and Applied Behavior Analysis (ABA) strategies are described. Experiences with this therapeutic combination are given through anecdotes from case studies.

Chapter 9 describes how Montessori can be applied to children with varying intellectual levels, including gifted and intellectually disabled children. The Montessori method, built on scientific principles, can be applied to the individual needs of children with all levels of intellectual functioning.

Chapter 10 details the three facets of assessment: observation, screening, and evaluation. This chapter summarizes the information that school staffs need to know in order to apply the Montessori method to various differences. As the knowledge of language learning and attention differences has increased, more precise assessments have been created to delineate the type of learning challenge the child is experiencing. More children are having assessments and more schools are receiving reports of the specific profile of the child as a learner, clarified by that assessment. The administrator and teacher must now know the terminology and statistical information used in these reports.

Montessori-Trained Educators

A good strategy for you would be to briefly review the headings and content in chapters 1 and 2 and then move on to the other chapters.

General and Special Educators

The best approach for both general and special educators who are not familiar with the Montessori method would be to start with chapters 1 and 2 and then choose other chapters of interest.

Parents and Guardians of Children Attending Montessori Schools

As the parent or guardian of a child attending a Montessori school or the parent of a prospective Montessori student, a good focus for you would be to start with chapters 1 and 2 to become familiar with the Montessori approach. Select chapters 3–9 to gain more information on any of the differences described in these chapters. Chapter 10, Assessment: Observation, Screening, Evaluation might also be helpful if your child is experiencing any learning challenges.

"The child has a mind able to absorb knowledge. He has the power to teach himself."

(Montessori, 1949/1995, pp. 5–6)

Chapter 1

Montessori History & Philosophy: A Medical — Scientific Pedagogy

Joyce S. Pickering, with contributions from Sylvia O. Richardson

Chapter 1 summarizes the life and work of Maria Montessori and notes the effectiveness of her educational method for all children.

Throughout her illustrious career as an educator, Dr. Maria Montessori worked with children across a wide spectrum of learning abilities. It was her early work with especially vulnerable children, however, that inspired her educational method. She spent decades investigating, with scientific rigor, the ways human beings learn. Her insights led to a philosophy, a method of education, and a thriving community of educators now practicing her methods. She placed an emphasis on early childhood education and included practical skills in her curriculum, recognizing that these skills foster independence throughout life. Today, Dr. Montessori's methods and techniques are used to educate children from toddlers to adolescents. Educators from other backgrounds continue to borrow from her work and confirm her findings.

Behaviorism and Constructivism: The Differences Between Montessori and Traditional Education

Traditional education, based on the theory of behaviorism, suggests that learning is best accomplished through textbooks and lectures. According to Angeline Lillard, a prominent Montessori researcher, author, and professor of psychology at the University of Virginia, behaviorist educators influenced our modern school system and helped design an industrial, assembly line-style education system (Lillard, A., 2005). The behaviorists believed there was little, if any, value to early childhood education.

Dr. Montessori observed that children carry within them vast unseen potential. She developed her method of education at a time when most authorities believed human potential was determined at birth.

Dr. Montessori succeeded in putting into operation the theory of constructivism, a theory to which some of her contemporaries ascribed, including Jean Piaget. Constructivism is based on the belief that children learn best and construct knowledge through interaction with the world. Dr. Montessori operationalized the theory of constructivism in many ways: by creating unique multisensory materials for children to explore as they learn; by matching lessons and curriculum to the developmental stage of the learner; and by creating a classroom environment where children are free to move and choose their work. She recognized that children learn best with individualized instruction and lessons that match their developmental stage, which she referred to as sensitive periods (the optimal time for learning a specific skill).

Dr. Montessori discovered that the sensitive period for language, for example, is between birth and 6 years, with the highest sensitivity being between birth and 3 years. She recognized that learning certain skills could take place after a sensitive period passed, but not as easily and efficiently.

Behaviorism and Constructivism: Testing and Assessment

A fundamental way behaviorist philosophy differs from constructivist philosophy is its approach to assessment and testing.

1. In the behaviorist model, two options are possible: success or failure. Many children simply fail. Passing or scoring well on a test leads to rewards, benefits, privilege, and/or opportunity; failure leads to feelings of frustration and discouragement.

2. In the constructivist model, observation and assessment reveals individual and unique learning abilities, which informs best practice and is essential for individualized instruction, remediation, and optimal learning.

The Montessori Classroom Environment

Dr. Montessori recognized the stifling inadequacy of the school environments of her time where, among other things, children sat at desks for long periods, worked on exactly the same lesson at the same time, and were forbidden to move about freely. Being aware of children's natural inclination to move their bodies and explore while learning, she developed a classroom environment in which children's movements and interests could be an essential and enriching part of their development and learning.

A Montessori classroom is a prepared environment. Furniture and open shelves are purposefully arranged. A space is reserved for each area of the curriculum, and within this space, activities are placed on the shelves. Montessori activities allow for multisensory learning. Many of the materials on the shelves are didactic or self-corrective, so children can check their own work for accuracy. Children can easily see the activities and make choices about the work they wish to do.

The Montessori curriculum for the 3- to 6-year-olds includes four main areas: Practical Life, Sensorial, Mathematics, and Language, as well as the Cultural subjects: geography, history, science, art, music, literature, and drama. Dr. Montessori delineated areas of learning, invented materials to present each percept/concept, and wrote detailed notes of how each activity could be demonstrated to children (Montessori, 1949/1995). Dr. Montessori recognized that young children learn by imitation. In the Montessori classroom, lessons are given slowly and carefully, engaging children's attention to increase their awareness of detail. The teacher presents activities and invites children to perform the task. Once children receive a lesson, they are free to choose that activity on their own. Often children will request a lesson that has not yet been presented. The lessons are always referred to as *work*, with the goal of helping children understand that work is satisfying and rewarding. An uninterrupted work period of 2 to 3 hours allows children time to concentrate deeply while working.

When introducing a new material to a child, the teacher presents the lesson without speaking, using slow hand movements so the child can concentrate on the steps of the lesson. The child then practices the lesson at this perceptual (hands-on) level. Language is attached in the ensuing lessons. The Montessori method builds on the work of Edouard Seguin, a 19th-century French physician and educator who utilized a three-period lesson for introducing vocabulary. (See pages 99–103 for more about the three-period lesson.)

In a Montessori early childhood classroom, children practice each activity, thereby refining their hand-eye coordination, fine motor skills, sense of order, organizational skills, and ability to sequence. In short, children are perfecting the skills necessary to go about a learning task.

The teacher takes detailed notes on the progress of each child and prepares reports for their parents; however, children do not receive grades and are not in competition with each other. They focus on building their own skills at their own pace.

Maria Montessori: A History and Legacy

Dr. Montessori lived an extraordinary life. She was a pioneering human rights activist. Her work broke gender barriers, challenged the status quo, and moved countless educators toward the goal of greater justice and peace on Earth through education. She traveled the world training teachers in her methods and was accepted by many in the upper echelons of society. As her success grew, she remained focused on her advocacy and work.

Dr. Montessori was born in the town of Chiaravalle, Italy on August 31, 1870. She was a precocious child. Recognizing her talents and potential, her parents moved to Rome to provide her with a better education. During her adolescence, she dreamed of becoming an engineer; however, her father advised her that this was not an appropriate profession for a woman.

Undaunted, she chose to pursue training as a medical doctor. Her father opposed this idea as well, but she persisted. When she was refused entry into medical school in 1890, she enrolled at the University of Rome to study physics, math, and natural sciences. She was successful and graduated in just 2 years, and was subsequently admitted to medical school.

Her years in medical school were extremely challenging. It was deemed inappropriate for a woman to perform dissections in the presence of men. Since she was the only female physician-in-training, she was required to do dissections alone at night in the morgue. Even with the challenges, she graduated in July 1896 and became one of the first female physicians in Italy. She began work at the San Giovanni Hospital, and in November 1896, became a surgical assistant. She was known as a compassionate physician.

As part of her duties, Dr. Montessori visited Rome's asylums for the insane. At the time, children who were diagnosed and labeled "idiots" or "imbeciles" were held in asylums. Her compassion for children grew. She studied all she could about child development, including the work of two French doctors, Jean-Marc Itard (who many consider the founding father of special education) and his student Edouard Seguin (Association Montessori Internationale [AMI], 2017). Itard studied language development and was known for his work with the "wild boy of Aveyron." This young boy was found in the woods at about age 10. He had no ability to speak. In the years Itard worked with the "wild boy," he was able to help him develop more skills, but he never learned to speak. Itard's work, however, provided important insights into human development and language acquisition.

In 1900, Dr. Montessori was appointed director of the Orthophrenic School for Defective Children, a model school for training teachers to work with children with disabilities. She employed many of the techniques devised by Itard and Seguin and experimented with making her own materials. Astonishingly, after 2 years of work, some of the children were able to pass exams to enter normal school. In 1901, she left the Orthophrenic School to study educational philosophy and anthropology (Montessori, 1913).

After Dr. Montessori completed her studies, apartment developers invited her to start a school in the San Lorenzo slum district of Rome. The purpose of the school was to keep children occupied so they would not damage the buildings while their parents were at work. In 1907, Dr. Montessori opened the Casa dei Bambini (Children's House). There she put into operation many of her ideas developed from observing how children learn (Standing, 1984, p. 38). Because of her education as a medical doctor, her ideas to educate young children were based on the scientific method. Beginning with hypotheses, followed by careful and critical observations, she developed her educational method. Within 3 years, word of the success of her method spread throughout Europe and beyond. Visitors from around the world came to observe the "new education."

In 1913, Dr. Montessori was invited to the United States, where she was received warmly. She enjoyed a reception at the White House. Alexander Graham Bell and his wife, Mabel, were so impressed that they formed the Montessori Educational Association to promote her methods. Thomas Edison was also interested in her work. Between 1912 and 1914, there were 187 English language articles and books published about Montessori education. At the 1915 Panama Pacific Exposition in San Francisco, a Montessori demonstration classroom ran for 3 months. Children worked behind a glass partition and hundreds of people watched in awe as children as young as 3 worked with focus and care. By 1917, over 100 Montessori schools were opened in 22 states in America. Although her trip was successful, Dr. Montessori never returned to the United States. By 1920, due to political uncertainty, all Montessori schools in the U.S. had closed.

Dr. Montessori continued her work in Europe. She lived in Barcelona, Spain where a laboratory school was created for her. She also lectured and trained teachers all over Europe. In 1939, Dr. Montessori and her son, Mario Montessori, traveled to India to offer a 3-month training course, followed by a lecture tour. In India they met Mahatma Gandhi, who became an admirer of Dr. Montessori and her method of education. In a letter to Dr. Montessori, Gandhi wrote, "If we are to teach real peace in this world, and if we are to carry on a real war against war, we shall have to begin with the children" (Gandhi, 1953, p. 33).

Because of World War II, Dr. Montessori and her son could not return to Europe until 1946. In 1949, after years of lecturing about education and peace, Dr. Montessori received the first of three nominations for the Nobel Peace Prize. Her last public appearance was in London at the 9th International Montessori Congress in 1951. Dr. Montessori died on May 6, 1952, and is buried just outside of Amsterdam (AMI, 2017).

In 1955, Dr. Nancy Rambusch, an American, visited a Montessori school in Europe and decided she wanted this method of education for her children.

She returned home, started Whitby School in Connecticut, and Montessori education in America was reborn.

In 1959, there was only one Montessori school in the U.S.—Whitby School. In 1967–68, the first Montessori program in a public school was opened in the Reading Community Schools in Cincinnati, Ohio by Dr. Robert G. Pickering (Gordon, 2005). By 1970, there were 355 Montessori schools in the U.S. and today there are over 5,000. Only China, with 6,000 schools, has more. Japan has 4,000, Canada has 1,000, and the United Kingdom has 750 (Whitescarver & Cossentino, 2008, pp. 2571–2600).

"Generalizing her discoveries with unparalleled mastery, Mme. Montessori immediately applied to normal children what she had learned from backward ones ... leading her to develop a general method whose repercussions throughout the entire world have been incalculable."

(Piaget, 1970, pp. 147–148)

Chapter 2

The Montessori Method & Curriculum

Joyce S. Pickering, with contributions from Sylvia O. Richardson

This chapter offers a brief description of the Montessori curriculum and the positive effect this method of education can have for all children. Photographs of Montessori materials and activities are included, as well as a detailed description of a teacher presenting a lesson to a child and an explanation of the child's work cycle.

It is remarkable that one person, Dr. Maria Montessori, could establish the principles and philosophy of such a successful education method, and also operationalize the theory with a detailed and innovative curriculum for every subject area. Those who read her writings may become astonished by the depth and breadth of her work, but for those working in Montessori classrooms, the results are appreciated every day.

The Montessori Method and Curriculum

The Montessori method includes materials that children use to investigate and explore, and a specially trained teacher within a prepared environment. The curriculum includes four main areas: Practical Life, Sensorial, Mathematics, and Language, as well as the Cultural subjects: geography, history, science, art, music, literature, and drama. All of the activities in these subject areas incorporate oral language development and vocabulary building.

The lessons for each subject are sequential and hierarchical. Lessons move from simple to increasingly complex. The curriculum uses special materials designed for multisensory learning, and the Montessori method integrates language learning into all activities and subjects.

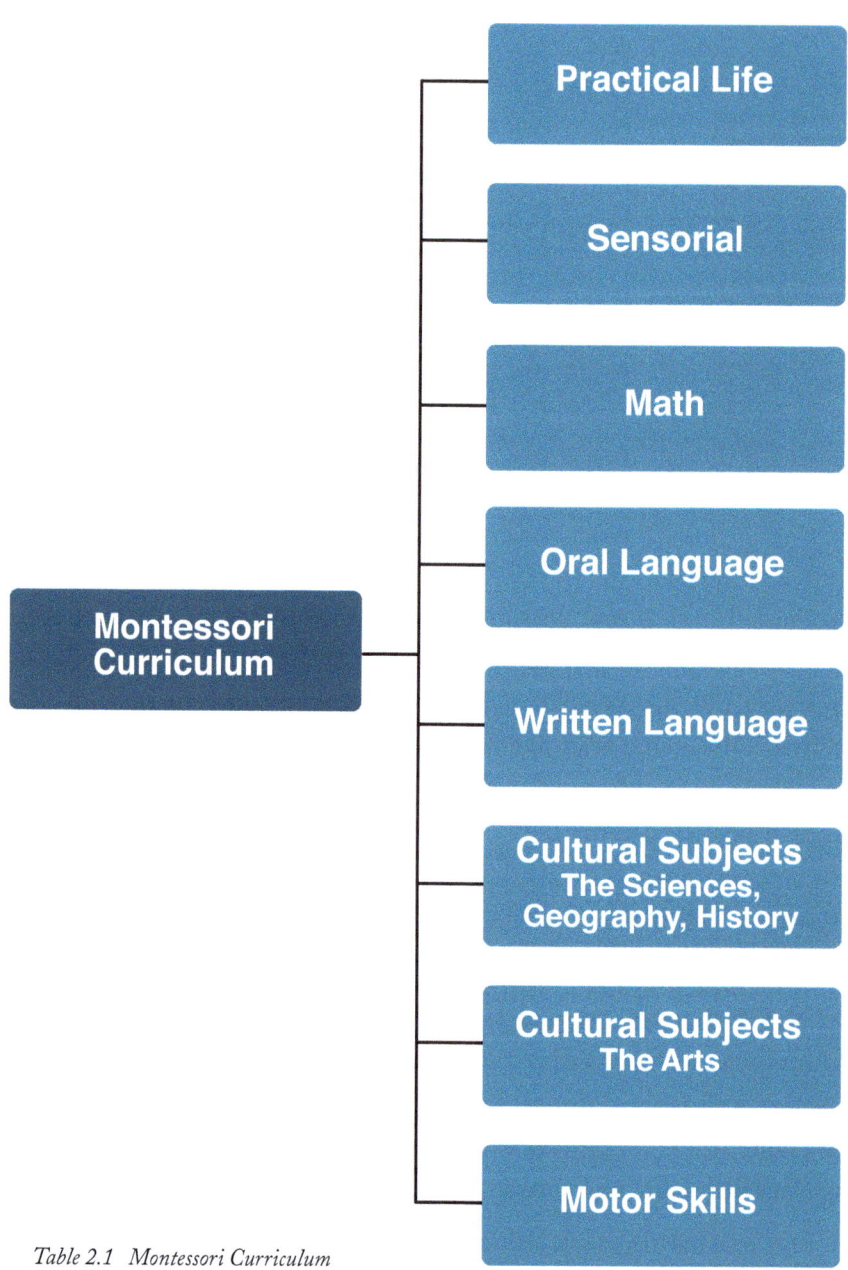

Table 2.1 Montessori Curriculum

The Montessori Teacher

One of the goals of a Montessori teacher is to be a kind, supportive person in the life of a child at school. According to Dr. Montessori, a teacher can be one of the most vital elements in a child's world. She recommended self-preparation as the first step a person takes towards becoming a teacher, and encouraged teachers-in-training to transform their inherited attitudes and behavior towards children in order to treat them with the respect they need and deserve.

Role modeling is essential in the Montessori classroom, and a committed Montessori teacher always strives to maintain a calm and dignified manner (Montessori, 1949/1995, p. 277). Montessori teachers model a soft "inside" voice and never talk across the room; rather, they move near each child and make eye contact before speaking.

Dr. Montessori suggested teachers attend to their appearance as a first step in gaining a child's confidence, and that Montessori teachers also train their bodies to move in a gentle and graceful manner, so children will also move in that manner (Montessori,1949/1995, p. 277).

The Montessori Lesson and the Child's Work Cycle

When a child or small group of children are ready for the presentation of a lesson, a teacher invites them to a small table or a work rug placed on the floor. Every presentation incorporates a work cycle: 1) selecting the activity; 2) choosing a place to work; 3) working with the materials; 4) returning the activity/materials to the shelf where they belong.

By setting up a work area and transporting the materials from the shelf to the work area, the child focuses and refocuses attention. Some activities are on trays and can be moved easily from the shelf to a small table or rug. Others have numerous pieces and require repeated trips to and from the shelf. As children carry materials of various sizes and weights, they develop body control and balance, while initiating and inhibiting motor movements.

If children choose to work on the floor, they first unroll a small rug to delineate their work area. Children are shown how to walk around these rugs on the floor, how to respect others' workspace, and how to ask if they may join another child in their work.

In an initial presentation, the teacher shows a child where an activity is located on a shelf and names the activity (for example, "This is the Pink Tower."). The teacher shows the child how to carry the materials from the shelf. After the activity is set out on the rug or table, the teacher requests the child's focused attention. The child will be better able to concentrate and follow the steps of the activity once their attention is focused.

Each lesson has a particular layout with consistent, sequential steps. The teacher uses only actions to demonstrate an activity. No words are spoken. Verbalization at this point might distract the child from watching the actions and learning how to perform the activity. The teacher always uses very slow hand movements, dramatically emphasizing each step required for the task. Children's attention, once attained, generally stays focused, but if it does not, the teacher's hands stop in mid-motion, drawing attention back onto the work. If necessary, the teacher says the child's name. If the child is unable to focus, the teacher may suggest pleasantly, "Let's put the activity away and try again another day."

After the presentation is complete, the teacher says to the child, "Would you like a turn?"

After the child's turn, the teacher may introduce specific language to attach vocabulary to the child's visual/tactile/kinesthetic perceptions of the materials. (For example, "This is *big*." "This is *little*.") The teacher observes the child's coordination, attention, order, perception, and understanding of the concept, and notes what the child cannot yet do. Those difficulties are addressed later, at a neutral moment, so the child is not discouraged.

After the child is finished with the work, the teacher demonstrates the steps for preparing the work for the next child who will use it (cleaning up, organizing the materials on the tray, etc.), and then returns the work to the shelf where it belongs. After a presentation, the child is free to use the material again to practice, explore, and discover new concepts.

Every presentation helps a child learn a specific skill or concept. For example, with the Pink Tower, the perception of size from largest to smallest is presented using 10 pink cubes. All cubes are the same color and the same shape. They vary only in size and weight. The language attached during this activity is large/small, larger/smaller, largest/smallest. (For a detailed explanation of introducing language using the Pink Tower, see Chapter 5, pages 99–101.)

Manipulative materials provide children with multisensory experiences, leading to perceptions that concretize abstract concepts. An emphasis on performing organized work teaches children how to go about a learning task (the work cycle). Hopefully the result is a lifelong work habit of investigation, organization, and completion.

Practical Life Curriculum

Practical Life is the bedrock of Montessori education and lessons may begin as early as a child is able (usually by age 2 or 3). Practical Life exercises help young children develop skills to care for themselves and their surroundings. Montessori classrooms have many Practical Life activities, such as water pouring, using a spoon, fastening buttons, cleaning, polishing, and food preparation. Practical Life exercises help young children develop independence, organizational skills, concentration, order, executive functioning, and work completion skills. Tasks such as mopping the floor or scrubbing a table develop gross motor skills. Tasks such as pouring juice or polishing metal develop fine motor skills (a prerequisite to the delicate manipulations and precise coordination required for more advanced activities, such as writing). As children perform these tasks, their concentration develops, preparing them for future academic work.

When presenting a lesson, the teacher always uses slow hand movements. As children watch the teacher's careful presentation, they begin to notice details. When children attempt to make each careful movement required for success, their hand-eye coordination improves and their motor movements slow. Children's attention and concentration become more focused as their motor skills refine (Zaporozhets, 1971, pp. 231–242). Practical Life skills learned in childhood, such as cooking, sewing, polishing, and arranging flowers help children feel independent and successful and are also useful skills throughout life.

Grace and Courtesy lessons help children develop interpersonal relationship skills and learn to relate appropriately with one another. The teacher models how to behave and introduces stories, role-plays, and related activities. (See Table 2.2). Activities and children's games improve perceptual motor skills. Examples include Dr. Montessori's Walking on the Line activity (for balance and coordination) and the Silence Game (in which children learn to sit still and become peaceful as they inhibit body movements). For a detailed explanation of the Silence Game, see Chapter 7, pages 144–147.

Chapter 2

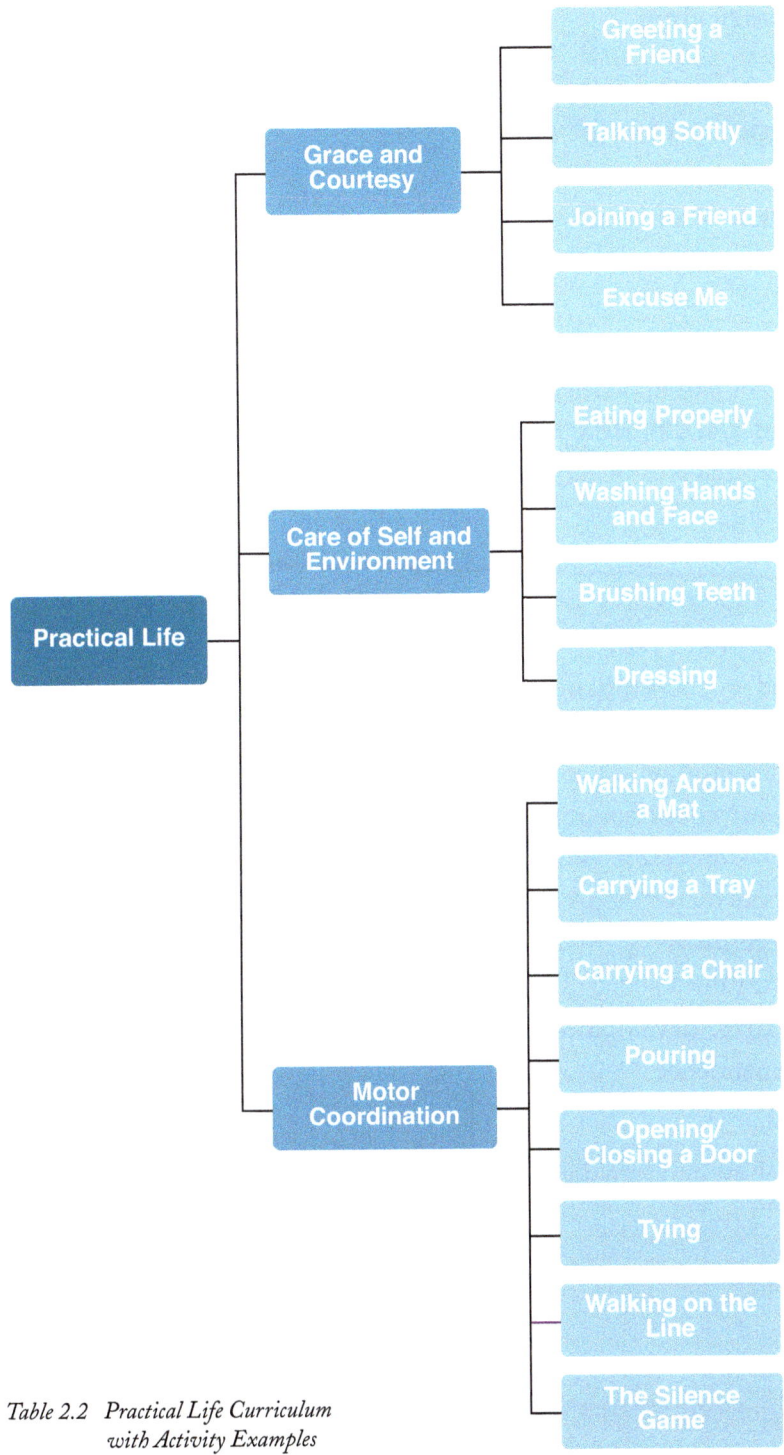

*Table 2.2   Practical Life Curriculum
with Activity Examples*

Practical Life Curriculum

    Goals:
- Independence in life skills
- Learning how to learn
- Enhanced self-concept
- Improvement of fine and gross motor skills

    Lessons include:
- Care of Self and Environment
- Grace and Courtesy—social values/social skills
- Perceptual Motor Skills—activities of coordination and balance

    Fosters:
- Fine motor skills
- Gross motor skills
- Hand-eye coordination
- Order/sequencing skills
- Organizational skills
- Executive functioning skills
- Work completion skills
- Sustained attention/concentration
- Self-control
- Social values/social skills
- Language development skills
- Independence

Figures 2.1–2.5 show children demonstrating tasks that are part of the Practical Life curriculum.

Chapter 2

Figure 2.1   Pouring

Figure 2.2   Spooning

Figure 2.3   Squeezing a Sponge

Figure 2.4   Sweeping

Figure 2.5   Hammering

Sensorial Curriculum

The Sensorial curriculum includes materials and activities designed to provide children with opportunities to experience the visual, auditory, kinesthetic, and tactile (VAKT) senses while learning, and also to investigate gustatory and olfactory identification and discrimination. This curriculum is unique in education and enables children to learn through all the senses.

Dr. Montessori wrote, "Our senses are the tools for the perception of our surroundings. The environment reaches the individual through the use of the senses" (1967, p. 6). The senses receive information, the brain interprets this sensorial information, and then the nerves transmit energy to the muscles that control movement. Through movement, information and learning are refined. This understanding of sensori-motor learning comes from the work of 19th-century physician and educator, Dr. Edouard Seguin, who wrote, "Perceptions are acquired by the mind through the senses not by the senses" (Seguin, 1907, p. 133).

Jean Piaget also placed a strong emphasis on the role of perception and the value of sensori-motor training in children's cognitive development, believing sensori-motor intelligence lies at the source of thought (Piaget, 1963/1966, p. 133).

With various Montessori manipulative materials, children develop visual perception and discriminate color (red/blue), form (circle/square), dimension (long/short), and tactile perceptions (rough/smooth, hot/cold, and light/heavy). As children become more sensitive to impressions from their environment, they are able to distinguish, categorize, and relate new information to what they already know.

The Sound Cylinders help children discriminate sounds from soft to loud. Working with the Montessori Bells, children learn to distinguish pitch, match the sounds of the bells, grade the sounds from low to high, and then to compose their own music. These activities expand auditory perception.

With the Tasting Bottles, children explore the gustatory sense and discriminate between the four basic tastes: sweet, sour, salty, and bitter.

With the Smelling Bottles activity, children contrast and match common scents and develop the olfactory sense.

Table 2.3 shows the Sensorial curriculum (page 22).

When learning with the Montessori Sensorial materials, children first perceive what matches, then notice contrast and gradation, as they develop the ability to distinguish sensory information. Working with the Knobbed Cylinders, for example, children discover that many gradations of dimensions are at the level of "just noticeably different." Refining and training their perception allows children to establish an order and to clarify what they sense. Their attention to detail is enhanced. These exercises teach the child to become a precise observer, to match, contrast, gradate, and generalize, leading to the abstraction of ideas and logical thinking, which is the basis of cognitive development.

This sensory work also expands children's vocabulary. Terms like "large, larger, largest" are introduced and learned in a concrete way, for example, by manipulating and feeling the differences of the cubes of the Pink Tower. For a detailed explanation of the three-period lesson used to introduce vocabulary, see Chapter 5, pages 99–103.

Figures 2.6–2.15 show children using various materials in the Sensorial curriculum.

Figure 2.6 Knobbed Cylinders

Figure 2.7 Color Box II

Figure 2.8 Pink Tower

Figure 2.9 Pink Tower — Size Discrimination with Labels

Figure 2.10 Knobless Cylinders

Figure 2.11 Geometric Solids with Bases

Figure 2.12 Geometric Cabinet Gradation—Circle Drawer

Figure 2.13 The Geometric Cabinet—Returning work to the shelf

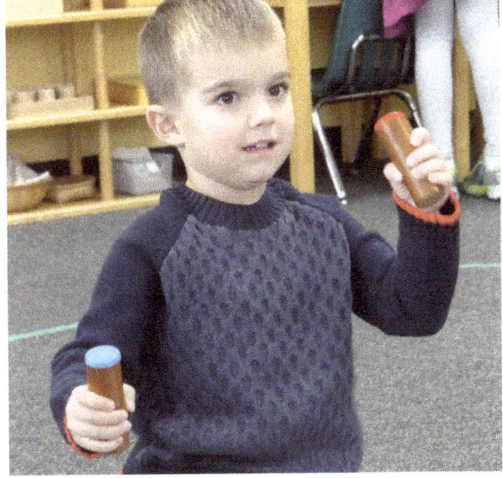
Figure 2.14 Sound Cylinders—Matching

Figure 2.15 Montessori Bells

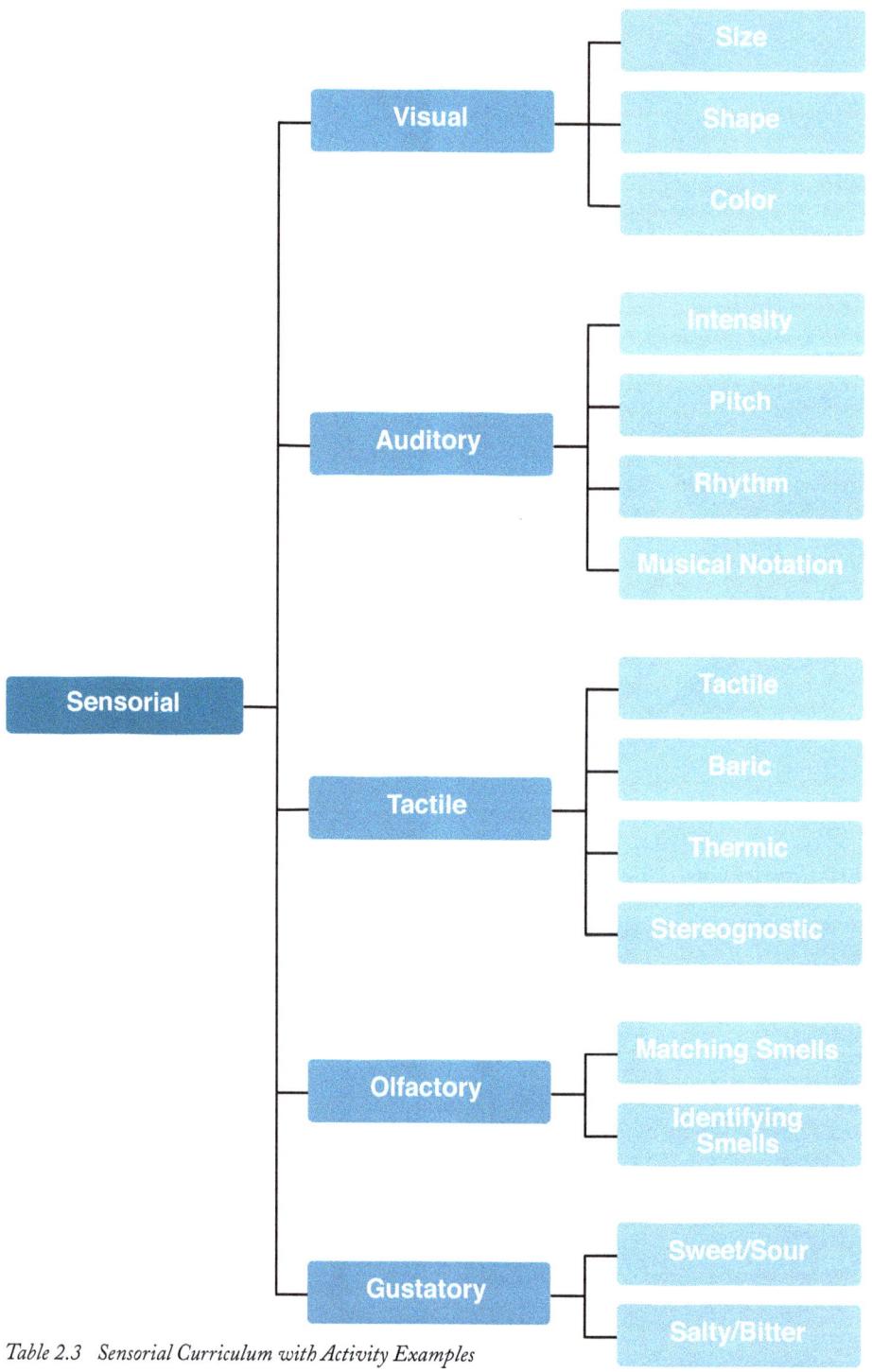

Table 2.3 Sensorial Curriculum with Activity Examples

Sensorial Curriculum

Goals:
- Categorization of the world through the senses
- Perception of sensory information from greatest contrast to finer and finer discrimination
- Language development

Lessons include:
Identification and discrimination of visual, auditory, kinesthetic, tactile, olfactory, and gustatory characteristics

Fosters:
- Sensory discrimination
- Sensory integration
- Language development/concepts
- Mathematical concepts
- Gross motor skills
- Fine motor skills
- Hand-eye coordination
- Order/sequencing skills
- Executive functioning skills
- Sustained attention/concentration
- Reasoning skills
- Independence

Oral Language Curriculum

The average 5-year-old has a vocabulary of 2,500–5,000 words and can use this vocabulary to express basic needs, wants, and ideas using expressive language. Although more sophisticated vocabulary and expression will be mastered, basic language skills are acquired before children enter first grade.

Oral language is a crucial part of human development. The Montessori curriculum is particularly well suited to help children develop oral language; every lesson in a Montessori classroom is purposefully presented so children can learn specific vocabulary. During lessons, teachers first present materials silently; then, after children have explored and worked with the material, language is attached, usually by using the three-period lesson. For a more detailed explanation of the three-period lesson, see Chapter 5, pages 99–103.

See Table 2.4, page 30, Oral and Written Language Curriculum.

The three-period lesson, originally developed by Seguin, takes children through the stages of *identity-recognition-recall*. In the *identity* stage, the teacher voices accurate language that describes a child's perception (verbally labels the object for the child); at the *recognition* stage, the teacher assesses receptive language (can the child point to what is named from a choice of two or more items?); and at the *recall* level, the teacher gauges the child's expressive language (can the child remember the label/name and give it verbally?). For each child this process varies in length of time; some children move through all three periods immediately and others work at the first and/or second stage longer. This careful presentation of *identity-recognition-recall* allows children to expand their vocabulary and expression and to become more precise in communication.

For example, after a child builds the Pink Tower by stacking the cubes in order from largest to smallest (Figure 2.8), the teacher asks the child to take the tower down and arrange the cubes in any order on the work rug. The teacher moves all the cubes, except the largest and smallest, to the side of the mat, and then presents a three-period lesson.

1st period:
Teacher, pointing to each cube: "This is *large*. This is *small*."

2nd period:
Teacher: "Show me *small*." (Pause. Wait until the child points to what they think is "*small*.") Then say, "Show me *large*." (Pause. Wait until the child points to what they think is "*large*.")

3rd period:
Teacher: "What is this?" Child: "*Large*" or "*Small*."

If the child cannot respond at any point, the teacher returns to the first period.

Each lesson begins with a silent, perceptual (hands-on) presentation; then the teacher presents language that describes the child's perception. This helps children gain understanding of their perception and gives children the language to express their perception as a concept. Children may work through all three periods during one presentation, or children may work through only one or two. In the Pink Tower activity, the child is using manipulative materials to understand the abstract concept of large and small and to gain the perceptual skill to gradate the ten pink cubes. This seemingly simple activity is actually the perceptual understanding of a major mathematical concept—greater than and less than.

Written Language Curriculum

Most children can blend sounds, then decode words, then begin to read quite effectively when exposed to sequential and explicit patterns of written language with the multisensorial materials the Montessori method utilizes. In Montessori schools, children often read at the second- or third-grade level when they enter the first grade. Table 2.4 plots the content of the language curriculum used in the Montessori classroom.

The first Montessori materials used to introduce letters and their sounds are the Sandpaper Letters (Figure 2.16). These have a colored background and a letter made of raised fine-grain sandpaper so children can see and feel the letter as they trace its shape with their index and middle fingers. Simultaneously they feel the movement of their hand and arm while tracing. Children learn to voice the sound of the letter (*mmm*), rather than the name of the letter (*em*), which is better preparation for blending sounds and beginning to decode. This activity integrates VAKT senses, and tracing letters with two fingers while voicing the sounds strengthens the sound/symbol association.

Dr. Montessori's original work used cursive Sandpaper Letters. Many Montessori schools teach cursive writing, starting with the initial introduction of the Sandpaper Letters. See Chapter 6, page 127, for more information on the benefits of cursive writing.

Montessori Strategies for Children with Learning Differences

Figure 2.16 Sandpaper Letters   Figure 2.17 Metal Inset

As presentations of Sandpaper Letters proceed, children also begin work with the Metal Insets. While working with the Metal Insets, children practice and develop fine motor control and pencil grip (both necessary skills for writing). Working with Sandpaper Letters (Figure 2.16) and Metal Insets (Figure 2.17) can also stimulate the desire to write. Developing sound/symbol association continues with the Object/Letter Sound Boxes (Figure 2.18).

Figure 2.18 Object/Letter Sound Box

An Object/Letter Sound Box is a small box containing objects or pictures that begin with one or two initial sounds (boy, boat, watch, wagon) and their corresponding letter cards (*b*, *w*). Children working with this activity develop the ability to identify the beginning sound of a word (Figure 2.18). Children say the word for each object and listen for the beginning sound, then sort the objects under the corresponding letter card. "Typically" developing children can distinguish the beginning sounds of words and start to identify them relatively quickly. Next they will be able to identify the ending sound, and finally the middle sounds (internal details) in words. This indicates readiness for the next activity, the Movable Alphabet—letters cut out of cardboard or plastic.

The Movable Alphabet features blue vowels and red consonants. Children choose a picture or object, say the name of the item in the picture, and then sound out the word, selecting the Movable Alphabet letter for each sound they hear. They place the letters next to each picture or object. The teacher does not correct spelling, because at this stage children learn reading and writing phonetically.

By this time, "typically" developing children are also "writing" the Sandpaper Letters by making letters in sand or on a chalkboard. They may begin to construct words spontaneously using the Movable Alphabet. Children are first presented with words with any of the five short vowel sounds in a consonant-vowel-consonant (CVC) pattern (cat, pot, bug). Word building then proceeds to four-letter, short vowel words (crab, gift, frog) and then long vowel patterns, including all of the phonograms of the English language. Finally, children learn words with other regular and irregular patterns, including sight words.

As children's word building skills increase, reading booklets, linguistic readers, and opportunities to copy words and sentences are offered to all children in Montessori schools.

Figure 2.19 Linguistic Books

Grammar is introduced with three-dimensional grammar symbols, one part of speech at a time. For example, the noun symbol is a black pyramid and the verb symbol is a red sphere (sometimes dramatically alluded to as a red ball of energy) (Dorer, 2016). There is a story for each grammar symbol, which engages and fascinates children, helping them remember what each symbol and part of speech mean. Pictures of Montessori grammar work are shown in Figures 2.21–2.23. Children move through the Written Language curriculum from word building to sentence building to reading/writing stories and books, to grammar analysis. Each new concept is presented with multisensory, hierarchical presentations and activities matched to each child's level. Each activity can be broken into reduced levels of difficulty or increased levels of abstraction as fits the needs of individual students.

Figure 2.20 Word Building with the Movable Alphabet

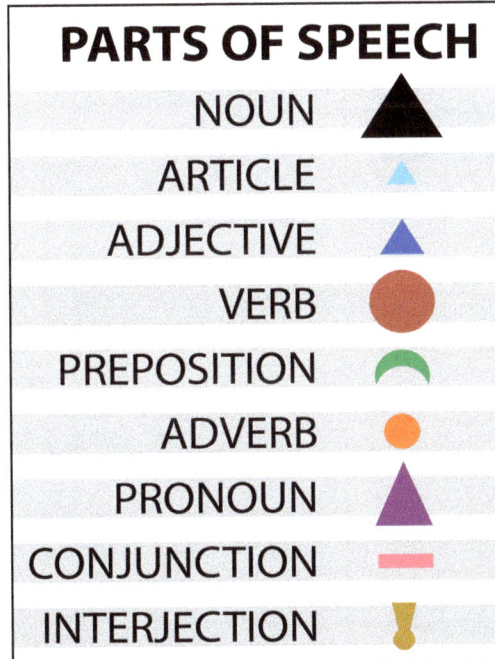

Figure 2.21 Montessori Grammar Symbols

Figure 2.22 Wooden Grammar Symbols

Figure 2.23 Grammar Symbols and Phrases

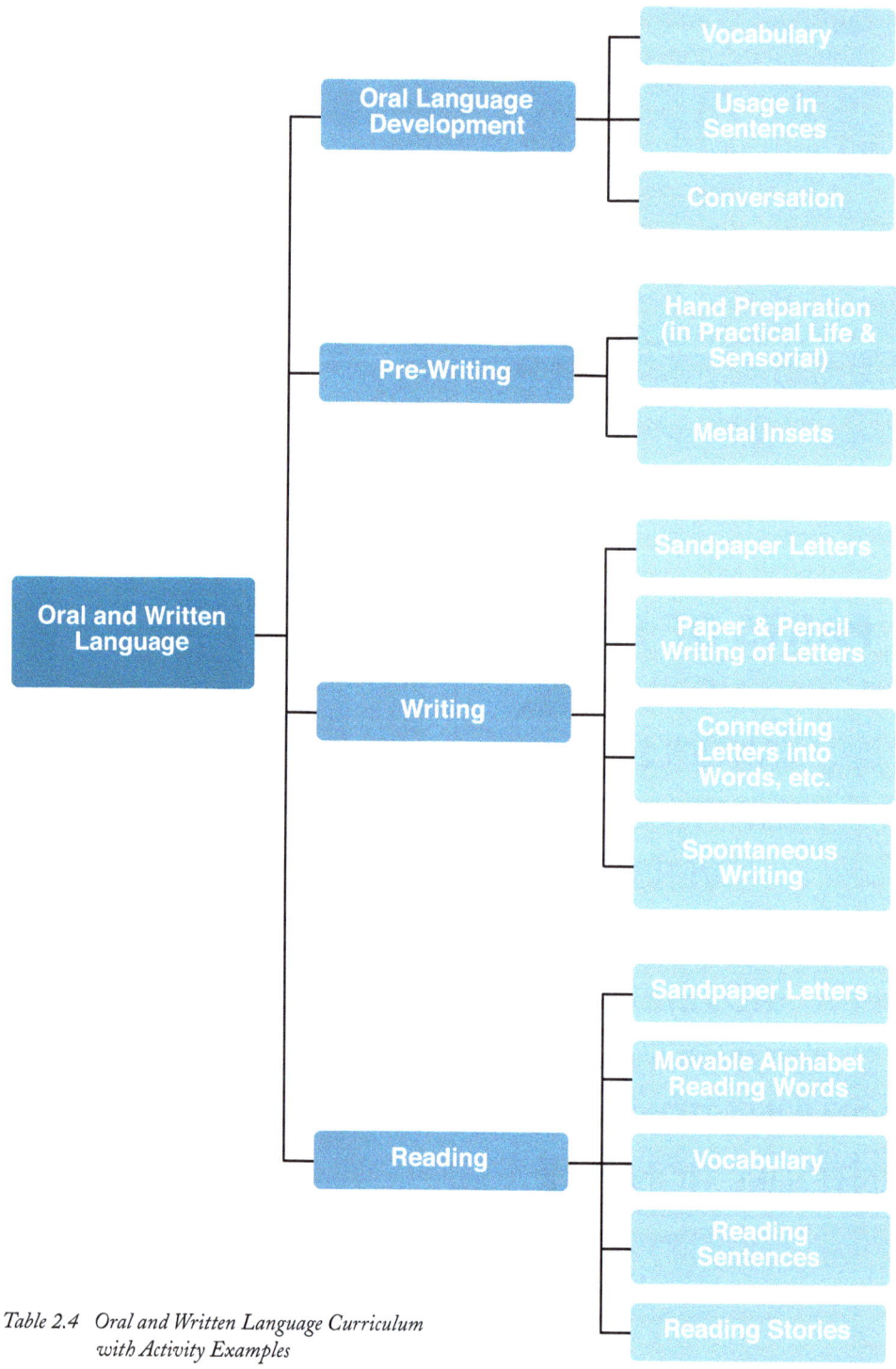

Table 2.4 Oral and Written Language Curriculum with Activity Examples

Oral and Written Language Curriculum

Goals:
- The acquisition of a wide range of vocabulary
- The acquisition of pre-writing, writing, pre-reading, and reading skills

Lessons include:
- Vocabulary building (using three-period lessons)
- Phonological awareness
- Visual recognition of letters
- Sound/symbol correspondence
- Blending
- Decoding/encoding
- Syllabication
- Fluency
- Writing sentences and questions
- Grammar

Fosters:
- Language development/concepts
- Conversational skills
- Reading skills
- Writing skills
- Spelling skills
- Grammar skills
- Fine motor skills
- Hand-eye coordination
- Order/sequencing skills
- Executive functioning skills
- Sustained attention/concentration
- Reasoning skills
- Independence

Mathematics Curriculum

Montessori Math features a vast array of activities and materials designed to facilitate acquisition of simple to complex concepts: numeral to quantity, zero, odd and even, the decimal system, and more.

The first activity in the Montessori Math curriculum is the Number Rods, which are designed to assist associating a numeral to a quantity. The Number Rods are ten rods of increasing length. The shortest is a red rod 10 cm in length. The second rod is 20 cm: half (10 cm) red, half (10 cm) blue. (Figure 2.25) The rods continue to increase in length and pattern up to 100 cm. Children are presented with the Number Rods after they have an understanding of the Red Rods in the Sensorial curriculum, with which they explored the concept of length from long to short.

To present the lesson, show a child how to carry the Numbers Rods one at a time, holding them on each end while carrying, and then placing them on the rug in random order. Next ask the child to arrange the rods from longest to shortest on the work rug (as done previously with the Red Rods). Observe the child at work, and when the child can order all 10 rods correctly, continue to the next step.

Introduce language/vocabulary by using a three-period lesson. (See pages 99–103 for the detailed description of the three-period lesson.) Introduce only two or three rods at a time. Holding the one-rod on each end, say, "This is one." Place the fingers of the right hand, palm-side down, on the rod and say "One." Then, holding the two-rod, say, "This is two." Count the sections of the rod ("one … two") by placing the fingers of the right hand, palm-side down, on the rod while counting.

When confident the child understands the counting activity, proceed to the second period of the lesson by saying, "Show me *two*." … "Show me *one*." Continue with the second period until confident the child can count and identify the rods that have been introduced.

Next, in the third period of the lesson, point to one of the rods and ask the child, "What is this?" Point to the other rod and ask the same question.

Continue in this manner with more of the Number Rods. First identify and count the sections of the rods. Then say the name of the rod and ask the child to find it. Finally ask the child to identify each rod.

The Sandpaper Numerals can be introduced around the same time that the Number Rods are presented. To use this material, children trace a Sandpaper Numeral with their fingers and then say its name (as in the Sandpaper Letters language activity, described on page 25).

After the child has acquired oral language to describe each rod, introduce language for the mathematical symbols (the names of the numerals). Use the set of wooden Number Cards printed with the numerals 1–10. Place the card for numeral 1 and numeral 2 on the work rug and proceed through the three-period lesson for as many presentations as necessary, until the child recognizes and can say the name when shown a numeral.

In the next lesson, the child matches the Number Rods and the Number Cards, first out of order and then in sequence. Place a rod on the work rug and ask the child to match the corresponding numeral to the rod. When the child can do this easily, ask the child to put the rods in order and then place the proper numeral card at the end of each rod.

In the Montessori setting, children are helped to progress and feel successful while moving at their own rate of learning proficiency. One child within a class may proceed through all of the steps in one lesson, while another may take many months to understand and master associating numeral to quantity. Through the use of manipulative materials, children move from concrete to abstract concepts. By matching presentations to children's developmental level, children concretize mathematical concepts and maximize their understanding. (See Table 2.5). Figures 2.24–2.32 show children using various materials of the Math curriculum.

Montessori Strategies for Children with Learning Differences

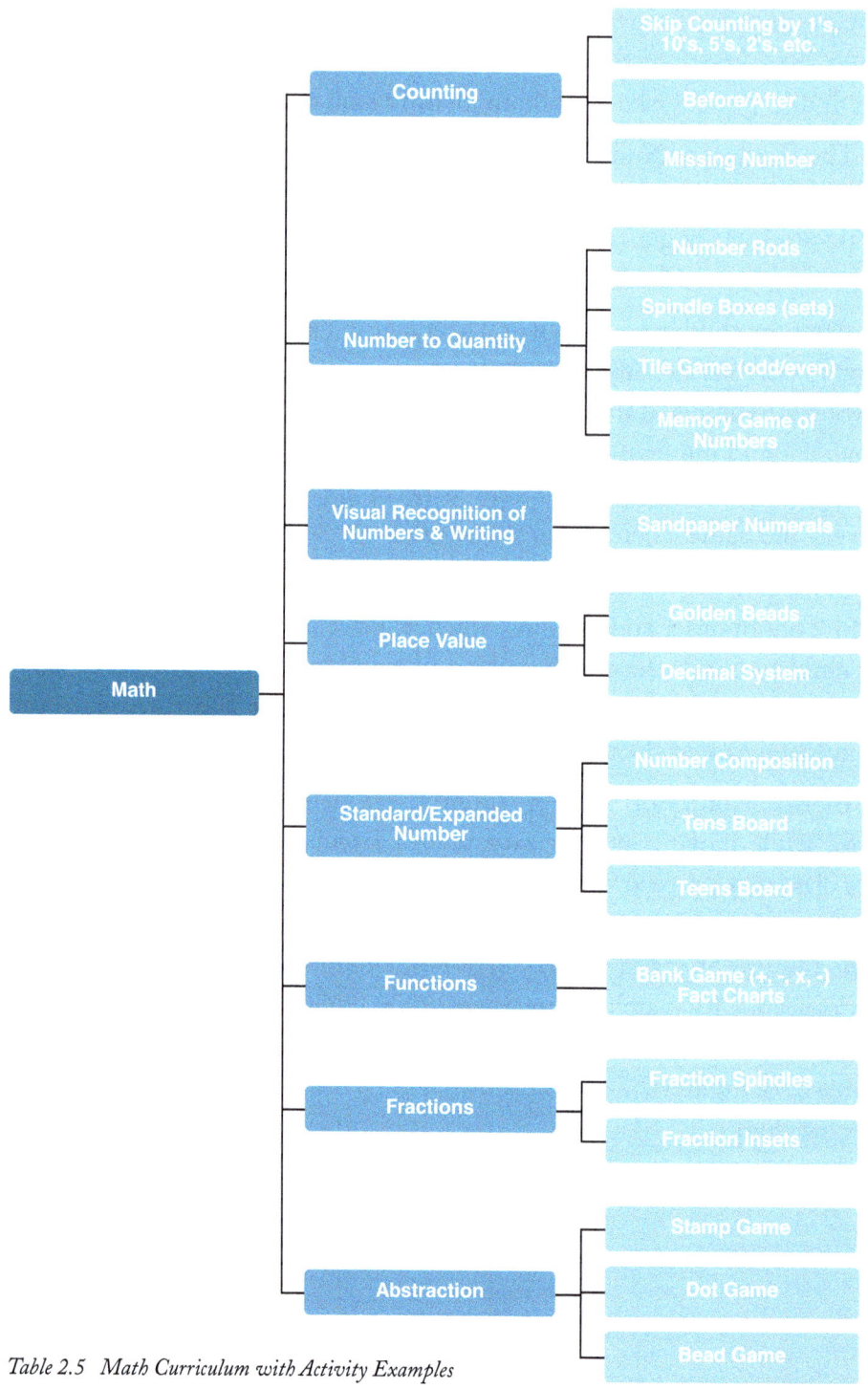

Table 2.5 *Math Curriculum with Activity Examples*

Mathematics Curriculum

Goals:
- The acquisition of mathematical concepts and functions

Lessons include:
- Counting
- Number to Quantity
- Visual Recognition of Numerals
- Numeral Writing, Place Value
- Standard/Expanded Numbers
- Arithmetic Functions
    (addition, multiplication, subtraction, division)
- Fractions
- Abstractions

Fosters:
- Mathematical concepts
- Language development/concepts
- Gross motor skills
- Fine motor skills
- Hand-eye coordination
- Order/sequencing skills
- Executive functioning skills
- Sustained attention/concentration
- Reasoning skills
- Independence

Figure 2.24 Colored Bead Stair

Figure 2.25 Number Rods

Figure 2.26 Desk Set Number Rods

Montessori Strategies for Children with Learning Differences

Figure 2.27 Numerals in Sequence

Figure 2.28 Sandpaper Numeral

Figure 2.29 Introduction to the Decimal System

Figure 2.30 Number Building— Numeral to Quantity

Figure 2.31 Short Bead Chains

Figure 2.32 Introduction to Fractions

Montessori Cultural Subjects: The Sciences, Geography & History

With the presentation of Cultural subject lessons (the sciences, geography, and history, as well as art, music, literature, and drama), young children in a Montessori setting have a wide range of topics to explore. By following their natural interest in the world around them, children develop their reading and writing skills as they gain knowledge. Oral and written language skills are integrated into every subject in the Cultural curriculum. (See Table 2.6.)

In the sciences curriculum (earth, physical, and life), hands-on materials help increase young children's awareness of the details of the world around them. Vocabulary is introduced so children can express what they experience. For example, children can match cards showing the parts of a leaf while looking at and touching a real leaf. With other card sets, children sort types of animals and plants or discover the difference between vertebrates and invertebrates. Prepared activities allow children to discover scientific concepts such as the properties of magnetic and non-magnetic objects, or the properties of objects that float compared to those that sink.

The social sciences (cultural geography and history) include materials created to give preschool children concrete experiences to enhance their understanding of the world around them. Materials include the Sandpaper Globe with a rough brown land surface and smooth blue water surface. Another material presents each land and water form (e.g., lake, island) using clay and water. Puzzle maps of the world and each of its continents lead to the study of geography, including countries and their flags and cultures. After a hands-on activity, precise terminology is given.

Time is a concept not fully understood by young children. The concepts of minutes/hours, day/night, and seasons, to name a few, are all introduced with concrete manipulative materials. Timelines are a useful tool to help children gain an understanding of the concept of time passing. The history curriculum begins with a timeline of a child's own life.

The sciences and physical geography help children begin to understand the larger world. Social studies, including cultural geography, history, music, and art, help children understand and feel connected to all of humanity.

Montessori urged teachers to give elementary-age children a "vision of the whole Universe" (Montessori, 1948/1986, p. 8) and help children discover the interconnected nature of existence. She called this "cosmic education," and it is the foundation and philosophy of her elementary curriculum. Elementary-age children study timelines of the major periods of history. These timelines are manipulative, giving children a visual image of how all living things (including humans and their civilizations) have changed and evolved over time. Children learn about the fundamental needs of all humans which include food, shelter, clothing, transportation, and more. As children research how the world works, they begin to appreciate the many ways humanity has benefited from all those who came before.

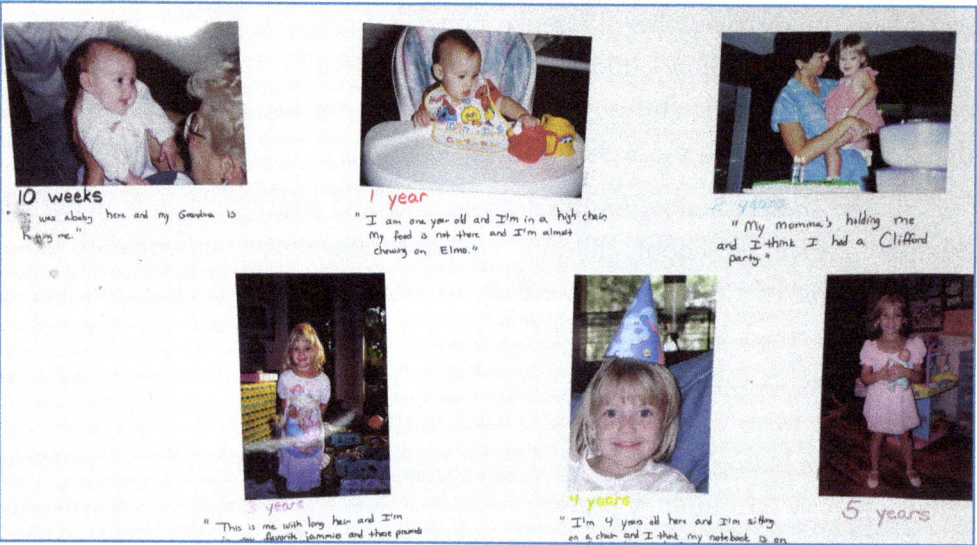

Figure 2.33 Child's Timeline

Chapter 2

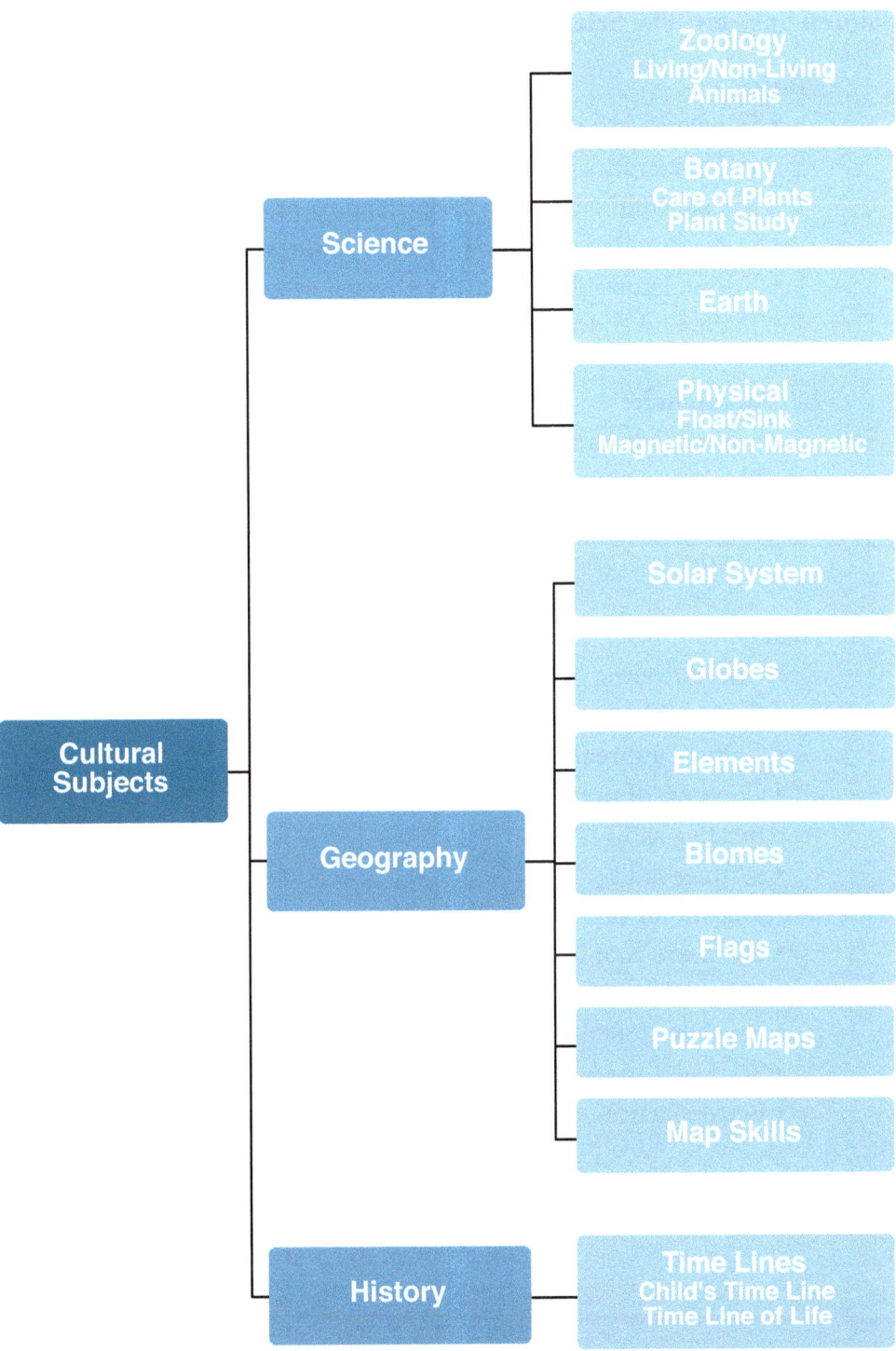

Table 2.6   Cultural Subject Curriculum

Cultural Subjects: The Sciences, Geography & History

Goals:
- To help children gain an understanding of their place in the world and humanity's place in the Universe
- To help children gain an understanding of scientific concepts
- To develop understanding of other cultures
- To gain knowledge of Earth's physical geography
- To develop concepts of time and history

Lessons include:
- Science (life, earth, physical)
- Physical geography (planets, globes, maps, continents, etc.)
- Cultural geography (food, dress, music, art, dance, etc.)
- History (starting with a personal timeline)

Fosters:
- Understanding of scientific concepts
- Geographical awareness
- Cultural awareness
- Concepts of time
- Reading skills
- Writing skills
- Fine motor skills
- Hand-eye coordination
- Order/sequencing skills
- Executive functioning skills
- Sustained attention/concentration
- Independence

Chapter 2

Figure 2.34 Land, Air, Water Elements

Figure 2.35 Globes and Planisphere Map

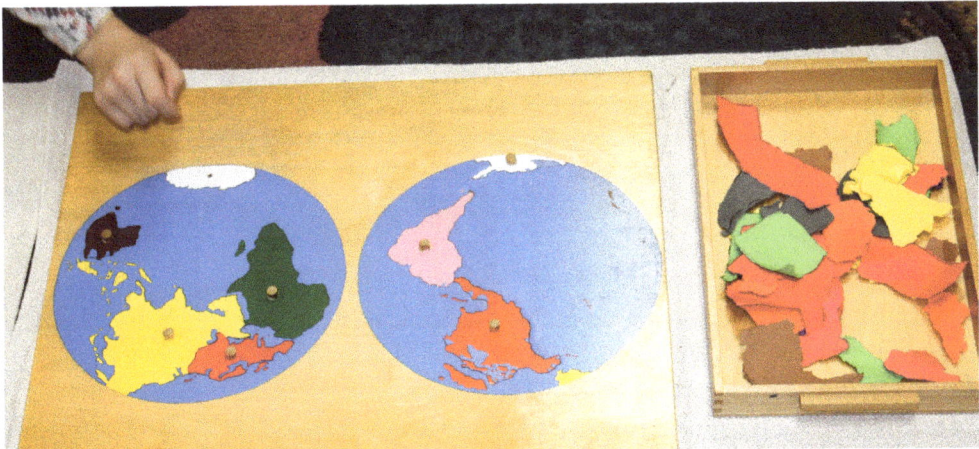

Figure 2.36 Planisphere (World Puzzle Map)

Figure 2.37 World Flags

Montessori Strategies for Children with Learning Differences

Figure 2.39 Map Made by Child

Figure 2.40 Box City Project Created by Student

Figure 2.42 Rock Matching Activity

Figure 2.43 Leaf Cabinet

Montessori Cultural Subjects: The Arts (Art, Music, Literature, Drama)

The Montessori Cultural Subjects curriculum also includes art, music, literature, and drama. See Table 2.7, page 44.

Art experiences in the Montessori classroom include sensorial explorations using color, texture, shape, and size in various mediums. Vocabulary building is integrated into the art curriculum.

Music begins with showing the child how to gently strike the Montessori Bells and then match and gradate the tones of the bells. Other activities help children distinguish degrees of loudness/softness and pitch. Music fosters auditory discrimination and a sense of rhythm. Songs help to build oral language and vocabulary.

Literature is presented through reading stories and poems. Drama is introduced through action and pantomime and proceeds to verbal role-play, skits, and short plays.

Conclusion

The Montessori curriculum provides a wealth of opportunities for children to explore the core Montessori areas: Practical Life, Sensorial, Language, and Math, as well as the Cultural subjects: science, geography, history, and the arts. Hands-on materials provide children with the means to explore and discover concepts such as big/little, loud/soft, rough/smooth, sweet/sour, and more. Rich vocabulary is attached to the materials and the concepts. Children work at their own pace and are not discouraged or frustrated because the lessons are individualized for each child.

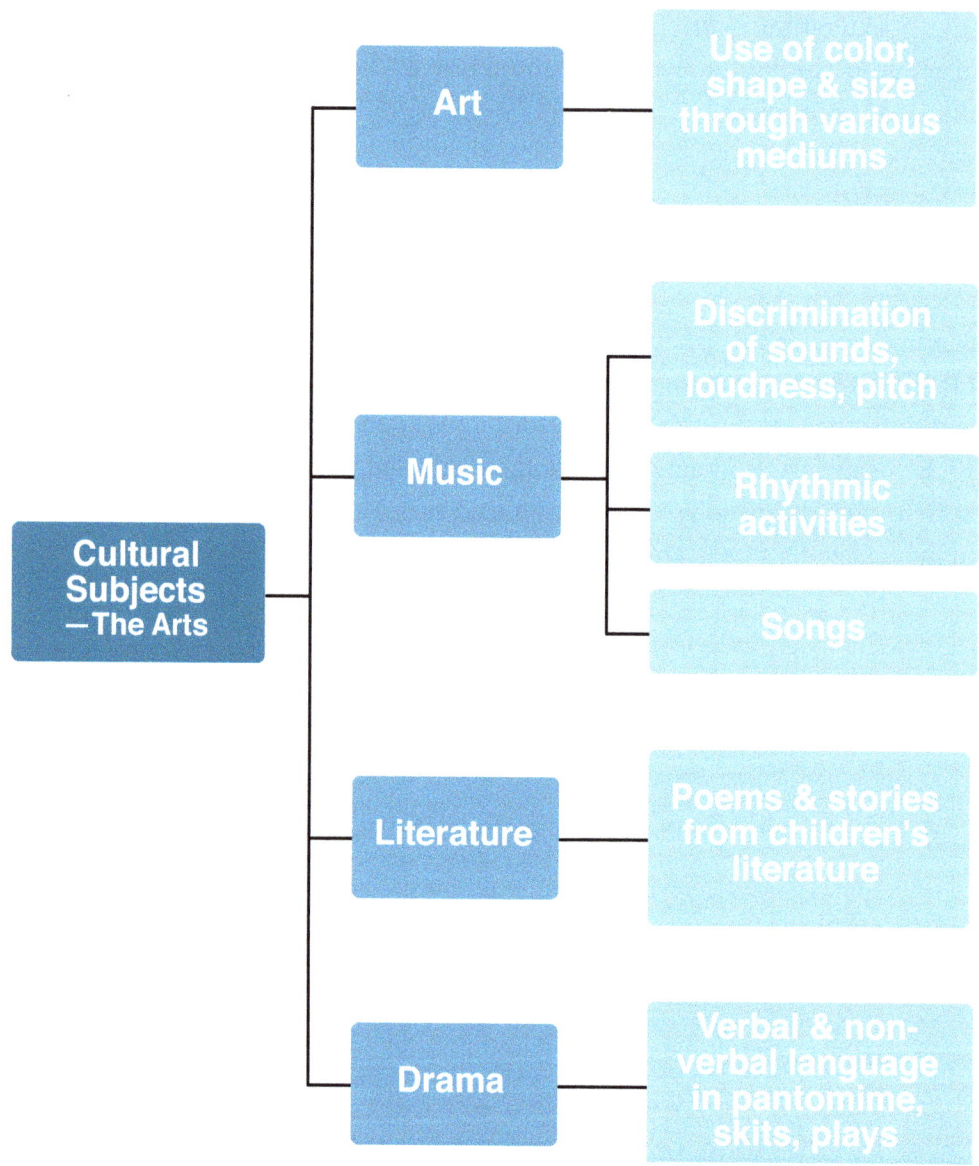

Table 2.7 Cultural Subjects—The Arts Curriculum

Cultural Subjects: The Arts

   Goals:
- Encourage creativity
- Provide opportunities to develop basic art, music, and drama skills

   Lessons include:
- Art—color, size, and shape in drawing, painting, etc.
- Music—activities of volume, pitch, notation, singing, playing instruments
- Literature—fiction and poetry
- Drama—verbal and non-verbal language in pantomime, skits, plays

   Fosters:
- Art, music, and drama skills
- Fine motor skills
- Hand-eye coordination
- Order/sequencing skills
- Sensory discrimination
- Sensory integration
- Sustained attention/concentration
- Language development/concepts

"Today it is this deviated child who occupies the center of the stage in scientific child psychology, which would better be called the psychopathology of childhood."

(Montessori, 1949/1995, p. 92)

Chapter 3

The First Plane of Development for "Typical" Children & Early Intervention for Children with Learning Differences & Varying Exceptionalities

Joyce S. Pickering, with contributions from Sylvia O. Richardson

This chapter describes Dr. Montessori's understanding of the Four Planes of Development for the "typical" child and then considers the differences in development found in children with language learning differences and varying exceptionalities. Definitions of learning differences, disabilities, disorders, and exceptionalities are clarified. The rate and frequency of learning differences and related disorders are presented. Signs of learning and attention differences are described at various ages and stages from early childhood to adulthood.

The Four Planes of Development and the Absorbent Mind

As a medical doctor and early childhood educator, Dr. Montessori observed and documented human development from a unique perspective. She began creating her method while working with children with disabilities, and she created a method that helps children develop many abilities, including, for most children, literacy, at an early age.

Dr. Montessori proposed the theory that human beings pass through four planes of development: the first from birth to age 6; the second, ages 6 to 12; the third, ages 12 to 18; and the fourth, ages 18 to maturity. She described development for "normal" children as smooth across the four planes.

Montessori Strategies for Children with Learning Differences

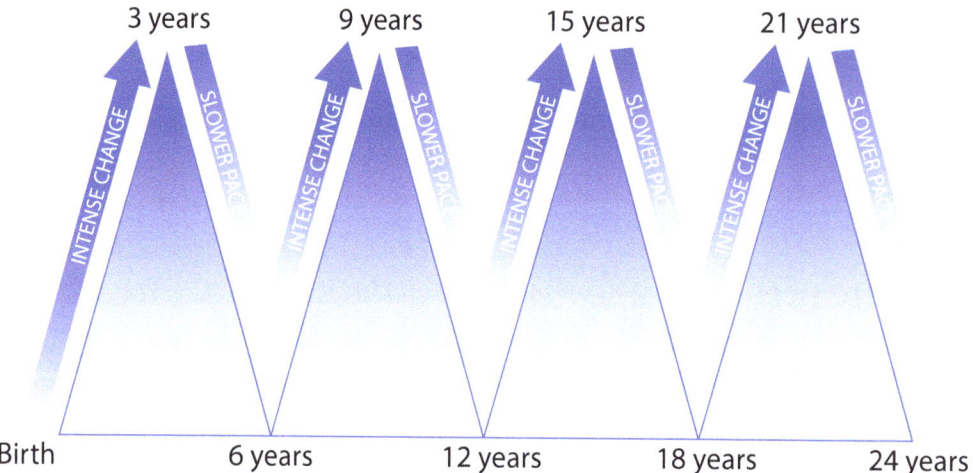

Figure 3.1 The Four Planes of Development for "Typical" Children from Birth to Maturity

Dr. Montessori described the first plane as the period of time when children have an "absorbent mind" (Montessori, 1949/1995). In the first plane of development, Dr. Montessori believed that children pass through two sensitive periods; during the first sensitive period from birth to age 3, children *unconsciously* absorb impressions from their environment. Among other abilities, children develop basic speech, a sense of order, and interest in small objects. This is a period of intense change and learning. According to Dr. Montessori, during the second sensitive period, from ages 3 to 6, children *consciously* absorb impressions from their environment and develop the ability to articulate expressive language. This is a period of change and learning at a relatively slower pace.

Dr. Montessori also believed that most children between the ages of 3 and 6 can learn written language when given an appropriate environment and system of education. She devised an ingenious early childhood program in which children work with manipulative materials while engaging multiple senses as they learn to read and write.

She described children's reactions to this method as "joyful." Her method was so effective that she asserted, "After all, writing is one of the easiest and most pleasant achievements for children" (Montessori, 1912/1988, p. 227). By age 6, the majority of young children in Montessori programs are on their way to being literate.

The first plane of development has two sensitive periods:

- Birth to age 3: Sensitive period for developing basic speech, a sense of order, and interest in small objects.
- Ages 3 to 6: Sensitive period for developing correct speech, reading, and writing. Children's sense of order develops further, and children exhibit a continued interest in small objects.

The First Plane of Development in Relation to Cognitive Ability, Executive Functioning, and Emotional Quotient

Throughout her career, Dr. Montessori worked with countless children and was known as a compassionate doctor. She began working with young children at the Orthophrenic School for Defective Children in 1897, and in 1900, Dr. Montessori was appointed director of the school. Today, the children she worked with would most likely be considered children with varying exceptionalities (learning and developmental disabilities).

Dr. Montessori's early work with vulnerable children with a variety of exceptionalities moved her to create a differentiated and individualized method of education. Much of her method focuses on children ages 3 to 6, and most of Montessori education today serves children in this age range. Dr. Montessori believed that during this period, certain developing "embryonic" parts of a human being begin to integrate. She also observed that at around age 6, this integration forms new abilities that are of service to an individual (Montessori, 1949/1995, p. 26).

> The embryonic development of each of its parts, which is at first carried on separately from birth till 3, must in the end become integrated, when it will be so organized that all these parts act together in the service of the individual. This is what is happening during the next period, from 3 to 6, when the hand is at work and the mind is guiding it. (Montessori, 1949/1995, p. 203)

Montessori Strategies for Children with Learning Differences

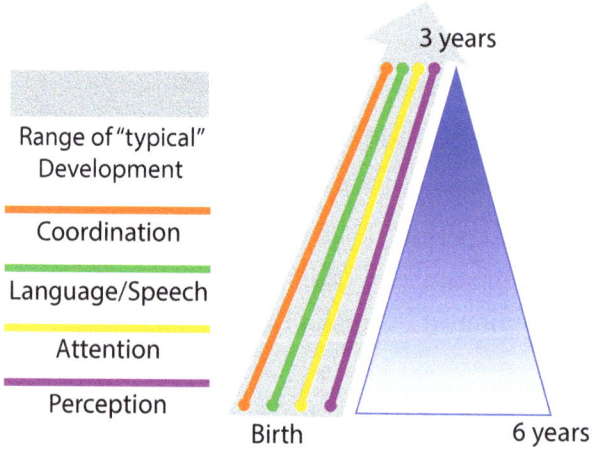

Figure 3.2 Development of Coordination, Language, Attention, and Perception Along Separate Tracks for "Typical" Children from Birth to Age 3

Dr. Montessori believed that certain parts of a personality develop separately during the first sensitive period from birth to age 3, and then, during the next sensitive period from age 3 to 6, those parts integrate. A more modern perspective indicates that from birth to age 3, children develop coordination, language, attention, and perception along separate tracks (Shedd, 1967; Brutten, Richardson, & Mangel, 1973; Critchley, 1947/1964/1984; Waites, 1990).

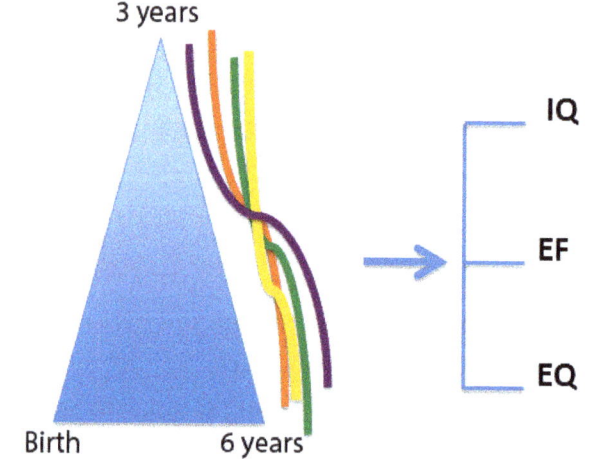

Figure 3.3 Integration of Abilities for "Typical" Children from Age 3 to 6 Leading to IQ, EF, and EQ

From ages 3 to 6, these areas integrate, which leads to cognitive ability (IQ), executive functioning (EF), and emotional intelligence (EQ). For most children, this development is fairly linear and smooth. According to Dr. Montessori, if children develop typically from birth to age 3, their development in the period that follows will be even. Dr. Montessori wrote, "To develop well in the second period, a person must have developed well in the first" (1949/1995, p. 194).

However, children who develop unequally from birth to age 3 may not integrate and consolidate abilities during the next developmental stage from age 3 to 6. Language, cognitive ability, executive functioning, and emotional intelligence may be affected by this unequal development, and this may further affect an individual's abilities throughout the rest of their life. In Figure 3.4, wavy lines represent this uneven development.

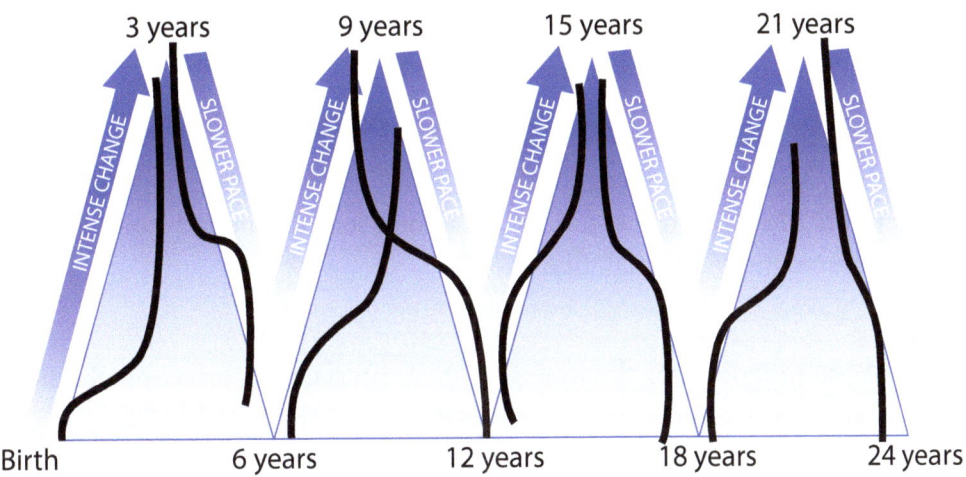

Figure 3.4 Four Planes of Development with Wavy Lines to Indicate Uneven Development

Children with autism, ADHD, dyslexia, and other learning and developmental disabilities often develop unequally and may struggle with coordination, language, attention, and perception challenges, and may develop typically in some areas, and not in others. For example, in the first plane, a child may have serious delays in language, but typical motor development. If this language delay is not remediated before age 6, it will most likely affect development in ensuing planes. Dr. Montessori voiced even sterner warnings. She described the behavior children with this unequal development might exhibit.

> If outer conditions prevent this integration from occurring, then the same energies go on urging each of the partial transformations to continue their activities apart from the others. This results in unequal development, divorced from its proper ends.
>
> The hand moves aimlessly; the mind wanders about far from reality; language takes pleasure in itself; the body moves clumsily. And these separate energies, finding nothing to satisfy them, give rise to numberless combinations of defected and deviated growth, which become sources of conflict and despair. Such deviations cannot be attributed to the personality itself. They come from a failure to organize the personality. (Montessori, 1949/1995, p. 203)

Dr. Montessori recognized the risk children face without early intervention. She advised that during the second sensitive period from ages 3 to 6, early intervention is crucial. She wrote:

> As to prognosis, or the hopes we may entertain of correcting children's defects, we may place those acquired in the postnatal period, from 0 to 3, as being curable in practice during the period from 3 to 6, when nature is still busy in the perfecting of many newly formed powers. (Montessori, 1949/1995, pp. 195–196)

Identifying children who are at risk, is a critical first step toward early intervention. During an acclaimed lecture at the Orton Dyslexia Society-Florida Branch in 1984, Dr. Sylvia Richardson suggested if you want to identify children at risk for learning disabilities, observe the development of coordination, speech-language, attention, and perception. (Dr. Richardson suggested an easy way to remember these developing systems was with the acronym CLAP.)

Education and early intervention are optimal during the first plane of development, and the results of early intervention can be a great benefit to an individual throughout their life. Today, Montessori methods continue to serve children with varying exceptionalities, and children who have atypical neurology or physiology are benefiting from instruction informed by modern science and blended with Dr. Montessori's original techniques.

What are "Deviated/Deficient" Children, Exceptionalities, Disorders, Learning Disabilities, and Learning Differences?

Dr. Montessori wrote extensively, using the language of her time, including the terms "deviated" and "deficient" to describe children with varying exceptionalities. It is no longer appropriate to describe children with these terms, though they still appear in Montessori's original writing.

The term **exceptionality** is an umbrella term that refers to a variety of challenges, including learning disabilities, developmental disabilities, and autism spectrum disorder (ASD).

Neurodevelopmental disorders include dyslexia, attention-deficit/hyperactivity disorder, autism spectrum disorder and intellectual disabilities. The Diagnostic and Statistical Manual, 5th Edition (DSM-5) describes neurodevelopmental disorders as:

> Neurodevelopmental disorders are a group of conditions with the onset in the developmental period. The disorders typically manifest early in development, often before the child enters grade school, and are characterized by developmental deficits that produce impairments of personal, social, academic, or occupational functioning. (American Association of Psychiatry [APA], 2013, p. 31)

Learning disability is a more specific term that describes dyslexia and various processing disorders. According to the National Center for Learning Disabilities (NCLD), in 2017 there were 2.4 million students diagnosed with learning disabilities in the United States (NCLD, 2018).

Dr. June Shelton preferred using the term **learning difference** instead of learning disability. Children with processing, learning, and attention challenges have brains that are different than most, both anatomically and functionally. Children with learning differences have average or above-average intelligence, adequate vision and hearing, no primary emotional disturbance, and have failed or are at high risk to fail when exposed to conventional educational techniques. With appropriate programs, they can learn and do not have to be disabled. Effective intervention will not cure a learning difference, but it can ameliorate learning challenges so children can cope in a classroom and succeed with some learning, especially if reasonable accommodations are provided.

Learning Differences: Rate and Frequency of Occurrence

The most prevalent learning difference is dyslexia. The American Speech-Language-Hearing Association (ASHA) describes dyslexia as difficulty with written language. About 15–20% of the national population shows the characteristics of dyslexia (Shaywitz, 2003). Children may be diagnosed with dyslexia when they are as young as age 6. Dyslexia may also be a part of a language learning disorder in which an individual has difficulty with spoken as well as written language (ASHA, 2018).

Another prevalent learning difference is attention-deficit/hyperactivity disorder (ADHD). A significant number of individuals with dyslexia also have ADHD as a co-existing condition. An estimated 5–7% of the national population exhibits ADHD symptoms (APA, 2013). According to the American Association of Pediatrics, children may be diagnosed with ADHD when they are as young as age 4 (Subcommittee, 2011).

Before children are diagnosed with dyslexia or ADHD, they may exhibit speech or oral language delays. Children may also show symptoms of dysphasia, dyscalculia, dysgraphia, and additional learning differences or developmental/neurological disorders. (See pages 113–114 for definitions of dysphasia, dyscalculia, and dysgraphia.) These may occur in combination with dyslexia or ADHD, or in isolation. In summary:

- Children may exhibit speech delays before they are diagnosed with dyslexia or ADHD.

- Dyslexia is the most prevalent learning difference.
- ADHD is also a prevalent learning difference.
- Additional learning differences or developmental/neurological disorders may occur in combination with dyslexia and ADHD, or may occur in isolation.
- According to the National Center for Learning Disabilities website (ncld.org), in 2017 there were 2.4 million students diagnosed with learning disabilities (learning differences).

Children with Learning Differences at Various Ages and Stages

Children with dyslexia often have close family members with dyslexia. They may have articulation errors in their speech. They usually have little difficulty in learning before the introduction of letters, sounds, and beginning reading activities. By the end of preschool, however, children who may be at risk for dyslexia still have difficulty with sound/symbol correspondence. As they proceed to first grade and beyond, they experience struggles with reading, writing, and spelling.

Children with ADHD may also have close family members with this learning difference. From an early age, children with ADHD exhibit hyperactive and impulsive behaviors. ADHD inattentive type is more obvious once the child begins school. Early speech-language and motor skill delays, and challenges with reading comprehension and math, are common as well.

Early Childhood

Delays in coordination, language, attention, and perception are early predictors of learning differences. During their first 5 years of life, children develop and refine gross motor movements. On average, children support the weight of their head by 4 months, sit by 6 months, crawl by 8 months, stand by 10 months, and walk by approximately 1 year. As large motor coordination improves, children begin refining fine motor movements in their hands and learn to grasp, pick up and hold objects, and feed themselves. As children's motor systems develop, the combined use of the hands and eyes becomes more accurate.

As babies hear the sounds of language, they first perceive the melody of language. Babies begin articulating language sounds by cooing, babbling, and echoing. Finally they arrive at their first meaningful word around age one (usually "mama" or "dada"). In the first 5 years of life, the average child's vocabulary grows to between 2,500 and 5,000 words, and children achieve basic mastery of their mother tongue.

When stimulated with sensory input and information, the minds of infants and toddlers become saturated. Every sight, sound, smell, taste, and touch is absorbed. At this age, children cannot inhibit sensory perceptions. By age 3, most children begin developing inhibition and are able to prioritize some perceptions of information. They can filter out extraneous information, focus on the important perceptual information, and organize that information in a meaningful way by means of their executive functioning ability. This develops the selective and sustained attention necessary for learning in school.

Children with ADHD, however, do not develop typical inhibition, and may be unable to focus on important communications like instructions, directions, or requests from teachers or parents. Beyond age 3, they continue to absorb all sensory stimuli in their environment; they cannot filter out extraneous perceptions. As preschoolers they may be inattentive, impulsive, and hyperactive.

From birth, babies refine their ability to perceive sound. By kindergarten or first grade, the "typically" developing child perceives many subtle differences in speech sounds. Children refine auditory perception to finer and finer details, until around age 5 or 6, when their auditory perception becomes more accurate. For the child with language learning and attention differences, the direct teaching of sound discrimination must continue for a longer period of time.

With typical development, children become "ready" for higher cognitive tasks such as reading, writing, and spelling (Pickering, J. S., 2012). Delays in coordination, speech-language, attention, and perception are early indicators of learning differences.

Elementary School
Because of auditory processing deficits, children with dyslexia have challenges with phonological awareness. They cannot perceive the discrete sounds in words, or locate those sounds accurately and consistently. A word is perceived as a glob of sounds. Often children's speech reflects how they perceive the spoken language of others. It may be mumbled or slurred. Younger children with dyslexia often have articulation errors (basketti/spaghetti) and confuse syllables (comtraval/comfortable). They also have difficulty perceiving the visual, internal details within words, so they frequently confuse words that start alike or look similar to others (then/there, for/from). They confuse short words more often than long words; longer words differ more distinctly from one another.

Because of processing deficits and challenges with phonological awareness, in early elementary grades children with dyslexia often compensate for their reading difficulties by memorizing words and using the pictures in early readers for contextual clues. Consequently they may not be identified as at risk for dyslexia, and subsequently may not be referred for assessment until the third grade or later.

For children in kindergarten through first grade, many parents, teachers, and diagnosticians believe processing deficits will improve with maturity. However, these deficits improve with maturity only in a small number of cases (about 1%, in my experience). In the majority of cases, these deficits are clear, early signs of dyslexia.

If these differences are not recognized by first grade, and if remediation is not begun as soon as possible, these deficiencies become stark. In the first and second grade, "typical" children learn how to decode written symbols, recognize words, and attach meaning to those words. Most children learn reading and writing with comparable ease; in some instances a rare 3-year-old may be an excellent reader, or a 7-year-old may be a slow, labored, and inaccurate reader.

By third grade, those who are still struggling and not making normal progress become more identifiable. Uninformed adults may assume a child is not trying or is not motivated. Motivation is rarely, if ever, the cause of a reading failure. The majority of ineffective readers have dyslexia, a specific learning difference.

If children with dyslexia do not receive strategic teaching, and are not given assessment and therapeutic remediation, their reading ability will continue to develop slowly, and they may become even more frustrated and confused. Some describe it as "swimming in alphabet soup." Often highly intelligent students with dyslexia experience greater frustration. To distract others from their weaknesses with reading and writing, they may exhibit emotional and behavioral outbursts such as clowning, withdrawal, or hostility. As children with dyslexia grow older, the disparity in literacy between themselves and their peers becomes greater.

In school, children with ADHD often have difficulty with reading comprehension, math, and written expression. Their handwriting and their spelling may be inaccurate. Students with ADHD usually have motor skill issues, including challenges with balance and coordination. Teachers often describe children with ADHD as "extremely wiggly."

Middle School
In middle school, the struggles for children with learning differences only increase as work volume, time demands, and requirements continue to escalate. Students are now required to produce multi-paragraph essays, book reports, and research papers. While "typically" developing children are becoming independent workers, students with learning differences cannot finish their work in the same amount of time. Other students write with richer vocabulary and more varied sentence structure. Students with dyslexia know much more than they can express in writing. Note taking is challenging or impossible. Students with ADHD are unable to focus; their ability to selectively focus has not developed typically, and they are stimulated by everything in the environment, which can be exhausting and overwhelming for them. Frustration and self-esteem issues may worsen during these years, as students with learning differences produce work that is inadequate for their grade level.

High School
As students enter high school, even the mildest learning difference can be a major burden. Higher cognitive and perceptual functioning is needed for the

complex literary vocabulary and the increased levels of abstraction in reading. The pressure to write comprehensive, fluid papers overloads even the brightest student with learning differences. The volume of reading and writing within the time constraints allowed is overwhelming. Many students with learning differences suffer from depression and anxiety and are at higher risk for alcohol and drug abuse. The potential for suicide increases as well.

College and Adulthood
Students with learning differences who have received no remediation may enter college, but many are unsuccessful. Those who persist and have an area of talent in which to major may attain a degree, but college is rarely easy or carefree. Often students with learning differences describe these years as highly stressful. Increasingly, colleges are providing support services and accommodations for those with identified learning disabilities.

At work, adults with learning differences may be bright and creative, but may also exhibit disorganized, slow, and erratic performance. Some find a niche in which their talents overshadow their weaknesses; others are not as successful. For some, problems with social skills or inattention persist and add to their difficulties.

The success of the adult with learning differences depends, in large part, on the severity of their processing disorder and the strength of their support system. A mildly dyslexic adult with strong math skills and above-average mental ability may be a dynamo in the business world—especially if they work with an administrative assistant who can write their letters and correct their spelling. Many companies have high-ranking executive officers who are dyslexic; they have visionary strength, can see the big picture, and predict trends—all skills needed to lead a company. They can hire others to attend to details. Individuals with attention deficits often think "out of the box" and may have strengths as entrepreneurs. If they partner with someone who can help channel their creativity, they may become highly successful.

The case histories of adolescents and adults have clearly illustrated the early signs of these differences. Delays in coordination, speech-language, attention, and perception are early predictors of learning differences. Early identification, strategic instruction, and therapeutic remediation are essential.

A Pioneering Article from
The American Montessori Society Bulletin 1966

In the early 1960s, Dr. Sylvia Richardson worked as the Director of the Child Study Center at the Oklahoma Medical Center with Dr. June Shelton. Their success educating children with varying exceptionalities using Montessori techniques was noteworthy. In 1966, Dr. Richardson published the following article, "A Pediatrician Looks at Montessori for Neurologically Impaired Children" in the American Montessori Society Bulletin (Vol. 4, No. 4).

A PEDIATRICIAN LOOKS AT MONTESSORI FOR NEUROLOGICALLY IMPAIRED CHILDREN

Sylvia O. Richardson, M.D.*

An Address given at the

1965 ANNUAL CONVENTION OF THE
NATIONAL ASSOCIATION FOR CRIPPLED CHILDREN AND ADULTS

November, 1965

Since each person speaks from a specific frame of reference, it may be helpful to explain that this pediatrician was first a speech pathologist, obtained the Masters degree in Education of the Exceptional, and taught speech and language to hard of hearing children in the public schools before going to medical school. For seven and one half years prior to our recent move to Cincinnati, I was the Director of the Child Study Center at the University of Oklahoma Medical Center. This was an evaluation center for children with learning disabilities and included a diagnostic or evaluation nursery where Montessori materials and techniques were used for both diagnosis and training.

Classically the pediatrician is said to be interested chiefly in the child's physical health. However, today he is also deeply concerned with the growth and development of the child's optimal mental health and function. Since the child is in a continuous process of creating his adulthood with its possibilities for optimal functioning, a handicapped child is any child whose ability to learn is seriously hampered by physical disability, intellectual subnormality or deviation, emotional conflicts and confusion, or crippling social environmental pressures.

The child who has a serious learning disability is indeed a handicapped child. A youngster with a neuro-motor disability, one with chronic disease, one who is an amputee, for instance, may have a particular disability to cope with, but he would be even more seriously handicapped if he could not learn to learn, learn to compensate, if he could not learn to develop social and personal autonomy to make his own choices and feel responsible for his own choices. Regardless of anything else, the child's *basic* concern and function from birth is in the process of learning and discovering, in creating the adult that he is to become.

For purposes of this presentation I should like to elaborate a bit on Dr. Montessori's often generally overlooked but immeasurable contributions to the education of the child with minor neurological dysfunction—one who has difficulty in learning.

---

* Assistant Professor of Pediatrics, University of Cincinnati, School of Medicine, Cincinnati, Ohio; Editor, *Children's House* Magazine; formerly Director of Child Study Center, Assistant Professor of Pediatrics and Psychiatry, University of Oklahoma Medical Center, Oklahoma City, Oklahoma.

First let us keep in mind Dr. Montessori's concept of the Prepared Environment. Essentially she points out that, since the child has only his immediate environment from which to gather his basic building materials, we must provide a learning environment for him that possesses order, one that disposes the child to develop at his own level, according to his own capacities. "Let the environment reveal the child," she said, "not mold him." As she pointed out, the child brings in from the external world a myriad of sensations and impressions (William James called this "a big booming buzzing confusion")—processing them through the central nervous system and expressing them in movement, language, and various forms of self-initiated activity. In an environment prepared for the child some order and structure can be given to these sensations and impressions which will facilitate learning. For the neurologically handicapped child, such order and structure are imperative!

The manifestations of "minimal cerebral dysfunction" which are described in the literature include one or more of the following:

1. Mild dyskinesia or choreoathetosis
2. Isolated hyperreflexia
3. Excessive clumsiness or irregularities in gross and fine coordination
4. Mild or minimal intellectual **disability**
5. Specific **disability** of speech development (dysphasia)
6. Specific developmental dyslexia and dysgraphia
7. Strabismus or monocular vision
8. Mixed laterality or Ambilaterality
9. Impaired form perception
10. Impaired spatial concept, and
11. Other perceptual-motor disturbance
12. Hyperkinetic behavior with distractibility, short attention span, emotional lability, impulsiveness and irritability

Most are said to have "general or specific learning disability." Since children with central nervous system dysfunction vary widely in learning ability, it is not possible to formulate a teaching program which will apply to them all. However, we have found that early diagnosis and early treatment, using primarily Montessori materials and techniques, have been associated with relatively good results, for children with minimal neurological dysfunction.

Where perceptual-motor disorders are involved, emphasis should be placed on training in the motor bases of behavior such as posture, development of laterality and directionality, and the development of body image; training in perceptual skills such as form perception, space discrimination, stereognosis, recognition of texture, size and structure; training in auditory perception (listening), in visual perception (looking), and in kinesthetic perception (muscular memory of movements, positions and postures).

The term "retardation" has been replaced with "disability."

For muscular education there are exercises which are intended to aid the development of physiological movement, such as breathing and walking. These are presented by Montessori as "Exercises in Deportment and Discipline" and assist the child in developing balance, posture, directionality, control and economy of movement. Children particularly like "Walking the Line," where they walk heel-to-toe along a line about two inches wide; there are innumerable variations that can be utilized in this exercise.

In order to assist development of independent function, Montessori provides "Exercises of Practical Life." These utilize materials that are normally found in the child's everyday environment and provide practice in the care of the person and care of the environment, as well as exercises in coordination. These exercises are important in providing order, sequence and temporal integration of motor activity. Indirectly they also provide enrichment of perceptions and vocabulary.

Of importance, as the child is taught each activity, such as washing hands or polishing shoes, each step of the operation is presented by the teacher in logical orderly sequence—almost as one would program a computer. Thus the child learns to focus attention and to analyze each of his body movements each time he repeats the sequence. Perfection of each step within an activity leads to economy of movement and gradual decreasing of clumsiness and extraneous activity—as well as better establishment of body image.

Zaporozhets, a student of Vygotsky, states that the essence of voluntary behavior is in *feedback*. He finds that to teach a child how to carry out a complex task, one must make sure that he is also taught how to organize his orienting responses (attention). He must learn what to look at; his action must be directed to the right cues, both external and proprioceptive. Thus, he must learn to make use of feedback both from the external situation and from his own action, and the teacher must train him to do this. Several experiments have shown that a task can be learned more rapidly if orienting behavior (attention) is specifically trained. This principle is demonstrated clearly in the Montessori method, though not stated in the same terminology. The functions of attention *do* respond to training, and the value of this for many children with CNS dysfunction cannot be over-estimated.

We have seen children with (mild) choreoathetosis and those with gross and fine motor incoordination show remarkable improvement as they mastered the exercise of pouring rice or pouring water, for example. Further, some of the most hyperkinetic and disorganized children begin to quiet down and to concentrate as they learn to exercise their motor drives in directed and purposeful activity. Experiences are taken in through the senses and the child works out meaning through his activity.

Learning requires concentration and these children will learn to concentrate by fixing their attention on some task that they are performing with their hands. Dr. Montessori pointed out that all through his development the hand is the child's teacher.

The Montessori material for "sense training" represents a selection from material used by Itard and Sequin in their attempts to educate mentally deficient children, from objects used as tests in experimental psychology, and from material designed by Dr. Montessori.

These materials are grouped according to sense: auditory, visual, tactile, baric, taste, smell, and stereognostic. They are also sub-grouped according to specific qualities such as sound intensity, pitch, form, dimension, color, texture, weight, taste, and odor.

Each sense is trained in isolation. There is no order of presentation according to a particular sense. However, there is an order in the psychological method of presentation. Contrasts are always presented to the child first, then identities are presented through matching, and finally, gradations of quality. Although Dr. Montessori emphasized this method of presentation 60 years ago, we still need to be reminded that children learn differences before they can classify by similarities.

When we "train" the senses we are not trying to make the child see better, we are helping him to know what he sees. By providing strongly contrasted sensations followed by a variously graded series of sensations, these materials teach the child to discriminate. For example, if we show him first red and then blue, then later, several shades of blue or red, he is learning what is red and what is blue. At the same time he is learning to compare, to contrast, to discriminate; that is to distinguish different sense impressions and to put them in some sort of order. This is the beginning of a conscious awareness of the environment as opposed to the unconscious knowledge he already may have. And as he isolates the sense impressions and the qualities perceived, he is gradually building up abstract conceptions: first the general category of "color," then redness and blueness, darkness and lightness. This is the beginning of the development of the intellect.

Isolation of a single quality in the material is as important as isolation of the sense being trained, so that in many sets of exercises the objects are identical among themselves in all respects except for gradation. Since these youngsters have difficulty in the organization of incoming stimuli we must present the sensory stimuli in an orderly way. By isolating one sense, the mind can give attention to a particular quality and can learn to create mental order. The apparatus is designed to give the knowledge systematically, so the order becomes apparent.

Of major importance in working with these youngsters, even the Montessori "sensorial materials" allow for the motor activity of the child. The possibility of arousing the child's attention and maintaining it depends less on the quality belonging to things than on the opportunities which they offer of doing something with them. These youngsters may not be able to concentrate on *things* but they will learn to develop a focus of attention that is sometimes remarkable in the *doing* of a specific activity.

Montessori materials are available for training the tactile sense, the baric sense, the stereognostic sense, even taste and smell. The solid insets and blocks are used for recognition of dimensions by visual and stereognostic means. For the sense of color there are the color tablets in eight colors, and for each color there are eight corresponding shades varying in intensity. Plane insets and geometrical shapes are used for the distinction of form. There are also cards on which are printed the geometrical figures corresponding to the geometrical shapes so that the child can match them and interpret visually the graphic symbol for the wooden geometrical shapes.

The same principle is used in the education of auditory discrimination. Developmentally, a child must first learn to distinguish between noises and sounds as apart from silence. Since this training starts with strongly contrasting differences and passes on to almost imperceptible differences, part of "auditory training" includes training in silence. This has many advantages which may be obvious!

The analysis of sounds relative to speech are essentially auditory-visual-tactile-kinesthetic exercises connected with the learning of the alphabet. Sandpaper letters are used which the child looks at and traces with his fingers as he voices the sound of the letter simultaneously, thus utilizing a multi-sensory approach. Later he uses the movable alphabet to build words; these are letters which the child can hold in his hand and manipulate himself.

Vocabulary building and perceptual development are assisted by training the neuro-motor functions through the activity of the child and his spontaneous interest in learning. All these processes go on day after day, side by side, all invisibly converging towards one end. The hand is being prepared for fine motor movement and writing indirectly through sensorial materials such as the cylinder inserts, the touch boards, the baric tablets, the pouring exercises, the dressing frames, etc.; the eye is also being prepared for finer discriminations through the sensorial materials. Through practice, the hand learns to control the pencil with the metal insets, and the sandpaper letters provide the kinesthetic sense with the memory for forms pertinent to language, at the same time that the sounding of the letters increases auditory discrimination and auditory memory and assists the child in the final perfection of speech itself.

In this brief time it is impossible to give more than a small bird's eye view of the techniques used. However, the purpose of this presentation has been to point out the value of the Montessori materials and techniques for the child who has a learning disability, and to stress that these techniques are very much in line with a "neurophysiological approach" to learning.

For me, personally, Dr. Montessori's greatest contribution is in the area of child psychology. She saw the child as totally separate and different from the adult —they are two different forms of life. She had an inspiring respect, a reverence, for the child and his work. A well-trained physician, she learned about children from her own observations, without first imposing on them a theory of behavior that they must be made to fit. She taught that the child himself creates the man he is to be, that he must use for this the materials provided in and by his environment. In order to prepare the appropriate environment for any child, we must come to understand the functions, purposes and needs of this busy little creature. Montessori saw each child as a unique individual, a person in his own right, not as a miniature adult. Moreover, in an age when child labor was exploited and when discipline in the schools was often brutal, Maria Montessori truly paid her respects to the child and his work; she gave him not only love, but dignity.

The American Montessori Society Bulletin is published quarterly for distribution to members of the Society. Address inquiries to the American Montessori Society, 175 Fifth Avenue, New York, N. Y. 10010. Additional copies 20¢.

"Pedagogy teaches that the environment must offer less resistance; so avoidable obstacles which the environment contains are diminished more and more, or perhaps removed entirely."

(Montessori, 1949/1995, p. 92)

Chapter 4

The Montessori Method Combined with Inclusion Strategies for Children with Learning Differences & Varying Exceptionalities

Joyce S. Pickering, with contributions from Sylvia O. Richardson

Chapter 4 presents Montessori techniques for enhancing learning for children with learning differences and varying exceptionalities. The Montessori method is an educational method for all children. "Typically" developing children discover information through the use of didactic materials. Children with learning differences and varying exceptionalities need careful presentations and direct teaching with these materials.

In 1968, Sylvia Richardson recommended that I consider the Montessori method as a way to help children in preschool who were showing signs of being at risk for language learning differences. Sylvia, a pediatrician, speech-language pathologist (SLP), and Montessori-trained teacher at the early childhood level, used the Montessori techniques while working with children with intellectual disabilities at the Child Study Center at the University of Oklahoma Medical School. She referred me to Dr. June Shelton, who employed Montessori techniques to educate children with learning differences. Sylvia recommended I contact June for training in Montessori techniques. One phone call led to a meeting with her.

That meeting convinced me this was the method I needed to help children in the early intervention program I was directing. Once trained, I encouraged my staff to use Montessori techniques to offer early intervention to children who struggled with reading and writing and had additional learning differences.

Children with varying exceptionalities need closer direction by the teacher, avoid work they sense they cannot do, and do not develop independence as "typically" developing children do. A teacher must help instill work habits, limit work choices, or choose work for children with varying exceptionalities until they can do so for themselves.

Montessori noted the differences she discovered between "typically" developing children and those she considered disabled. One marked difference was the "typical" children did not require a one-to-one relationship with their teacher while exploring the Sensorial materials. Children with varying exceptionalities needed more individual attention.

The traditional Montessori method includes individualization, attention, structure, organization, manipulative materials, gross and fine motor development, oral language development, social skills, and an environment of encouragement. These components, embedded within the Montessori curriculum, help the child who has a learning difference.

The Montessori teacher can use additional therapeutic strategies in helping children with processing and attention challenges. Some of these strategies include partnering with the child to maintain focus. For some children, more physical movement is needed to increase attention. Because of executive functioning challenges, children with learning and attention differences need to be taught a cycle of work. Reducing a lesson's difficulty to match the child's developmental level is always necessary. More repetition and multisensory reinforcement are necessary as well. Some children with processing challenges may be unable to understand if they have completed a task correctly. For these children the teacher must offer acknowledgment and validation for their efforts and their successes. Rules of the classroom must be explicit and followed consistently, and children with varying exceptionalities may require positive feedback when adhering to these rules.

The Montessori Method and Enhancements for Children with Varying Exceptionalities

Embedded in the Montessori method are procedures and presentations that enhance the development of attention, order and organization, gross and fine motor skills, visual and auditory perception, oral language development, the academic skills of written language and mathematics, and personality growth. This is accomplished through a hierarchical curriculum and a trained and skillful teacher who, through careful observation, can match lessons to the child's developmental level. Children feel successful in school because the lessons are matched to their developmental level and they can see themselves as competent.

The following list enumerates the parts of the Montessori approach that especially support children with varying exceptionalities. These features of the traditional Montessori classroom enhance learning for all children—"typical" learners as well as children with varying exceptionalities.

- Classroom structure
- Individualization/differentiation
- Training attention
- Specific classroom procedures with clear limits and privileges
- Work organization
- Manipulative materials
- Motor skill development
- Oral language development
- Social skills development
- Environment of encouragement

The following sections explain the parts of the Montessori approach that especially support children with varying exceptionalities. Dr. Richardson and I implemented a number of modifications to traditional Montessori strategies to better support the needs of these children. These sections, describe how children with varying exceptionalities might function in the Montessori environment, why this feature is important, or what additional modifications can be made to better support the needs of children with varying exceptionalities.

69

Classroom structure

The Montessori classroom structure is an orderly prepared environment. Each area of the curriculum is set up in a distinct area of the classroom. All the materials for the lessons are meticulously arranged on trays and organized on shelves. The classroom is attractive and free of clutter. Each lesson has a sequence and order, and is carefully presented to the children. The structure of a Montessori classroom quickly guides children who are "typical" learners towards self-control and a cycle of work within weeks.

- The calm, uncluttered, and organized environment itself is part of the remediation for children with a variety of processing challenges.

- Children with learning differences need help learning self-regulation and a work cycle. Self-directed learners in a Montessori classroom generally only need a teacher to present new work before they can work independently. This leaves teachers with more time to give individual lessons to those with learning challenges.

Individualization/differentiation

The Montessori method provides individualization. The lessons are planned carefully to meet the specific needs of each child and can be presented one-to-one or in small groups. A major tenet of the Montessori philosophy is respect for children. The teacher respects children by observing their developmental levels and following their needs in selecting lessons for them. Detailed individual records allow the teacher to track each child's progress. The child always experiences some success in each lesson. This creates a safe environment for children to explore.

- Most children are interested in learning something new, so they join in eagerly when a teacher invites them to a lesson. Children with learning differences may be reluctant if the lesson involves a skill in which they feel unsure. Teachers can make shorter presentations or reduce the number of materials used in order to ensure the child's success in challenging areas.

Training attention

The Montessori method provides specific procedures and techniques for developing attention. Dr. Montessori wrote, "Normalization comes about through 'concentration' on a piece of work" (Montessori, 1949/1995, p. 206). (See Chapter 7 for more about children with attention deficits and/or hyperactivity.)

Howard Gardner, a highly regarded researcher in the field of psychology in the 1960s, observed that the Montessori method was particularly well suited to help children develop attention.

> We were impressed with the variety of ways in which the Montessori method develops effective inhibition of irrelevant motor activity, while at the same time developing both focal attention and concentration upon sequences… involved in complex tasks. This operation interested us particularly because we have long been impressed with the notion that specific forms of selective attention… are among the most valuable and uniquely human of our evolutionary gifts. (Gardner, 1968, p. 78)

"Typical" children can filter out extraneous sights and sounds. Attention, focus, and concentration are all functional. The presentation of materials provides the child with a demonstration of sequential steps to achieve a task. As the child watches the steps to conclusion, the teacher's slow hand movements focus attention.

Each lesson teaches organization and sequence, directly enhancing executive function. Attention, focus, and concentration are required in all steps of each lesson. The teacher's physical presence and movements help children with attention deficits to focus. Presentations with high-quality materials stimulate children's desire to investigate, learn, and complete activities. In Montessori schools, teachers encourage inhibition by helping children learn to wait for their turn, walk slowly, talk in a quiet voice, clean up after themselves, and control their bodies and behavior. In essence, these are the skills needed to function in a work environment.

- Children with attention differences must be taught how to attend. The teacher must help them reach an attention level so they can maintain learning throughout a range of activities. The teacher must help them learn to make choices or they may wander, doing little meaningful work. Work ribbons and work plans can help a child learn how to make choices. For more information and resources about training attention, see the Appendix.

- Techniques for developing attention are found in the Montessori classroom structure, three-period lesson procedures, and in the Montessori Silence Game. The Silence Game is an exercise in which children practice inhibition of motor movements and practice focusing attention. With practice and one-on-one instruction of the Silence Game, children with attention differences can develop an increased ability to concentrate. See Chapter 7, pages 144–147, for more about the Montessori Silence Game and attention-deficit/hyperactivity.

- After an initial lesson is complete, the teacher shows the child the steps for returning the work to the shelf where it belongs. For children with varying exceptionalities, one enhancement that can help support their success is to mark each shelf with a symbol, which matches the symbols on the materials that belong on that shelf. This is particularly helpful to children with attention, memory, directionality, and/or spatial problems. Symbols help the child find where things belong. Symbols also direct the child's attention in the final step of each activity they complete.

- These careful presentations increase the executive function skills of organizing and prioritizing, which are especially challenging for children with attention deficits.

Specific classroom procedures with clear limits and privileges
The rules of the classroom are taught explicitly through the Montessori Grace and Courtesy lessons, so children respect other children's work, respect boundaries, choose their own work, and work without interruption. Based on respect, children learn how to behave toward others and how to carefully treat

the materials in the classroom. Grace and Courtesy lessons must be repeated as necessary. Role-playing is an effective method for teaching how to return materials to the shelf and how to tuck in a chair so others do not bump into it. Most children soon develop self-control and respect for the people and learning materials in the environment.

Work organization
An emphasis on work organization gives children a model for learning how to set up and go about work tasks. Each lesson has a particular layout with consistent, sequential steps. The result is a lifelong habit of investigation and completion. Specific classroom procedures, with clear limits and privileges, help children with inhibition control challenges. The classroom is a prepared environment with ordered calm, which supports children with attention deficits and hyperactivity. See the Appendix for information about the MACAR manual, *Empowering Children for Self-Control*, that describes inappropriate behaviors and how to help children gain appropriate behavior.

Manipulative materials
Working with manipulative materials gives children multisensory perceptions and helps them form defined concepts. All lessons progress from concrete materials to abstract concepts and from simple movements and ideas to complex movements and understanding. All of the materials in the Practical Life curriculum allow children to explore each life skill with attractive, age-appropriate materials that fit their small hands, offering visual, tactile, and kinesthetic sensory feedback. The auditory sense is engaged at the end of each presentation, when teachers attach language to the perceptual learning taking place.

The entire Sensorial curriculum provides precise activities to isolate the quality being taught and teaches vocabulary such as long/short or large/small, as well as comparatives and superlatives. The multisensory activities provide controlled perceptual presentations of visual, auditory, kinesthetic, tactile, olfactory, and gustatory information to stimulate perceptions of size, shape, color, sound, weight, texture, smell, and taste.

The Montessori Math materials build on the Sensorial curriculum, relating numeral to quantity and the functions of math leading toward abstraction. The Cultural curriculum uses multisensory activities to teach geography, history, science, and the arts.

Motor skill development

As children move around the room, to and from the shelves, while carefully circumventing the mats on the floor, they carry materials on trays of various sizes and weights. This requires practice in motor coordination and balance. These specific techniques increase gross motor skill development, eye-hand coordination, and fine motor skills. Fine motor skills are developed initially in Practical Life and Sensorial work. Many of these activities require coordination of the hand and, more specifically, the three fingers used in grasping a pencil for writing. In most areas of the curriculum, hand-eye coordination is continued through the use of manipulative materials. See the Appendix for information about the Perceptual Motor Skills manual for additional motor skills training.

Oral language development

Montessori presentations, in small sequential steps with scientifically researched materials, enhance skill development in language, as well as math, geography, history, art, music, and the physical and biological sciences. Careful presentation of each activity in each area of the curriculum enhances learning for all children and helps children develop accurate and definitive vocabulary to describe people, objects, ideas, their attributes, and their functions. For more information on oral language development, see the Appendix for the MACAR Oral Language Development Manual.

- For children with oral language weaknesses, repetitions of the vocabulary of all attributes and functions of materials in each presentation should be labeled (named). The amount of vocabulary introduced in each lesson needs to be matched to the child's level of language ability. For example, after a presentation of a Practical Life pouring activity, the teacher can introduce the vocabulary that describes each object on the tray: "This pitcher is small. It is white and it is round." Adding the vocabulary that describes the function of the object, the teacher could say, "The pitcher is for pouring water." The teacher could then ask, "What do we do with a pitcher?"

Social skills development
Social skills are practiced and enhanced in a Montessori prepared environment. Montessori teachers model considerate behavior and teach children grace and courtesy. Children have a role model for emotional intelligence and absorb and practice these grace and courtesy skills. Basic skills include: helping others when they spill something; respecting a child's wish to work alone; saying "please," "thank you," and "excuse me."

- Children with varying exceptionalities may have delays in social skills and may need direct teaching, in addition to the many opportunities afforded in the Montessori classroom. The *Choices* program is a proven curriculum that Dr. Laure Ames and I developed; it includes direct instruction and training to help children develop social skills and greater social competence. For more information, see the Appendix.

Environment of encouragement
An environment of encouragement and de-emphasis of failure encourages the child's desire to be independent. A mantra in Montessori education is "*mistakes are not bad; they are the way we learn.*" If we try one way and do not succeed, let's try another way. There are no grades, just progress reports; no tests, just observations. The teacher knows what the child needs next.

- This atmosphere is healthy for all children and critical for children with varying exceptionalities.
- Children with special needs require more support from the teacher than "typically" developing children. When they complete work correctly, they need validation from their teacher, such as, "That is accurate. You have done that work correctly." These comments are not praise but rather an assessment that work was done correctly. Montessori believed praise was unnecessary for most "typical" children who achieve inner

satisfaction from their work. Children with varying exceptionalities may not perceive when their work is accurate or inaccurate; hence they do not achieve the inner satisfaction from learning that other children experience. To help these children stay engaged in work, the teacher's validation is critical.

Contrast of Typical Development and the Development of Children with Varying Exceptionalities; Montessori Strategies that Enhance Learning for Children with Varying Exceptionalities

Development of "Typical" Child	Development of a Child with Varying Exceptionalities	Montessori Strategies that Enhance Learning for a Child with Varying Exceptionalities
Adaptive Children perceive their world accurately and learn through imitation. With typical development the child's neurological system matures and self-control and sustained attention are attained.	**Adaptive** Children with varying exceptionalities may have distorted or overwhelming perceptions of the world. Perception may be inaccurate and so intense it may cause discomfort.	**Adaptive** The order and calm within a Montessori environment is supportive for children with varying exceptionalities.
Coordination: Gross Motor Walks, hops, runs, jumps, skips, throws, and catches ball by approximately 5 years of age if offered the opportunity to learn these movements.	**Coordination: Gross Motor** Uncoordinated body movements sometimes observed in classroom.	**Coordination: Gross Motor** **Manipulation of Materials:** Carrying/using multisensory materials of various sizes and weights. **"On the Line"** procedures: Moving to rhythms, marching, hopping, skipping to music.
Coordination: Fine Motor Cuts on a line, cuts out shapes, holds pencil, maintains line and pressure, makes corners by age 5 if offered the opportunity to learn these movements.	**Coordination: Fine Motor** Has challenges maintaining patterns, jerky cutting motion results in jagged cutting. Holds pencil in awkward fashion, has challenges maintaining a line, pressure, making corners, even if offered a model and instruction.	**Coordination: Fine Motor** **Eye-Hand coordination:** Manipulation of materials in all areas of curriculum. **Hand coordination:** Preparation of the hand for writing; use of thumb, index, and middle fingers working together for grasp and release. Particular training in the pre-writing activity of Metal Insets.

Development of "Typical" Child	Development of a Child with Varying Exceptionalities	Montessori Strategies that Enhance Learning for a Child with Varying Exceptionalities
Oral Language The average 5-year-old has a vocabulary of approximately 2,500 to 5,000 words and usage of this vocabulary or basic communication with appropriate sentence structure.	**Oral Language** Nominal vocabulary. Often seen as a quiet child, child who is confused by simple directions. High incidence of articulation and rhythmical difference in speech. Some children with varying exceptionalities may have normal vocabulary development.	**Oral Language** All lessons presented silently to allow child to process the perceptual information being demonstrated, and then the labels, the language concepts, are associated. Specific vocabulary covered. Curriculum for the at-risk child must be extended from vocabulary development to effective oral communication. Three-period lesson.
Written Language If presented, has mastered most of the letters and the basic sounds of the language. Usually can blend these sounds and decode. Often is beginning to read by age 5.	**Written Language** Inconsistency learning letter symbols and sounds. Variable performance with all written symbols activities, and has challenges in perceiving the patterns of words.	**Written Language** Presentations begin with the multi-sensory Sandpaper Letters with which the child can receive visual, auditory, kinesthetic & tactile information to increase the sound/symbol correspondence. Several activities presented after the Sandpaper Letters give repeated practice through varied materials in sound/symbol association. The Movable Alphabet provides the child with 3-dimensional letters that the child can manipulate to practice word building by using his sound/symbol knowledge. This activity gives the child a beginning reading activity at the word level before presenting the challenge of reading in a book. All activities reinforce the left to right progression of language. Reading, spelling, and writing proceed at the child's rate through a hierarchy of simple to complex word patterns.

Development of "Typical" Child	Development of a Child with Varying Exceptionalities	Montessori Strategies that Enhance Learning for a Child with Varying Exceptionalities
Attention Inhibition control begins to develop at 2 to 3 years of age. Focuses on activity presentation and concentrates. Works with activities for periods of 10 minutes or longer.	**Attention** Attention deficits may be present. Behavior often noted as hyperactive, hypoactive, or distractible. Inhibition control does not develop in a normal manner; therefore, focus and concentration are faulty.	**Attention** Prepared Environment: Organization of materials, areas prepared for children's use. Classroom Atmosphere: Ordered calm. Order in Presentation: Assists focus, child waits for completion. Silence Game: Teaches inner calm, concentration, and focus. Classroom Structure: Clear limits/freedoms, teacher accepts role to help children develop inhibition techniques, and central focus.
Perception Matches and discriminates sensory information. Perceives patterns in shape, color, numbers.	**Perception** Matching is usually within normal limits. Challenge with discrimination of sensory information noted. Discrimination/memory difficulties in math or letter symbols frequently seen. Often difficulties with association of symbol to name.	**Perception** Through the Sensorial curriculum, the teacher can assess the child's ability to perceive, discriminate, and gradate visual, auditory, tactile, olfactory, and gustatory information. These sensorial discriminations and the associated language concepts are significant in the progression to higher cognitive functions such as categorizing, generalizing, and the beginning of reasoning. All areas of the curriculum utilize VAKT to assist the child in perceptual discrimination & memory required in language and math.

Development of "Typical" Child	Development of a Child with Varying Exceptionalities	Montessori Strategies that Enhance Learning for a Child with Varying Exceptionalities
Organization Order and sequence learned by imitation.	**Organization** Has challenges in ordering work tasks and working in sequential way.	**Organization** All activities have specific sequence. The teacher helps the child refine work habits which helps the child gain the skills of analysis necessary for organization.
Work Cycle Chooses one activity after another varying the challenge of choices.	**Work Cycle** Does not establish a true work cycle without teacher support.	**Work Cycle** The teacher can enhance the work cycle by teaching the child how to make choices, set up the work, choose areas appropriate for work, complete an activity, and return the activity to its location.
Work Choices Chooses variety of work, usually proceeding to more difficult concepts.	**Work Choices** Chooses simple work that has been mastered, avoids work that is perceived as "harder." Avoids letters and/or numbers, avoids written work, needs teacher guidance for choices.	**Work Choices** Procedures allow the teacher to guide the child in learning to choose their work. A teacher may allow choice, limit choices, or make choices for the child until the child can do this task independently.
Work Habits Chooses work, uses procedure with purpose, replaces the work on the shelf.	**Work Habits** Avoids work, often insecure due to lack of successful learning experiences. When chooses, often replaces the work without using it or leaves work and wanders the room.	**Work Habits** The structure of the classroom and the procedures for working with the activities foster organized work habits.

Development of "Typical" Child	Development of a Child with Varying Exceptionalities	Montessori Strategies that Enhance Learning for a Child with Varying Exceptionalities
Math Gains number to quantity concepts, math symbols, math concepts, and beginning computation by age 5.	**Math** Variable performance on number to quantity concepts, longer work time for mastery, erratic performance on symbol/numeral association, math concepts often superior to computation, challenge with immediate recall of facts, challenge with patterns as seen in odd/even, writing to 100, skip counting, challenge with 1:1 correspondence.	**Math** Materials are manipulative and multisensory. Many number to quantity activities including Number Rods (1-10), Spindle Box (concept of 0), Tile Game (1-10 odd/even). Teen Boards and Tens Boards allow for language of teen numbers & tens numbers to be introduced by number to quantity. Introduction of the decimal system (language of number to quantity 1, 10 , 100, 1000) provide child repetitions of building various quantities from 1-9,000 with the golden beads & matching the numerals. Addition, multiplication, subtraction, and division introduced with golden beads. Writing of numerals introduced with Sandpaper Numerals. Skip counting introduced with the manipulative bead chains. Functions practiced with additional multisensory materials: addition strip board, subtraction strip board, multiplication board, division board.
Cooperative Behavior Usually has gained inhibition control by age 5 which enables cooperation with peers and teachers. Given encouragement enjoys the acceptance of responsibility and independence. Follows a model of consideration of others.	**Cooperative Behavior** May not have neurological maturation that enables inhibition control. May lack self-control. Needs direct instruction in inhibition, how to accept responsibility, how to persevere, and how to act in a considerate manner.	**Cooperative Behavior** A classroom teacher must accept their role as explicitly teaching appropriate behavior and social skills, and guide the child towards inhibition of impulsive behavior, as well as self-control, acceptance of responsibility, perseverance, and consideration of others.

Montessori Practical Life and Additional Supports for Early Childhood

Montessori Practical Life activities help young children enhance attention and develop motor skills. While doing Practical Life activities, children must coordinate their hands and eyes while focusing on a task. For all children, developing hand-eye coordination, focusing on a work task, and lengthening attention span are important, but for children with varying exceptionalities, many hours of practice are needed and this work is critical.

A child with more severe challenges may need a limited activity adapted to their level—for example, a pouring activity limited to three large beans poured from one small pitcher to another of equal size. An additional assist is placing a red circle in the bottom of each cup, giving children a place to aim. The pouring activities may slowly increase in difficulty as children progress. Students with varying exceptionalities benefit from practicing these activities for very long periods of time.

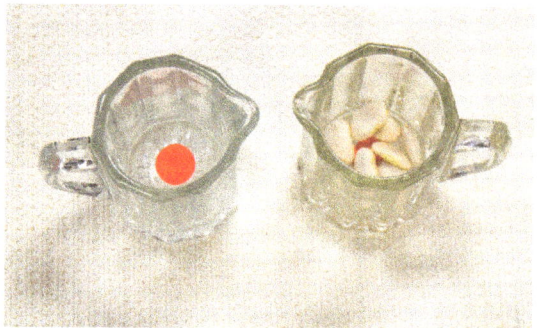

Figure 4.1 Pouring with Red Dot for Aiming

Figure 4.2 Pouring Liquid

Montessori Practical Life and Additional Supports for Elementary and Adolescents

Children can continue practicing Practical Life skills in elementary and middle school with science experiments, projects, and cooking. Continuing these activities also allows the interspersing of more demanding academic activities with less demanding and tiring tasks, while keeping children involved productively.

Consider the following activities for children based on their age and appropriateness:

- Food preparation
- Cleaning and maintaining the classroom
    — washing and polishing items and furniture
- Polishing (silver, copper, brass, pewter)
- Packing a suitcase
- Organizing a locker, notebook, folder
- Making models (aircraft, ships)
- Sanding a table
- Changing a tire
- Manicuring
- Gardening
- Presenting Practical Life activities to younger children

Some activities are the same as in the early childhood classrooms, but are presented at a higher level of difficulty as a chance to further refine a skill. In some cases, a child may come to a Montessori school after age 6, and may not have had the benefit of previous Montessori Practical Life experience. Attention to detail and careful completion of work is still necessary at this level. If an Elementary teacher feels these works are inappropriate for the children, so will the children. However, if the teacher believes the essence of the work ethic and pride in all tasks done well is introduced through Practical Life activities, then the older children's attitude will usually mirror the teacher's and they will often perform tasks such as pouring activities.

Continuation of the Practical Life activities over a longer time period provides an opportunity to master hand-eye coordination, fine motor skills, order and sequence, and improve sustained attention. All of these skills are critical for success in academic work. Children should practice Practical Life activities in every Montessori classroom, regardless of their age.

Montessori Sensorial Curriculum and Additional Supports

The Sensorial curriculum helps children learn to classify and categorize their world through their five senses. This curriculum is unique in education. Sensorial materials are auto-educational and can make education possible for children across a wide spectrum of learning abilities. Most preschool programs assume children will automatically develop abilities to perceive differences, discriminate, and classify. The Montessori method offers a curriculum for assessing these abilities, addressing areas of importance, and giving informed lessons to children.

Children with varying exceptionalities may have dysfunctional perceptual discrimination, and without accurate discrimination ability, they may be unable to categorize and classify. The Montessori Sensorial curriculum can help children with varying exceptionalities improve their perceptual discrimination, so they are better prepared to move toward reasoning skills.

With direct instruction children, with varying exceptionalities can manipulate and feel the contrasts and sensations of the unique, specially-designed Sensorial materials and expand their vocabulary; they can become more sensitive to the impressions of the environment, and can learn to distinguish, categorize, and relate new information to what they already know—this is cognitive development.

At all ages, Sensorial work is beneficial and can offer amelioration to children. A child who enters a Montessori program during the elementary years and who has not had the advantage of early childhood Montessori, can benefit from Montessori's early childhood methods adapted with additional supports; this can close developmental gaps and be therapeutically crucial.

Preschool-age children with varying exceptionalities process sensorial information differently and have challenges attaching language to their perceptions. The Montessori Sensorial curriculum offers teachers a way to observe the development of perceptual skills and the development of language defining those perceptions. The Sensorial curriculum is used to diagnose processing or perceptual delays and lessons with Sensorial materials are a way to remediate children whose development is not proceeding typically.

Montessori teachers have a rigorous understanding of child development and the materials and methods to help at-risk children to progress from delayed development to more age-appropriate development, and can work successfully with children with learning and attention differences. To do this, Montessorians need to be aware of the following additional support techniques (Pickering, 1976):

- Break presentations into even smaller steps (for example, use three pink cubes (the largest, smallest, and a mid-size) to illustrate the concept of size gradation if necessary, then move to five and then ten at a rate at which the child has success).

- Encourage the child to feel the material as well as look at it. For example, feeling each cube carefully to get a sense of the size and deciding which cube goes next can help facilitate learning through more than one sense, which is more important for children with varying exceptionalities.

- Reduce the difficulty of the task (for example, use three color tablets for shading: darkest, middle, and lightest until the child grasps the concept, then add more shades).

Figure 4.3 Color Shading Control Chart

- Make control charts to assist children with spatial perception challenges (for example, make a control chart to build the red rods on until the child perceives the gradation task, and then, as the child becomes successful, challenge them to remove the chart).

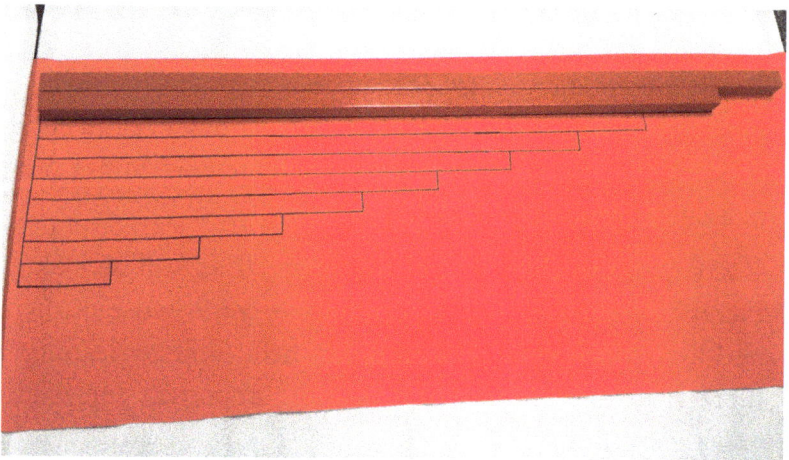

Figure 4.4 Red Rods Control Chart

- Analyze through your observations:
  - Why is the child having challenges?
  - What can I do to structure this activity for success?
- The key to teaching children, especially children with varying exceptionalities, is to structure every presentation for success, so they will keep trying.
- Attach further language to every presentation after the child has mastered the perceptual task (for example, using the three-period lesson to introduce and practice all the language of the Sensorial curriculum). Children will acquire greater vocabulary.
- Continue Sensorial work in the upper elementary grades and beyond. Children who have varying exceptionalities need exposure to these activities for a much longer time frame. To ease a Montessori teacher's burden, older children can give lessons to younger children with varying exceptionalities.

Chapter 4

- Any and all Montessori Sensorial activities may be adapted for older children.
- To develop perceptual discrimination ability, and to help familiarize children with pencils and paper, children with varying exceptionalities can work with three-dimensional multisensory materials, take that work to a two-dimensional level, and then to a paper and pencil level. This as an additional way to encourage children who might otherwise avoid written work activities. (Figures 4.5 and 4.6.)

Figure 4.5 Pink Tower Three Dimensional to Two

Figure 4.6 Transfer to Paper—Large, Small

Whether through Practical Life or Sensorial work, when children, interact with self-corrective materials they learn mistakes are not bad, but are the way we learn. In the spirit of investigation, the teacher reinforces this concept as well, and engages the child in dialogue:

- "How do you think you can do it?"
- "Try it."
- "It's okay if it's wrong, then you can try it another way."
- "If we can't figure it out today, maybe we can tomorrow."

This experience minimizes children's negative reaction to something they try and cannot do. Frustration, anger, giving up, rushing through, cheating, or avoiding a difficult task need not occur when the child is given direct instruction.

Montessori Mathematics and Additional Supports

The Sensorial materials are a prerequisite to mathematics. The child learns to discriminate greater than and less than through varying size dimensions in the Sensorial curriculum before beginning to deal with the more abstract concept of relative quantities represented by numbers. This preparation benefits children with varying exceptionalities.

Children with varying exceptionalities often have weaknesses in abstract reasoning and need longer one-to-one lessons in math. For children with varying exceptionalities, the use of three-dimensional models demonstrates patterns and functions in mathematics. The two most critical components of learning math are visual-spatial ability and the language of math (Krasa & Shunkwiler, 2009). Children with challenges in math may have different visual spatial perception and will understand math more clearly by working with these three-dimensional models as well.

For detailed math presentations for the child with learning differences see the MACAR math manual, listed in the Appendix.

Conclusion

Using traditional Montessori practices, as well as additional strategies based on an understanding of children's special needs, teachers can deliver strategic instruction to help children achieve their potential. By providing additional support, children with varying exceptionalities can experience the benefits that Montessori education offers.

Children who struggle with motor coordination, oral language development, reading and spelling, and the maintenance of attention often develop anxiety about school. One of the most significant advantages of the Montessori method is that when children with special needs interact with self-corrective materials, they learn that mistakes are not bad; rather, mistakes are the way we learn.

The major motivation for learning is success. Using the Montessori method, small levels of task difficulty can be matched to the child's ability level. Therefore, presentations can be structured for success, eliminating emotional problems such as hostility, bullying, bossiness, and/or withdrawal. Experiencing success can be the difference between a child growing into a person with inadequate school performance and damaged self-esteem, or a person who is productive, coping well, and contributing to society.

"Language lies at the root of that transformation of the environment we call civilization."

(Montessori, 1949/1995, p. 108)

Chapter 5

Montessori Applied to Communication Disorders, Including Speech & Oral Language

Joyce S. Pickering, with contributions from Sylvia O. Richardson and Amy Kelton

This chapter provides teachers with information about speech and oral language development. With this knowledge, the educator can prepare to better serve children with language learning differences and begin to implement basic remedial strategies of instruction. In addition, many children who are learning a second language benefit from additional language instruction with the same strategies.

Maria Montessori based her methods firmly on language pedagogy, scientific, and medical understanding. She described children's ability to absorb language effortlessly, until around age 6, as the "absorbent mind." It is one of her most enduring and noteworthy theories. Language learning is an essential part of her early childhood program.

To understand how children develop language, it is helpful to understand two developmental milestones from a speech-language perspective.

- By age 2, "typically" developing children can produce expressive language through speech.
- At age 5 or 6, "typically" developing children acquire a basic mastery of their mother language and are able to produce clearly articulated speech. They are not as able to learn language effortlessly and can no longer simply absorb language from their environment.

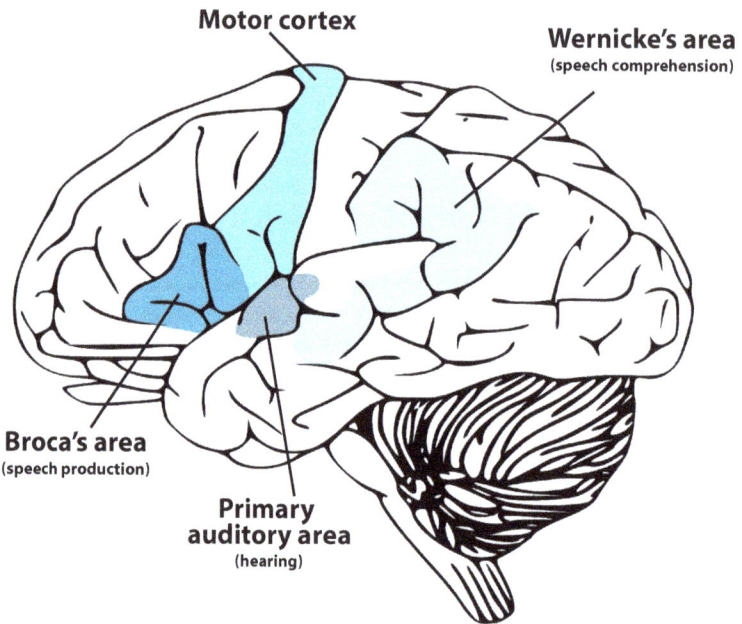

Figure 5.1 Graphic of the Brain Areas for Language

Speech and Oral Language

Speech and language are two different abilities. Speech is the ability to use the speech musculature to produce words, phrases, and sentences. Oral language is the ability to give meaning to words (receptive language) and to express oneself with words (expressive language). Speech and language, however, are highly related. Speech is determined by development of the human brain areas that allow for retrieval of words and the motor ability to express oneself; oral language is a system that includes the development of the brain that brings meaning to the words and associates those words with people, objects, and ideas.

Speech and oral language are the foundation for written language, and difficulty articulating spoken language is an indication that a child may be at risk for dyslexia or other difficulties with written language.

Speech and Oral Language Development

According to Dr. Montessori:

> To follow a child in his language development is a study of the greatest interest, and all those who have devoted themselves to it agree that the use of words, of names—the first elements of language—falls at a fixed period in the child's life, as if a precise time keeper were superintending his activity. (Montessori, 1949/1995 p. 6)

Even in the womb, children hear language. During the first year of life, children are absorbing language as they are exposed to language in their environment. Speech begins to develop for "typically" developing and hearing children over the first year of life.

Between birth and 3 months, children hear language, but they only cry and coo to communicate. Infants coo soft sounds, almost as if by accident, as they discover they can make sound. For parents or caregivers, a baby's unique cry is noticeably different than cooing and can mean several things depending upon the circumstance: for instance, is the baby overtired, in pain, or uncomfortable because of a dirty diaper?

Between 3 and 6 months, children begin to babble. At first many sounds, including sounds that may not be present in the baby's mother language, may be heard during babbling; however, toward the end of this period, the sounds of the child's mother language are increasingly present. Babblings are not words, but a way for children to exercise their speech musculature in an attempt to reproduce their auditory perception of sounds.

By 6 to 9 months, children can echo sounds they hear from others. This period is called echolalia. As children with accurate perception attain control of their speech musculature, they repeat what they hear (for example, when a child hears a parent saying "ba-ba-ba," they repeat it).

Between 9 and 12 months, children are internalizing their receptive language and begin to understand the meaning of the words they hear. For example, if Mom says, "Let's go bye-bye," the child looks at the keys or moves toward the door. Receptive language is developed before children can produce words and communicate with expressive language.

At 12 months, "typical" children make various vowel sounds, various consonant and vowel combinations, speak their first words, and show evidence of social-skill reciprocity by looking at and responding to the person with whom they are speaking. Most children say their first meaningful word by 12 months, although some speak earlier and some speak later. If children have not produced speech by 18 months to 2 years, their speech is considered delayed.

At age 2, most children are communicating with expressive language. This is a milestone. Children can ask for items by name, answer "What's that?" by using accurate and basic vocabulary to indicate objects, and describe objects or experiences with combinations of two or three words, such as "more juice." Most children at this age still have some articulation errors.

At age 3, a child can ask questions, answer questions with prepositional phrases like "Where is it?", and speak with functional sentences that carry meaning: for example, "me go store" or "me hungry now." As their auditory perception develops, children begin to self-correct articulation errors.

At age 4, children can respond to questions like, "Which one do you want?" and "What do you do when you are hungry?" with clear and specific answers. They can speak in grammatically correct sentences like, "Go to the store" and "I want a big cookie." The child can also answer questions about functions: for example, "What are books for?" … "Books are for reading." Articulation becomes more accurate for most children.

Most preschool children have some articulation distortions, substitutions, omissions, or additions of sounds in words (wed/red, balantine/valentine, thun/sun). Most children self-correct these errors by age 4 or 5. At age 5, children ask "how" questions, answer verbally to "Hi" and "How are you?", and can speak about something using past and future tense. Children can also use conjunctions to string words together: for example, "I have a cat and a dog and a bed." Children continue to improve their articulation accuracy. Around ages 5 or 6, another milestone is achieved. By this age, "typical" children have acquired a basic mastery of their mother language, have acquired basic grammatical structures including plurals, verb tenses, and conjunctions, and are able to produce clearly articulated speech.

If children are not discriminating between sounds and not perceiving the location of sounds in words they hear, articulation errors will remain. These errors most likely indicate phonological awareness dysfunctions. Because older children are not able to learn language as effortlessly as when they were younger, they may not be able to self-correct errors and will likely not "outgrow" their condition. They may need therapy to improve their speech.

Following the typical acquisition of these abilities, children communicate using increasingly complex descriptions in conversations, and for those with typical language skills, speech sounds are articulated with increasing accuracy. In social interactions, children begin to recognize nonverbal and verbal information (pragmatics of language) and continue to develop effective communication through their elementary, middle, and high school years.

Speech and language are separate yet related abilities. For "typically" developing children, speech develops effortlessly. "Typical" children absorb language from their environment and produce language along a developmental path achieving two significant milestones along the way. The first milestone is using speech to communicate expressively by age 2. The second is at age 5 or 6, when language development reaches a pinnacle, after which children are no longer able to learn language as effortlessly.

Human beings are the only species to possess the unique ability of spoken language, and there is no clear limit to our potential to express ideas in meaningful ways. Language is an extraordinary ability. Written language allows human beings to record and gain vast knowledge in an efficient manner. Reading and writing are requirements for education. Oral language is the foundation for reading and writing. For children with oral language delays or disorders, the risk of written language disorders, like dyslexia, are significant. Early intervention should begin with oral language development.

Reasons for Speech-Language Delays

Reasons for speech and language delays include: hearing impairments, chronic ear infections, oral language disorder (aphasia/dysphasia), apraxia of speech, speech dysfluencies, multiple language acquisition, and lack of exposure to language.

Because of deficits in hearing acuity, children with **hearing impairments** lack exposure to language. The earlier these deficits are recognized, the sooner treatment can begin. Whether treatment is hearing aids and therapy or cochlear implants and therapy depends on the severity of the impairment. With treatment, children with hearing impairments at all levels can learn to communicate with spoken words.

Chronic ear infections can result in mild to moderate hearing loss. Children with chronic ear infections may not receive exposure to language and may not develop the capacity to discriminate the sounds of human speech.

A body of research suggests that ear infections can have a negative effect on language, speech, and academic development (Birsh, 2011, pp. 48–49). Common treatments are prescriptive antibiotics to eliminate any infection or surgical insertion of tubes to drain and prevent fluid blocks. The nature of hearing loss as a result of ear infections can be evasive. Because this type of hearing loss is often unrecognized by adults, consultation with an ear, nose, and throat physician (ENT) and audiologist is highly recommended to garner a thorough evaluation of hearing and discrimination capacity.

Children with **aphasia** or **dysphasia** can hear words but cannot bring meaning to what they are hearing. The association of meaning to words is perceived by the brain in the Wernicke's area, an area which processes spoken language. To learn spoken and written language, children with dysphasia or aphasia need specific therapy, such as the DuBard Association Method.

Children with **childhood apraxia of speech** understand what is said to them, yet do not make progress in expressive language because they cannot coordinate the speech musculature to make specific sounds and words. These children benefit from early and intensive intervention with a speech-language pathologist (SLP).

Some children with severe hoarseness must be referred to an ENT for assessment of vocal nodules on the vocal chords.

Other speech difficulties in young children include **speech dysfluencies**. These are characterized by repetitions of sounds in words, like "b-b-baby." This is often believed by teachers to be stuttering. At a young age of 2 or 3, however, dysfluencies are common. Children are learning to talk and communicate and may hesitate on words and repeat sounds. When hesitations become a speech block, in which a child has tension in their speech musculature and cannot produce a word until it seems to explode out of their mouth, then the child has moved to the level of stuttering, and an SLP should be consulted.

In the authors' experience, children who learn two or more languages in their preschool years have the advantage of being bilingual, but they may acquire each language more slowly than monolingual children. Generally, if children learn multiple languages before age 3, they absorb those languages more easily than older children. After their mother language is established around age 3, children will learn additional languages more slowly.

Some children can learn two languages very well, but sometimes they know one language better than the other. The language a child knows better is called the dominant language. Over time, the dominant language may change, especially if a child does not use one of the languages regularly. Speaking two languages is like any other skill. To do it well, children need lots of practice. Without practice, it may be difficult for children to understand or talk to people in both languages (ASHA, 2015). Children learning two languages benefit from many multisensory structured language (MSL) learning techniques.

In extreme conditions, children who lack exposure to language will have delays in language or may not develop language ability at all.

Characteristics and Frequency of Occurrence of Oral Language Disorders

Most children self-correct speech errors by age 4 or 5. Those who continue to make articulation errors, or have many sound omissions or substitutions, have a speech disorder. Speech disorders include phonological disorders that are characterized by problems in making accurate sound production (dat/that). These difficulties are often called articulation disorders (APA, 2013). In their attempts at spoken communication, children with speech/articulation disorders can be difficult to understand, which can be very frustrating for them. They may exhibit withdrawal from speaking, as well as behaviors such as growling, crying, and even hitting.

Stuttering, another speech disorder, is characterized by a break in fluency, where sounds, syllables, or words may be prolonged or repeated (APA, 2013). Stuttering is diagnosed when the speaker has prolonged blocks on words with tension seen in the lips and jaws. Preschool children may have periods of dysfluency (breaks in fluency) while their speech skills are developing. These repetitions are not considered stuttering, and often disappear with maturity.

Expressive language disorders are characterized by a limited vocabulary and difficulty expressing oneself beyond simple sentences. The individuals with this difficulty understand what is said to them but are unable to organize and retrieve words and get their ideas across at a level expected for their developmental stage.

Mixed receptive-expressive disorders are characterized by difficulty comprehending the speech of others, as well as difficulty with oral communication (APA, 2013).

The National Institute on Deafness and Other Communication Disorders (NIDCD) has reported that in the United States, there are 7.5 million people with a voice disorder, 3 million with a stuttering disorder, and 6–8 million with a language disorder. The NIDCD also estimates that 5.95% of the national population is Severely Language Impaired (SLI), 8–9% of preschool children in America have speech disorders, and by first grade that figure only drops to 5% (nidcd.nih.gov).

Modern assessment can reveal a child's unique "learning profile," which can inform strategic classroom instruction and guide therapeutic remediation. See Chapter 10 for information about assessment.

The Three-Period Lesson and Language Learning

During children's first year of life, they develop an understanding of language that is not yet ready for expression. When children begin attaching words to perceptions, their "inner language" becomes expressive language. Around age 1, most children begin to define and express their perceptions and then express those perceptions as concepts; they begin speaking. Edouard Seguin recognized this development and created the three-period lesson, which eventually became a critical part of Montessori education (Seguin, 1907).

The three-period lesson offers teachers a way to observe children's perceptual development as well as their ability to attach language to their perceptions. The three-period lesson also allows children to expand their vocabulary and expressive abilities and become ever more precise in their communication. Any teacher can use the simple and effective three-period lesson. First, present a lesson silently, with slow hand movements, so children can perceive and focus on the presentation. Then use a three-period lesson to attach the relevant vocabulary so that children can formulate the concept. To expand children's learning in subsequent lessons, more vocabulary words that refer to the attributes of the materials can be attached to the concepts.

The three periods are: *identity-recognition-recall*. Children may work through all three periods during one presentation or children may work through only one or two.

- In the *identity* stage, the teacher verbally labels (names) the object.
- At the *recognition* stage, receptive language is assessed (does the child know the object, if the teacher names it?).
- At the *recall* stage, the teacher gauges the child's expressive language (can the child remember the name and repeat it?).

For example, during a presentation of the Pink Tower, a teacher silently and slowly demonstrates the precise movements that are required to build the tower in gradation, from the largest cube to the smallest. The teacher then takes the tower down, places the cubes in random order on the work rug, and says to the child, "Now it's your turn." The teacher observes how the child performs what was demonstrated. Do they perceive the gradation? Can the child build it in gradation or partial gradation? The teacher notes the child's ability to perceive size, and either determines that the child needs additional presentations to develop the concepts, or proceeds with attaching language to the percept so a language concept can be formed. Then the teacher places all cubes, except the largest and smallest, to the side and the three-period lesson begins.

Figure 5.2 Pink Tower Built Horizontally

Three-Period Lesson

- **First Period: Labeling (identity)**
  The teacher points to the largest cube.
  – "This is big."
  The teacher points to the smallest cube.
  – "This is little."

- **Second Period: Receptive Language (recognition)**
  – "Show me little."
  The teacher waits until the child has pointed to one of the cubes.
  – "Show me big."
  The teacher waits until the child has pointed to one of the cubes.

- **Third Period: Expressive Language (recall)**
  – "What is this?"
  The teacher points to one of the cubes.

If the child understands, the child indicates verbally if it is big or little. If the child does not answer, or if the child's answer is inaccurate, the teacher does not correct the child or indicate the child has made a mistake. Instead the teacher either returns to the first period or notes what to review in another lesson on another day. The beginning language attached to the concept (big/little) can be expanded to secondary language (large/small) and to the comparatives and superlatives (larger, smaller/largest, smallest).

For younger children or children with learning differences, a simple response such as "little" in the third period, is appropriate. As children develop language, they will usually begin to reproduce complete sentences, such as "This is little." As children develop and explore increasingly complex materials, the language in presentations and three-period lessons can progress to more complex sentences.

For example, during the initial presentation of a puzzle map, the teacher removes each differently colored continent one by one, and then places them back into the map frame one at a time. The teacher asks the child, "Would you like a turn?" The teacher observes the children's hand-eye coordination as they remove and refit the pieces back into the puzzle frame. The teacher observes if this is done through visual perception or by tactile perception (by feeling around the edges of the puzzle). If the child completes the puzzle, the teacher moves on to the three-period lesson, using two continents.

- "This is North America." ... "This is South America."
- "Show me South America." ... "Show me North America."
- "What is this?" ... "What is this?"

The goal is for the child to answer in a complete sentence: "This is North America" and "This is South America." If the child answers correctly, but with just the names of the continents, not in a sentence form, the teacher says, "Yes, you are right," and then repeats the complete sentence, "This is North America." .... "This is South America."

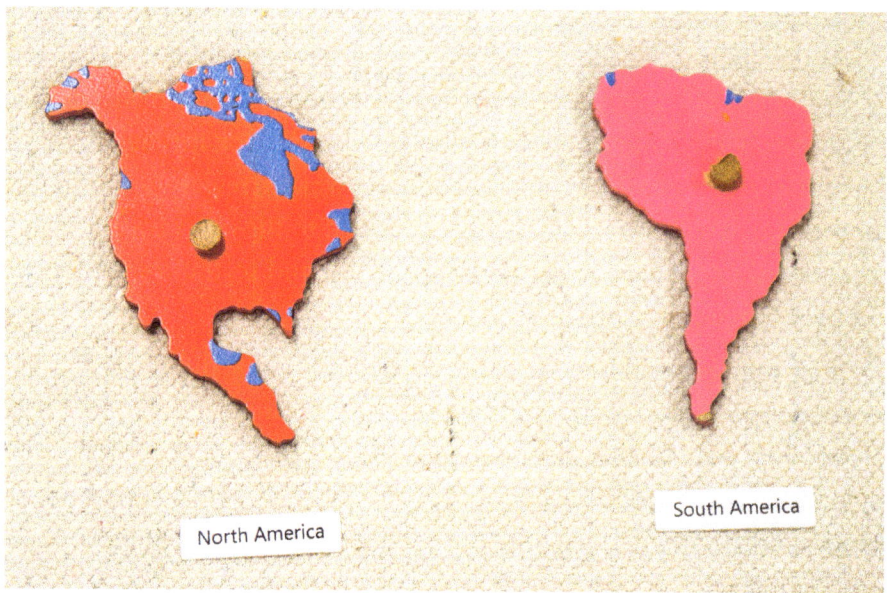

Figure 5.3 North and South America—Three-Period Lesson

If the child remembers the names of the continents and is able to repeat the complete sentences, the teacher can present a three-period lesson with two other continents. If the child does not remember the names of the continents first introduced, the teacher returns to the first period of the lesson and repeats, "This is North America" … "This is South America." The teacher may return to the first period immediately, or take note to present this lesson again another day. In this way, the teacher follows the child's development.

Each activity in each area of the Montessori curriculum stresses sensory input, leads to comprehension of multisensory information, and results in a perception. Attaching language to the perception during three-period lessons defines the child's perceptions and helps children develop concepts. For more information about Montessori Sensorial work and additional supports for children with perceptual discrimination challenges, see Chapter 4, pages 84–88.

Presentations with Montessori multisensory materials allow teachers to offer strategic, remedial instruction and match each child's work to their developmental level. Montessori methods can reveal whether a child's perceptual and oral language skills are typical or below expectation. The Montessori materials and the three-period lesson are ideal for remediating students with language learning differences. For each child, the three periods may vary in length; some children move through all three periods immediately, while others may work longer in each period.

The Three-Period Lesson and Additional Therapeutic Strategies

For children with learning differences, the three-period lesson can offer significant opportunities for oral language development. In addition, the three-period lesson allows a teacher to observe and make an informal assessment of a child's perception and language ability, and then to present remedial lessons. Using the three-period lesson to label (name) a perception, gauge receptive language ability, and then observe a child's ability to reproduce expressions, allows a teacher to guide language development.

Especially for children with more severe language learning differences, it can help if everything a teacher says during a three-period lesson is also referenced in writing on a notecard. (The teacher says, "This is…" and points to the words on the notecard while speaking.) This helps the child understand that there are separate and distinct words in the flow of the auditory information they are hearing.

In the Montessori curriculum, grammar is modeled by the teacher's speech. Moving from simple vocabulary to sentence form benefits all children, but offers children with language learning differences incredible developmental opportunities.

Montessori teachers should be aware that at any age, children with learning differences may have underlying oral language weaknesses. To help a child with language learning differences increase their vocabulary, a teacher can name all the bits and pieces in a presentation and then ask the child for the attributes and functions of each. For example, in a pouring activity, after the first presentation, a teacher can name the objects on the tray: pitcher, cup, sponge, etc. Then the items can be described by their attributes: color, size, shape, texture, weight, etc. When the pouring activity is being presented and the child is exploring and improving this skill, the teacher may sit with the child and discuss the attributes:

- This is a pitcher. What is this object?
- This pitcher is blue. What color is the pitcher?
- This pitcher is small. What size is the pitcher?
- You pour from a pitcher. What do you do with a pitcher?

For each activity in each area of the curriculum, strategies for expanding vocabulary can be implemented. Children with language learning differences may need a significant number of additional presentations. They will benefit when a teacher or therapist guides them through as many hours of direct instruction as needed.

Generally, the teacher should:

- Give the student the label (name) of the activity/object.

- Have the student repeat it.

- Give the child labels (names) for various attributes of the objects (color, size, texture, etc.). Ask the child questions about an object that describe the object (color, size, texture, etc.).

- Describe a function of the object. "This is what you do with a ___." Ask the child the function of the object: "What do you do with a ___?"

Additional Vocabulary and Expression Support

Children between birth and age 6 are in a sensitive period for language acquisition. During this sensitive period, children with language learning differences benefit from as much exposure to language and as many opportunities to develop vocabulary as possible. From 18 months to age 3 is a particularly critical time for the development of language.

It must be recognized that children with language learning differences come to preschool lacking the characteristic oral language development of "typical" 3-year-olds. Their language development is different, and their vocabulary may be nominal. Additional oral language support is important.

In addition to the vocabulary development built into the Montessori curriculum, providing children with additional oral language development opportunities benefits children with learning differences. There are many activities that are appropriate in a Montessori environment that work well for children with language learning differences and can help them fill in vocabulary gaps.

Alice Feltus and I created an oral language development curriculum to provide additional support and to help children expand their expressive ability, vocabulary, and word knowledge. In our activities, teachers present word games and pictures. These activities can blend seamlessly with the Montessori curriculum. For more information about this oral language development program, see the Appendix.

Our oral language development curriculum includes the following subjects:
- Body
- Family
- Clothing
- House
- Community
- World Regions
- Animals
- Plants
- Foods

Strategic Teaching and Partnership

The greatest warning signs of dyslexia and other language learning differences are evident in children's speech and language development. Warning signs for other exceptionalities and developmental disabilities may be evident in children's speech and language development as well.

Before assessment and remediation, Montessori teachers are in the unique position to offer basic strategic teaching if speech-language delays and other signs of language learning differences are present. Teachers can add additional oral language development material to their classroom and can offer strategic instruction through partnership with therapists.

Children with articulation errors need an accurate model. Children benefit when teachers articulate sounds accurately, articulate words clearly, and ensure that their production of the final sound of each word is articulated rather than dropped. For example, production of unvoiced sounds like /t/ at the end of words should be emphasized and clearly articulated. Montessori teachers strive to model precise language to children. By partnering with a speech-language pathologist to instruct for the remediation of sound errors in a child's speech, teachers can help children with language learning differences "fill in" language gaps.

According to Dr. Montessori, children can learn to read and write almost effortlessly with her method (Montessori, 1912/1988). The joy and empowerment this brings can last a lifetime. Children diagnosed with dyslexia may not be able to access the benefits of Montessori written language learning, and therapeutic remediation may be essential. A teacher can complement that therapy by working with a therapist to coordinate developmentally appropriate lessons in their classroom.

In an ideal scenario, a student with dyslexia or any other language-learning difference will have an informed teacher and access to an academic language therapist and a speech-language pathologist. Remediation would begin as early as possible, and all parties would work together in partnership to offer the child as much chance for success as possible. In any scenario, an informed classroom teacher who offers strategic language instruction to a child will make a positive impact on that child's life and future.

Conclusion

Dr. Montessori was firm in her belief that early childhood education could make an enormous impact on the lives of all children, especially those between ages 3 and 6. She developed her method while working with very poor children and children with special needs. Paula Polk Lillard describes the impact of Dr. Montessori's method for this population:

> … with these children, where many steps usually taken for granted have been missed in earlier years, it can make the difference between the success and failure of a human life. (1972, p. 144)

For children with speech delays and speech disorders, early intervention with Montessori techniques and additional therapeutic strategies can make this difference.

"By reading I mean the interpretation of an idea by means of graphic symbols."

(Montessori, 1912/1997, p. 230)

Chapter 6

Montessori Applied to Written Language, Dyslexia & Related Disorders

Joyce S. Pickering, with contributions from Sylvia O. Richardson and Amy Kelton

This chapter highlights the definitions and characteristics of dyslexia and related learning differences and describes how a Multisensory Structured Language (MSL) approach can be combined with the Montessori curriculum to offer strategic teaching and remediation.

Dyslexia and Related Disorders

Dyslexia is the most common learning difference, and it simply means difficulty with reading and writing. In the *Diagnostic and Statistical Manual of Mental Disorders* (DSM-5), published by the American Psychiatric Association (APA), dyslexia is called Learning Disability in Reading (2013).

Attention-deficit/hyperactivity disorder (ADHD) is also a common learning difference, and is often a co-existing condition with dyslexia.

Educators are moving towards a more enlightened understanding of dyslexia, ADHD, and other learning differences. Still, many are confused or in disagreement about the rate of occurrence, reasons, and potential remedies for these challenges. With specific instruction and additional supports, children with learning differences can be highly creative, contributing members of society, but children who do not receive early childhood intervention may be at a disadvantage as adults. In some situations, educational challenges during childhood can even become mental health problems later in life.

Characteristics of Dyslexia

Individuals with dyslexia possess normal or above-average intellectual ability. They can be quite verbal and may do excellent oral work in school. Their main challenges are reading, decoding, spelling, and written expression. Their comprehension is usually better than their decoding accuracy.

Individuals with dyslexia may read and write at a slower rate because their processing speed is slower than the typical student and their visual and auditory processing deficiencies cause them to make errors while reading and writing. They also have challenges differentiating words that look similar, (then/there; party/pretty). Other characteristic errors include: omission of vowels in words (respt/respect), confusion of sounds (m/n; mam/man), and omission or addition of sounds or endings in words.

While writing, an individual with dyslexia may spell the same word three to five different ways in the space of two paragraphs, demonstrating variable processing of the sounds they perceive in words. They may read or write a word several times correctly, but then reverse, jumble, or omit letters in that same word, moments later on the same page. Fifteen to twenty percent of our national population struggles with dyslexia (Shaywitz, 2003).

Definition of Dyslexia

According to The International Dyslexia Association (IDA), dyslexia is:

> … a specific learning disability that is neurobiological in origin. It is characterized by difficulties with accurate and/or fluent word recognition and by poor spelling and decoding abilities. These difficulties typically result from a deficit in the phonological component of language that is often unexpected in relation to other cognitive abilities and the provision of effective classroom instruction. Secondary consequences may include problems in reading comprehension and reduced reading experience that can impede growth of vocabulary and background knowledge. (National Institute of Child Health and Human Development [NICHD], 2016)

This definition, also used by NICHD, was adopted by the IDA Board of Directors on November 12, 2002.

Neurophysiology and Anatomy of Dyslexia

Phonological awareness is the ability to discriminate one sound from another, as well as the ability to locate the position of each sound in a word. Individuals with dyslexia have impaired phonological awareness, have difficulty telling where sounds are located in words, and confuse words because they do not perceive sounds accurately.

Difficulty reproducing shapes with internal detail is evident in the way children and adults with dyslexia read and write. In the 1960s, my teacher Dr. Charles Shedd helped create a visual motor performance test, during which he showed Gestalt figures (simple geometric shapes with and without internal details) to test subjects with dyslexia. Children with dyslexia did not perceive internal details well. This research helped confirm what was, at the time, a groundbreaking discovery; children with dyslexia perceive words as a whole form or shape and struggle to reproduce and recognize the internal details of words. If a child perceives a word as a shape and does not perceive the internal detail, they will have difficulty with reading and writing and will decode inaccurately. (Shedd & Drake, 1967).

In tests of auditory perception, the inability to perceive discrete sounds within a word is evident as well. Children with dyslexia perceive speech as globs of sounds, and their attempts at reading and writing reflect their visual and auditory deficits.

In the 1990s, with the advent of functional magnetic resonance imaging (fMRI), it became possible to effectively perform brain imaging studies to observe the anatomy and brain function of people with dyslexia (Eden, 2003). Since then, researchers have confirmed that the dyslexic brain is anatomically and functionally different than the brain of the average reader.

> The brains of people with developmental dyslexia are different in subtle but distinct ways. Scientists have discovered gross anatomical differences

as well as cellular and connectional differences in autopsied brains. These structural differences correspond with functional differences found in neuroimaging studies. (Sherman & Cowen, 2003, pp. 9–13)

There are two noteworthy anatomical differences that distinguish brains of individuals with dyslexia from those who are "typical" readers. First, before the sixth month of gestation, cells migrate to the cortex on the left side of the dyslexic brain. These ectopia cells do not exist in typically developing brains. This cell migration is believed to be generated by a genetic code, which supports the hypothesis that dyslexia is genetic and inherited (Sherman & Cowen, 2003).

A second anatomical difference is in the planum temporale area of the brain. In "typical" readers, the left planum temporale area is larger than the right. In the brains of those with dyslexia, these areas are equal in size.

There are noteworthy functional differences that distinguish the neurophysiology of individuals with dyslexia. Sally and Bennett Shaywitz, working with a team at Yale, performed neurobiological and longitudinal epidemiological studies and identified the parts of the brain used in reading. Their research indicates that typical readers first learn to decode words by primarily using Broca's area of the brain. With repetition and practice, the "typical" reader begins using the parietal and occipital lobe as well. As word form recognition ability develops, the occipital lobe becomes the main area used when reading (Shaywitz, 2003).

Individuals with dyslexia primarily use Broca's area for word recognition and do not use the parietal or occipital lobes. This is a neurological signature of dyslexia (Shaywitz, 2003). Dyslexic errors are caused by neurological differences in the areas of the brain where symbols, letters, and sounds are processed and integrated.

A vast body of research indicates that people with dyslexia have different brain anatomy and functioning than people with typically developing brains. Dr. Jeff Gilger (2003, pp. 6–8) reports that dyslexia is familial, genetic, and inherited. Dyslexia is not caused by a family's lack of support or a child's lack of effort or level of maturity. Dyslexia runs in families because of nature, not nurture (DeFries & Alarcon, 1996; Smith, 2002).

Dyslexia, ADHD, and other learning differences are being identified much earlier than in the past. Children as young as age 5 can be assessed for these learning differences. Dyslexia and ADHD affect language development in a variety of ways, and individuals with dyslexia or ADHD may also have additional learning differences that can combine to affect learning as well. Therapeutic strategies have been developed, and early intervention and remediation can make a critical difference.

Other Related Disorders

The differences described below fall under the broader category of learning and communication disorders. Children with communication disorders may have a family history of the specific difference, though some are caused by injury or insult to the brain.

ADHD refers to a family of chronic neurobiological disorders that interfere with the capacity to attend to tasks, regulate activity, and inhibit behavior in ways appropriate to age and circumstance. The essential features of ADHD are inappropriate degrees of inattention, impulsiveness, and hyperactivity (APA, 2013). Increasingly ADHD is believed to affect executive functioning. There are three types of ADHD: Inattentive, Hyperactive/Impulsive, and Combined (APA, 2013).

Some children may have other communication disorders that can cause language and social skill challenges. When dyslexia, ADHD, and other learning differences occur in combination, learning can be affected in a variety of ways.

Children with **receptive language** disorders have difficulties in attending, processing, comprehending, retaining, or integrating spoken language. They process only part or none of what others speak (Hunt & Marshall, 2005).

Children with an **oral language** weakness or an oral language disorder such as **dysphasia** or **aphasia** are unable to bring meaning to spoken language. Children with this disorder do not easily comprehend the meaning of spoken words. They also display difficulty with reading comprehension and written expression, since both require language facility. Diminished communication skills may impact their social interactions.

Children with **expressive language** disorders struggle to speak or write, have limited vocabularies, and often repeat the same words and/or phrases in conversation (Hunt & Marshall, 2005). Children with expressive language disorders have difficulty expressing themselves beyond simple sentences. Individuals with this difference understand what is said to them, but are unable to organize and retrieve words, or to get their ideas across at a level expected for their developmental stage. Mixed receptive-expressive disorders occur as well, and include problems comprehending the speech of others and difficulty with oral communication (APA, 2013).

Speech disorders, phonological disorders, and articulation disorders are all characterized by problems in making accurate sound production. Stuttering, another speech disorder, is characterized by a break in fluency, where sounds, syllables or words may be prolonged or repeated (APA, 2013).

Children with **reading comprehension** difficulties have oral language weaknesses and struggle to bring meaning to reading.

Children with **dyscalculia** have challenges processing numeric symbols correctly, difficulty with number fact recall, and exhibit spatial misplacement of numbers in math equations. They also have challenges with language in the context of mathematics and may misprocess mathematical signs. Some may perform these math skills without challenge but may be unable to process math concepts within a normal range for their age and IQ.

With certain **written expression** weaknesses, children may face different challenges than those associated with dyslexia. Their intellectual ability may be brilliant, but their compositions may contain a free flow of ideas with no organization or sequencing, which can make it difficult for readers to understand their writing.

Children with **developmental coordination disorders** may have **dysgraphia**, i.e., the inability to use hands and fingers in precise movements. Dysgraphia affects fine motor development and handwriting. This is evident when children grasp writing instruments and utensils. Gross motor disorders may be evident when a child attempts rhythmic movements (marching to a musical beat) or alternating movements (walking up or down stairs, or skipping).

Maintaining balance on a balance board is a challenge for some children with developmental coordination disorders. Spatial judgment can also be challenging; for example, children with developmental coordination disorders may find it challenging to navigate through a room and not bump into other children or furniture.

Children with any of these disorders may also have social skills weaknesses. Students with oral language disorders face challenges communicating and, therefore, in expressing themselves to others. Children with ADHD are often impulsive and interrupt others, and may also have social skill weakness. They want friends and try to develop friendships, but some of these characteristics get in the way of making and keeping friends.

Children with nonverbal learning disorder (NVLD) have major challenges with social skills. NVLD is a neurophysiological disorder that impairs reception of nonverbal or performance-based information in varying degrees, due to difficulties with visual-spatial, intuitive, organizational, evaluative, and holistic processing functions. Nonverbal learning disabilities include difficulties in dealing with cause-and-effect relationships, a marked reliance on overdeveloped rote verbal capacities and memory skills during communication (which can bore others), as well as significant deficits in social perception, judgment, and interaction.

Children with NVLD can have difficulty identifying and expressing their feelings and may experience stress reactions in ordinary situations. They may struggle to read facial expressions and body language of other children and teachers. They may have difficulty making friends and getting along with others. They benefit from direct instruction in social skills.

An assessment will clearly indicate the developmental abilities of a child, can inform an appropriate program of therapeutic remediation, and may be the greatest assistance a person receives in life. Chapter 10 describes both informal and standardized speech-language assessments that can be performed by professionals.

Multisensory Structured Language (MSL) Learning and Sequences

A Multisensory Structured Language (MSL) approach in combination with Montessori methods can significantly help children with dyslexia and other learning differences. The MSL approach was first created by Dr. Samuel T. Orton, a neuroscientist, and Anna Gillingham, a psychologist, working with Bessie Stillman, an English teacher. The three worked together to create the Orton-Gillingham (OG) approach for the treatment and remediation of children with dyslexia. MSL methods, such as the original OG approach, teach reading and writing by "building letter sounds into words, like bricks into a wall" (Gillingham & Stillman, 1960, p. 40). In the MSL approach, children develop sound/symbol correspondence while working with VAKT senses.

The Montessori written language curriculum is a multisensory, sequential, explicit language approach. As children trace Sandpaper Letters and voice the sounds of the letters, sort small objects in Object/Sound Boxes for sound discrimination, and build words using the Movable Alphabet, they employ the visual, auditory, kinesthetic, and tactile (VAKT) senses. Lessons are presented in a sequential way, and children move through a sequential hierarchy of skills: from sound discrimination and sound/symbol correspondence, to word building, and then reading and writing. Children progress at their own individual rate.

When combined with the Montessori written language curriculum, an MSL approach supports remediation and strategic teaching of children with dyslexia. MSL programs have been used effectively for over 70 years.

Sequential English Education (SEE) is an MSL approach that I developed with colleagues over the course of my career. It blends seamlessly with the Montessori curriculum, and is known for offering written language remediation to children with characteristics of dyslexia who are as young as 5 years old. The SEE program uses word families to teach decoding and blending.

With any MSL approach, the structure and sequence of language presentations is crucial. The beginning sequence for teaching letters and sounds in SEE is:

a, t, p, h, c, n, l, b, f, s, g, m, j, v, r, d, i, k, w, wh, z, th (unvoiced) u, sh, e, th (voiced), y, ch, q, o, x

The reason for this sequence is so children can begin blending sounds to the /at/ word family to create words in a simple consonant-vowel-consonant (CVC) pattern. A CVC pattern can be perceived as two parts: a beginning sound and a word family sound. For example, the word cat is taught with the beginning sound /k/ and the word family /at/. For children who may have dyslexia, who do not perceive internal details in words, blending a beginning sound to a word family makes word blending easier.

Word families are introduced sequentially. Teachers first present beginning consonant sounds (*t, p, h, c, n,*) and all word families with the same short vowels (*at, ap, an*) to make words, such as *pat, hat, cat; tap, cap, nap; tan, pan, can*. Children should learn all the words with the /*at*/ word family before moving on to the /*ap*/ family and then the /*an*/ family, etc.

Teachers choose words that are regularly spelled, with each letter voicing its own sound. Children first master the word families with the short /*a*/ sound, (*at, ap, an, al, as, ag, am*) before moving on to different word families with other short vowel sounds. Word families with long vowel sounds are introduced later, after children master certain sequences and patterns with short vowels.

Throughout my career, I have offered remediation to countless children with dyslexia and other language learning differences. I have trained Montessori teachers to complement therapeutic remediation and to implement strategic MSL supports for children with dyslexia, and I have trained special educators to work with Montessori techniques in combination with MSL therapeutic remediation. Both methods are rooted in language pedagogy, child development theory, and medical understanding, which combine to produce best practices for children with dyslexia.

Montessori and Handwriting Preparation

In Montessori education, pre-writing skills are developed through Practical Life and Sensorial activities and prepare children's hands for writing. Working with the Metal Insets (metal frames and insets of various geometric shapes)

helps children develop the ability to manipulate and properly grip a pencil. In tracing the shapes and shading the internal part of the designs, children practice all essential movements of handwriting. Metal Inset work enhances fine motor skills.

To best help children with dysgraphia (the inability to use hands and fingers in precise movements to develop fine motor coordination), begin with the rectangular Metal Inset. Place the inset on a piece of paper and trace around the edges of the shape with a colored pencil. Choose a different color pencil for filling in the shape. Children who have challenges with hand-eye coordination should be encouraged to fill in the entire rectangle by using short pencil strokes, beginning at the top left, ending at the bottom left, and continuing top to bottom all the way across the shape, until it is completely colored. This activity gives children practice initiating and inhibiting a fine motor movement. It can take some children several days to fully shade the rectangle, but children can file this work in their folder and work on it for several days until it is complete.

Of all the insets, the rectangle is unique. The reason the rectangle is presented first is because the rectangle gives children practice making short, even strokes; all of the lines between the top and bottom are the same length. Children can move on to the other shapes as they progress and need more challenge. For the square, all lines are the same length, but the distance is greater. For the other shapes, such as the circle, the lines are shorter at the beginning of the work, then increase and decrease in length again. Shading those shapes requires greater fine motor skill control. The essence of writing is to make the pencil start where it should and move how it should. Metal Inset practice increases children's ability to coordinate the movements necessary for writing.

Children with learning differences benefit from additional work to develop fine motor skills and writing instrument control. In addition to the Montessori Metal Inset activities to refine their fine motor skills, children can use an eye dropper, spoon rice, pour beans, work with knobbed puzzle pieces, tear paper into strips, crumble paper with the dominant hand, cut snippets, do push-pin work, and cut on straight and curved lines.

Chapter 6

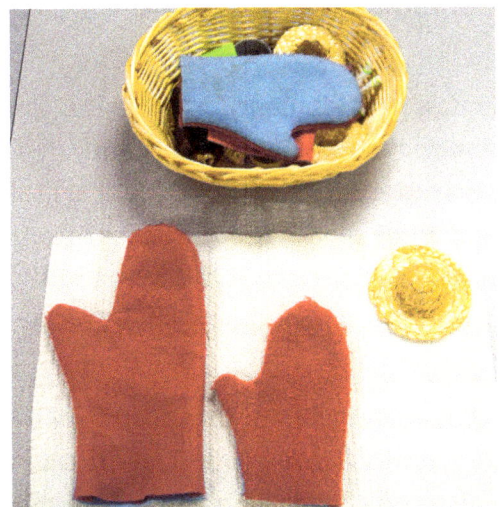

Figure 6.1   Patting Out Sounds with Mittens

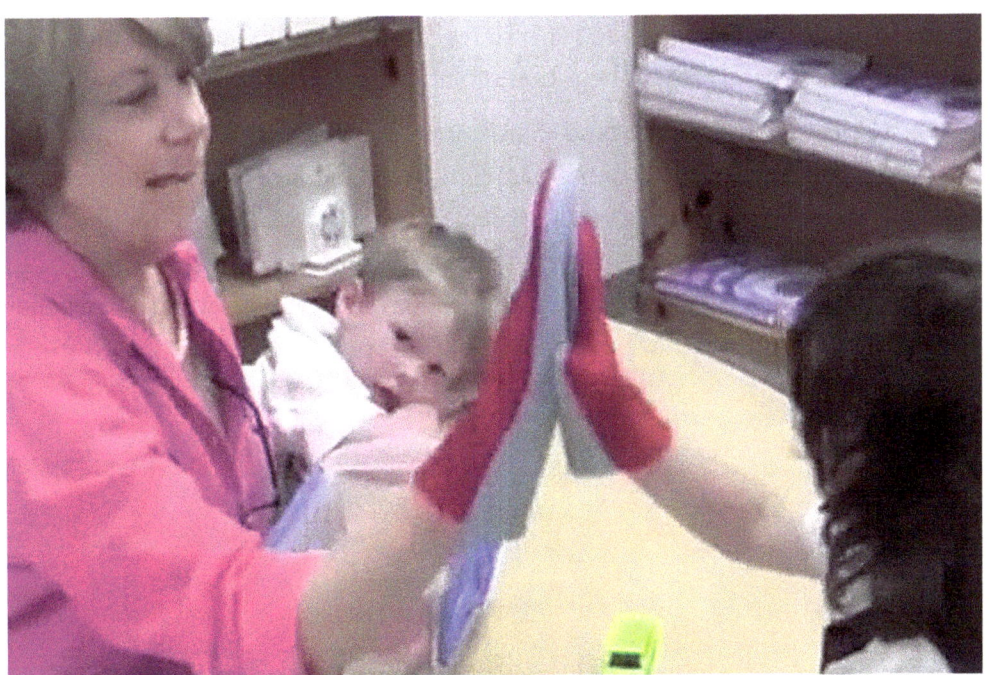

Figure 6.2   Patting Lesson

MSL Strategies Combined with the Montessori Written Language Curriculum

By combining Montessori techniques with MSL strategies, Montessori teachers can offer strategic teaching to children with dyslexia. In a Montessori environment, children who are at risk for dyslexia benefit from direct, structured teaching (with presentations modeled on the sequence of an MSL approach) while working with Sandpaper Letters, Object/Sound Boxes, and the Movable Alphabet. Children who are at risk for dyslexia also benefit from additional phonological awareness activities.

Before the introduction of the Sandpaper Letters, patting out each sound in a word in rhythm delivers tactile-kinesthetic information about the number and order of those sounds. This additional phonological awareness activity helps children develop the necessary phonological skills to work with the Sandpaper Letters—and to learn to read and write. If young children use a mitten for the patting, it will help them maintain interest.

Object/Sound Boxes and Sandpaper Letters may be combined for structured language presentations. Children with language learning differences benefit from structured support and instruction. Show children how to trace a Sandpaper Letter, say its sound, and then place appropriate objects next to it. These pairings may be modeled on the sequence of an MSL approach to further assist children who may have dyslexia.

Figure 6.3 Sandpaper Letters and Object Sound Boxes arranged in order of introduction in the SEE program

In a Montessori classroom, the first step children take toward developing sound/symbol correspondence is using the Sandpaper Letters. While tracing the letter, children voice the sound of the letter. In this way, children see the letter (visual) and hear the sound (auditory), while exercising arm muscles (kinesthetic) and feeling the shape with their fingers (tactile). In essence, they experience all the VAKT senses while developing sound/symbol associations (Montessori, 1914/1966). The original OG approach utilized a similar, multisensory technique to teach children sound/symbol association.

Most children love to work with the Sandpaper Letters and will explore them until they know all the sounds and symbols. "Typically" developing children may choose the letters in any order. Children who have dyslexia may require more presentations and direct instruction with Sandpaper Letters in a structured, sequential manner modeled on an MSL approach.

Before moving on to word building with the Movable Alphabet, it is crucial to provide opportunities for children with language learning differences to practice discriminating the sounds and locations of sounds in words. Children with language learning differences can begin blending sounds into words with an additional graph and indicator activity. In one variation, a child sounds out the word and places a token in each box for each sound.

Figure 6.4 Placing a token for each sound in the word

Montessori Strategies for Children with Learning Differences

In another variation, children place a token on the circle, voice the word, and then move the token to each of three squares while speaking each sound; then they repeat the word. While working with this activity, children see a visual representation of the number of sounds in the word which helps develop their phonological awareness. (Figure 6.6a.)

Figure 6.6b shows a variation of this phonological awareness activity in which a child identifies a beginning sound and a word family, then blends the two together. It is a simpler task to blend two sound units (c-at) rather than three (c-a-t). Blending by word family helps children who may have dyslexia because they struggle to perceive the internal detail of words.

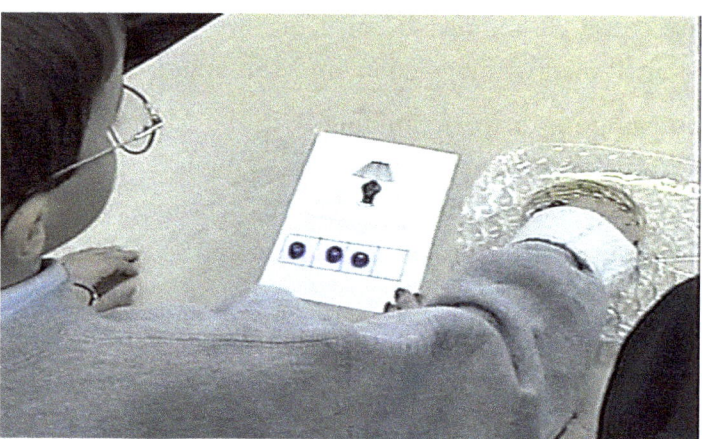

Figure 6.5   Sound cards with tokens

Figure 6.6a   Blending activity with token, sound-by-sound

Figure 6.6b   Blending by word family

Figure 6.7a Phonological awareness activity (c-a-t)

Figure 6.7b Blending the beginning sound to the word family (c-at)

The Movable Alphabet is a set of individual letters a child can manipulate to spell words. Children are ready for word building with the Movable Alphabet after they begin blending sounds. The "average" child can begin working with the Movable Alphabet by building words with all five short vowels. For children who may have dyslexia, it is better to begin work with simple CVC patterns, using only one short vowel (pat, hat, cat). The presentation of phonograms is best modeled on the sequence of an MSL approach.

For children who may have dyslexia and have difficulty with sound blending, presenting a word family model is also more effective. With the SEE approach, the child blends a beginning sound to a word family (c-at) instead of blending the individual sounds of each letter.

For children who are at risk for dyslexia, word building may proceed at a measured pace. They may struggle to master simple reading and writing tasks, but when Movable Alphabet work is modeled on a structured approach with word families, they should experience remediation and avoid much confusion and frustration.

Figure 6.8 Word Building by Word Family

As children's word building skills increase, reading booklets, linguistic readers, and opportunities to copy words and sentences can be offered.

From word building with the Movable Alphabet, children in the Montessori classroom move to learning the parts of speech. In Montessori classrooms, grammar for written language is taught with a unique system in which each element of grammar is represented by a geometric symbol. Sentence patterns are represented graphically, with these symbols drawn or placed above each word in a sentence, so the child can see the pattern of syntax. There is a story for each grammar symbol, which assists memory (Dorer, 2016). Montessori grammar symbols make grammar more understandable and enjoyable.

In the Montessori classroom, children learn to read and write with multisensory, manipulative materials. Sandpaper Letters allow children who may have dyslexia to learn through VAKT senses. Children with auditory processing deficits can develop phonological awareness by working with the Object/Sound Boxes. The Movable Alphabet allows children who struggle with writing to practice language patterns by manipulating and moving letters with their hands. Montessori grammar symbols provide visual representation of the parts of speech.

The Montessori curriculum offers effective materials and activities that can be used by any educator who works with children with dyslexia. Children with dyslexia benefit a great deal from the environment of encouragement within a Montessori classroom, and can also benefit from the multisensory materials used to teach literacy. When Montessori language presentations are modeled on the structure and sequence of an MSL approach, a great deal of remediation can be accomplished before children move up to elementary.

But even with informed strategic instruction and language lessons modeled on the sequence of an MSL approach, children with dyslexia may struggle to blend beginning sounds to word families using the Movable Alphabet. They will most likely leave their early childhood Montessori classroom without being able to read and write proficiently and will benefit from additional MSL therapy.

Multisensory Structured Language Therapy

Children generally begin MSL therapy around age 7, but in Montessori classrooms, children have the unique potential to begin when they are learning to blend sounds together into words, around age 5 or 6. For these children in your classroom, you will know their ability to blend words has been achieved through great effort, because you took the time to offer them the best strategic teaching possible. You worked with them on additional phonological awareness activities; you modeled your language presentations on an MSL approach; and to ensure your students with dyslexia learned how to decode and blend, whenever possible you gave them additional one-on-one instruction.

To begin assisting children with dysgraphia, therapists help students develop a correct pencil grip, which helps children develop the ability to write better and for longer periods of time. Metal Inset work (described previously in this chapter) is a great opportunity for children to practice the proper pencil grip. Most MSL approaches offer additional activities to enhance this skill. (Figure 6.9)

Sequential English Education (SEE) features many pre-writing exercises similar to the Metal Insets. Children generally enjoy these pre-writing exercises, which also indirectly help them develop control of a writing instrument. (Figure 6.10)

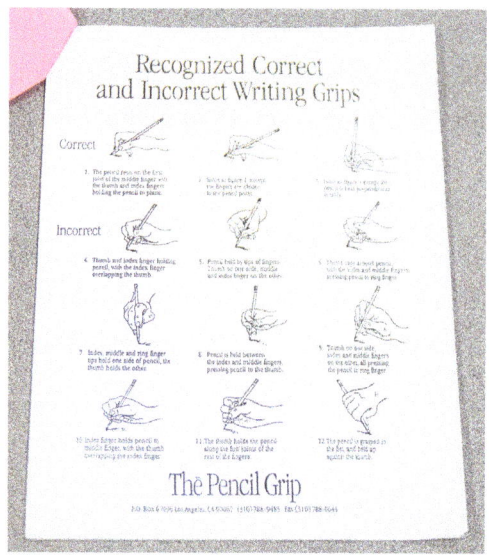
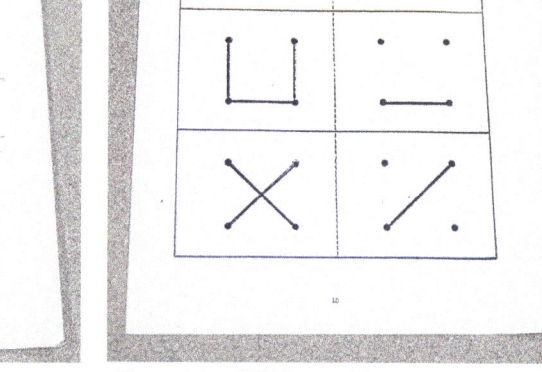

Figure 6.9 Pencil Grip   *Figure 6.10 SEE Pre-writing Example*

Dr. Montessori described the hands as the "instruments of man's intelligence" (Montessori, 1949/1995, p. 27). She believed cursive writing assists learning to read (Montessori, 1912/1997, p. 230). In many Montessori classrooms, children learn to write in cursive before learning to read and write in print. Cursive writing is used in Montessori classrooms because letters in words are connected. Printing requires more coordination because children must lift their pencil in between every letter.

Some children with language learning differences demonstrate challenges with directionality and spacing in their written work. Cursive writing can assist these students in developing legible writing, and most MSL approaches use cursive to teach students how to write as well. With cursive, children tend to exhibit less spatial and directionality errors in their writing than they do when printing (Bounds, 2010; Garrison, 2014; Phillips, J. 2013; Press-Register Editorial Board, 2012, Wofford, 2015).

In SEE Book I, children voice the sound of written letters three times, while tracing the letter with their index finger on their dominant hand. Children trace the letter with their finger on the textured side of a memory board, an 8- by 11-inch piece of Masonite, thus experiencing multisensory learning with simultaneous input through VAKT senses. Next, they attempt to write the letter with a pencil three times on unlined paper. Prior to this lesson, the child worked with the Montessori Sandpaper Letters. (Figure 6.11 and 6.12)

Figure 6.11 Tracing Sandpaper Letters and SEE Model

Figure 6.12 Writing Letters

After children can write the letter correctly, they practice with the rainbow letters exercise. In this exercise, the student writes on the letter model with three different colored pencils, one at a time. (Figure 6.13)

Figure 6.13 Rainbow Letters

All 31 short vowel, consonant, and consonant digraph sounds of the English language are presented in SEE Book I. The additional 13 English sounds are taught in Books II and III. SEE is a pattern-based program and features word patterns from simple to complex and regular to irregular. It also features a word family model which is imperative for children with dyslexia.

The lessons in Book I are for children ages 5 to 7. Book II introduces consonant blends and sight words for students age 8 to adult. Book III covers long vowel and other vowel sounds. Book IV includes homonyms, homographs, root words, prefixes, and suffixes. All 44 sounds of the English language are presented. This series includes auditory exercises to improve auditory discrimination and memory. (Figures 6.14, 6.15, 6.16, and 6.17)

Figure 6.14 SEE Book I Lesson

Figure 6.15 SEE Book I Lesson — Pointing to Print and Cursive Letters

Figure 6.16 SEE Book I Lesson — Reading Sentences

Figure 6.17 SEE Book I Lesson — Writing Lower Case Cursive Letters

Additional MSL Approaches

With study, any MSL method can be combined with the Montessori Language curriculum and materials to offer strategic instruction to children. Other MSL approaches, for which there are multiple accredited training courses, may be found on the IMSLEC or IDA websites (see the Appendix for more information). To be considered an MSL program, seven areas of content must be present: phonology and phonological awareness, sound/symbol association, syllables, morphology, semantics, syntax, and fluency. The principles of instruction must include simultaneous VAKT, systematic and cumulative language instruction, direct instruction, diagnostic teaching to automaticity, and synthetic/analytic instruction.

Conclusion

Learning to speak is a high-level neurological task requiring auditory processing of sounds, as well as the motor skills to produce those words in speech. To write, children must integrate their motor system with their auditory and visual systems. Learning to read is an even more complex neurological processing task. The visual and auditory processing of letters, sounds, and words must be integrated at a rapid rate to decode written text.

Written language skills are among the highest level skills our brains can process, but many take this for granted and simply hope by age 5 or 6, children will develop these abilities. However, 15 to 20 percent of the population has dyslexia and may struggle if not offered additional support (Yale Center for Dyslexia and Creativity, 2018).

Montessori recognized the advantage of a multisensory approach for learning both spoken and written language. Educators have confirmed over and over again the power of her approach. For children with language learning differences, Montessori techniques in combination with an MSL approach and therapy can be instrumental.

"It is high time that movement came to be regarded from a new point of view in educational theory."

(Montessori, 1949/1995, p. 136)

Chapter 7

Montessori Applied to ADHD & Delayed Attention Development

Joyce S. Pickering, with contributions from Sylvia O. Richardson

Montessori schools and their staffs are asking more and more questions about how to guide children with attention deficits and hyperactivity. They indicate that they are seeing more children who exhibit these characteristics in their classrooms and realize they do not have the training to best serve them. In my experience, parents of children with learning differences often look for schools with individualized/differentiated programs. Montessori programs appeal to these parents because they emphasize individualized learning. Montessori schools often include many children with attention deficits and hyperactivity.

Definition of Attention-Deficit/Hyperactivity Disorder

Attention-deficit/hyperactivity disorder (ADHD) refers to a family of chronic neurobiological disorders that interfere with the capacity to attend to tasks, regulate activity, and inhibit behavior in ways appropriate to age and circumstance. The essential features of ADHD are inappropriate degrees of inattention, impulsiveness, and hyperactivity (American Association of Psychiatry [APA], 2013). Increasingly, ADHD is believed to affect executive functioning.

A significant number of children with dyslexia also have ADHD as a coexisting condition. There are three types of ADHD: **inattentive; hyperactive/impulsive;** and **combined**. All three are displayed in varying degrees in a variety of manifestations. Most children who have ADHD possess normal or above-average intellectual ability. Children with the inattentive type can sit still, but their attention, focus, and concentration are erratic. They are "with you" one moment and then are not the next.

Children with the hyperactive/impulsive or combined type are never still, regardless of the situation, and hyperactivity is usually noticeable from birth. However, signs of the disorder may be minimal in novel settings, one-to-one situations, or when very strict control is present (e.g., being examined in the clinician's office, or interacting with a video game) (APA, 2013). While children with ADHD are described as distractible, they are actually absorbing all incoming sensory stimuli from their environment; they cannot filter extraneous perceptions. Five to seven percent of our national population exhibits symptoms of ADHD (APA, 2013).

ADHD: History and Characteristics

Throughout my career, the condition we now refer to as ADHD has been termed "hyperkinetic reaction of childhood" (APA, 1968), "attention deficit disorder" (APA, 1980), and, as of 1994, is referred to as "attention-deficit/hyperactivity disorder" (APA, 2013).

According to the American Association of Pediatrics, an ADHD diagnosis can be given to children as young as 4 years old (Subcommittee, 2011). However, in many circumstances, most young children exhibit some attention challenges and hyperactivity. Techniques to help children develop focus and inhibit movement are valuable for all children, and can be crucial for children who are at risk or diagnosed with ADHD.

It is generally agreed that symptoms of ADHD characteristically emerge during the toddler and preschool years. Diagnosis and remediation, however, do not typically occur until the elementary school years. The majority of children with ADHD continue to have symptoms as adults (Brown, 2005). For some, the hyperactive component may diminish, but attention deficits can last a lifetime. Adults may continue to struggle throughout their entire life, even though they have "outgrown" their most obvious symptoms.

The development of inhibition control (the ability to sustain attention and filter out extraneous information) typically begins around age 3. By this age, most children can inhibit extraneous information from their environment and selectively attend to the most important information, such as a lesson a teacher is presenting or words an adult is speaking. ADHD impairs inhibition control in significant ways.

Dr. Charles Shedd recognized that some children do not develop inhibition control. Their ability to selectively focus and concentrate is similar to that of a younger child. He referred to this as "arrested development" (Shedd, 1968). Dr. Montessori made a similar observation:

> The difficulty of fixing attention, the general instability [uncoordinated movements], etc., are characteristics which the normal infant and the deficient child have in common. (Montessori, 1909/2008, p. 90)

Dr. Montessori created a method to help children train their attention and learn to control their movements. She described the remedial effects of her method that "deficient" children experienced as "normalization" (Montessori, 1949/1995, p. 206). I have also witnessed the highly effective and ameliorating way the Montessori method helps children with attention deficits develop selective focus and helps children with hyperactivity learn to control their movements. What Dr. Montessori described as "normalized" may not be something every child can achieve, but opportunities to focus on tasks and develop concentration can benefit all children.

Montessori, Movement, and Learning

In Montessori schools, children are free to move about in a defined space while observing reasonable rules of the classroom. Montessori recognized the role of movement in learning and concluded that children learn better when they are able to move freely.

The "freedom within limits" of a Montessori classroom helps produce an environment in which children comport themselves in an agreeable manner and take a spontaneous interest in pursuing enriching work. When this "normalization" occurs, the classroom is calm and peaceful. The children move about with purposeful steps. They speak softly to one another and often spontaneously help each other. Many children concentrate deeply on their work. When teachers have a moment to reflect on the situation, they often feel a tender happiness.

Or it can be chaos.

Often one of the first questions teachers ask me is: "Does ADHD exist, or is it just a stage?"

My answer is, "Yes. ADHD exists. No. It is not just a stage. It is a neurobiological condition."

There are individuals who struggle to sustain attention, focus, and concentration. Without the ability to concentrate and inhibit movement, children with ADHD may be unable to sit still during lessons or listen to instructions given by a teacher in a classroom.

In a Montessori classroom, children with ADHD may be unable to concentrate during individual and group presentations. They might not develop a cycle of work (choosing work, completing work, returning it to the shelf, and finding another interesting work). They may wander about the classroom. If they choose an activity, they may work for a short time, then leave the work and wander more. Children with ADHD may not "normalize" like others.

Montessori teachers might observe that these children's struggles are due to inattention or hyperactivity, and their executive functioning ability (their ability to organize and prioritize information being processed through the senses) is different than most. A Montessori environment and a Montessori teacher trained in additional strategies to help children with learning and attention differences can offer children with ADHD the opportunity to develop inhibition and self-control. To do this, the teacher must employ techniques to help children develop and maintain concentration during tasks. Dr. Montessori advised:

> Only "normalized" children, aided by their environment, show in their subsequent development those wonderful powers that we describe: spontaneous discipline, continuous and happy work, social sentiments of help and sympathy for others. (Montessori, 1949/1995, p. 206)

In a Montessori early childhood classroom, children learn to focus and control their bodies at an early age. This early intervention can be a significant influence in the life of a human being and can have lasting and positive effects for children with ADHD. A Montessori environment and a Montessori teacher can help children develop inhibition, self-control, and concentration.

> Mental order and co-ordination of movement guided by scientific standards are what prepare for concentration, and this, once it has occurred, "frees the actions of the child," and leads him to the cure of his defects. (Montessori, 1949/1995, p. 206)

In essence, the Montessori teacher can "free the actions" of the child with attention deficits and hyperactivity. To do this, the teacher must understand ADHD and how to prepare children to focus and inhibit movement.

ADHD: Executive Function

According to Martha Bridge Denckla, MD, "Executive function refers to a wide range of central control processes in the brain that connect, prioritize, and integrate operation of subordinate brain functions" (Denckla, 1996, p. 278). Children with ADHD have impairments in executive functioning.

As young children mature and begin to perform more complex tasks independently, the central management system of the brain becomes increasingly important. Many researchers have confirmed the consensus—individuals with ADHD have difficulty accessing self-regulation and higher-order cognitive processing (executive functioning) (Tannock and Schachar, 1996). ADHD affects executive function, which begins developing during early childhood and is crucial for learning. For years, Thomas E. Brown, clinical psychologist and expert on ADHD, has reported a broader view of inattention that includes challenges related to executive function (Brown, 2005).

Although people with ADHD struggle with executive function, they can sustain attention under certain conditions, such as an emergency or a situation with a high level of immediate, spontaneous interest. The main challenge a person with ADHD faces is that they are unable to activate and sustain attention in many situations where it is necessary or desirable to do so (Tannock and Schachar, 1996).

For example, an individual may be able to "hyperfocus" and sustain intense attention for several hours while playing a sport, building with blocks, or using a computer, yet they may be unable to sustain attention for more than a few minutes when reading or when sitting in a class or a meeting. The functions of paying attention, organizing, and recalling are intact, but they are simply not responsive to higher-order processing. That is, the individual is not readily able to activate, deploy, and utilize these functions as needed. These functions are not readily turned on or off, and are not responsive to "willpower." Executive function (the higher-order systems of the brain that activate, integrate, coordinate, and modulate a variety of other cognitive functions) is not always accessible to people with ADHD (Tannock and Schachar, 1996).

The 21st century has brought us an understanding of ADHD as a spectrum of executive impairments that may also coexist with many other psychiatric disorders. This leads to more research questions about the nature, etiology, assessment, course treatment, and outcome. The evolving understanding of ADHD, however, has led to increased awareness and accommodations.

Dr. Thomas E. Brown, the author of the Brown Executive Function/Attention Scales published in 2018 (Pearson) provides a model of executive function, which includes six clusters. These include:

    1. Activation—organizing, prioritizing, and activating to work
    2. Focus—focusing and sustaining effort and processing speed
    3. Effort—regulating alertness, sustaining effort, and processing speed

4. Emotion—managing frustration and modulating emotions
5. Memory—utilizing working memory and accessing recall
6. Action—monitoring and self-regulating action

As the understanding of executive function and its relation to ADHD evolves, early childhood intervention and remediation continues to offer great hope for the future success of many children (Barkley, 2017).

Coexisting Conditions

The teacher should be aware that various conditions can be comorbid or coexisting for children with ADHD. The more disorders present in the child's diagnosis, the more complex the learning and attention difference. Especially when in combination with ADHD, these coexisting conditions may be expressed by emotional and behavioral challenges. It is possible to help some children with combined disorders in a Montessori classroom; however, some may require an expert therapist. Staff and teachers at Montessori schools can work with parents and therapists or counselors to meet the needs of many children. Sometimes, however, an intensive intervention in an alternative clinical setting may be required.

Individuals with ADHD may also have comorbid oppositional defiant disorder, primary disorder of vigilance, and/or bipolar disorder (webmd.com, 2018). These disorders can occur in any combination or alone.

Oppositional Defiant Disorder

About half the children diagnosed with ADHD also have oppositional defiant disorder (ODD) (webmd.com, 2018). The most common symptom for this disorder is the child's refusal to follow any or all instructions or directives. In addition to displaying inattentive and impulsive behavior, these children demonstrate aggression, have frequent temper tantrums, and display antisocial behavior. Up to 25% of children with ODD have phobias and other anxiety disorders.

Primary Disorder of Vigilance
Primary disorder of vigilance is a term for a syndrome that includes poor attention and concentration as well as difficulties staying awake. People with vigilance disorder tend to fidget, yawn, and stretch, and appear to be hyperactive in order to stay alert; they typically have kind and affectionate temperaments. The condition is inherited and gets worse with age, but it is treatable.

Bipolar Disorder
A recent study found that as many as 25% of children diagnosed with ADHD may also have bipolar disorder, formerly called manic depression (webmd.com, 2018). Indications of this disorder include episodes of depression and mania (with symptoms of irritability, rapid speech, and disconnected thoughts), sometimes occurring at the same time.

ADHD Treatment

By age 3, most children can focus on the more important sensory information in their environment and are able to "shut out" less important sights, sounds, smells, tastes, and textures. They have developed inhibition control and can also control some of their body movements. Children with ADHD characteristically are not able to do these things. The minds of children with ADHD are being constantly bombarded by sensory input. Since these children cannot inhibit perception, they absorb it all. They are unable to use executive function or make their bodies still.

For children with ADHD who do not develop typical attention and concentration, treatment can make a crucial and critical difference. Although no one perfect treatment for ADHD exists, a healthy lifestyle, education, therapy, exercise, medication, and counseling can help children manage ADHD. Two treatments in particular have proven effective: strenuous exercise and medication.

In 2012, The Shelton School and Evaluation Center participated in the HOPE study, a program that investigated exercise as an innovative treatment for ADHD. Results indicated that for adolescents with ADHD, strenuous exercise can offer effective treatment. In the study, high school students rode spin bikes in their health class for 20 minutes with the goal of keeping their heart rate at 70%

of their maximum. During each semester trial, students reported physiological improvement and improvement in attention and focus. The students who were the most hyperactive reported the most dramatic improvement in attending and memory. Some indicated this experience taught them how to manage their ADHD (Hughes & Pickering, 2014). For more information about the HOPE project, see the Appendix.

The theory that inspired this study is described in the book *SPARK: The Revolutionary New Science of Exercise and the Brain* by Dr. John Ratey (2008); Ratey found that when physical exercise is paired with mental exercise, the effect on the brain is similar to the effect achieved with medication. Data supports the claim that children with ADHD benefit from strenuous exercise. At the Shelton School, students are offered access to the gymnasium or to trampolines placed outside their classroom, and also have the option of standing at desks in the classroom.

Strenuous exercise is one effective treatment for ADHD. Medication may also help. Every day, children arrive at schools on prescribed medication, and most often the decision to medicate is beyond the influence of a teacher. Although stimulant medications can negatively affect mood, appetite, and sleep centers of the brain, the benefits of medication can outweigh the side effects.

Exploring additional therapies and remediation is useful as well. Many other practices benefit those with ADHD, including adequate sleep, nutritionally balanced diet, regular exercise, meditation or prayer, and medication, if necessary (Hallowell, 1995; Hallowell, 2009).

Researchers and educators are beginning to understand how ADHD works and what treatments are most effective. Children benefit from treatment and management, and early intervention can be critical. For those who do not receive proper treatment, coping in this world can be a challenge.

Montessori, Inclusion, and Children with Attention-Deficits/Hyperactivity

In inclusive classrooms, teachers strive to meet the needs of all children. Although most Montessori classrooms are highly organized, children with attention deficits may be overwhelmed by the number of choices available and may be unable to choose work productively. In order to include for children with attention deficits to function in the classroom, they must learn how to complete a cycle of work. Having a system to assist in decision making helps children develop a work cycle.

The teacher may limit the choices children have by suggesting to a child that they choose work from just one shelf. Sometimes the teacher must make the choice for a child. Teaching children to use a filing system helps them develop organizational skills. Lessons on how to complete and file work in a work folder establish a system for organizing ongoing and completed work. This skill can be of lifelong value.

To work successfully with children with attention deficits in an inclusive classroom, Montessori teachers must help them sustain and develop attention during one-to-one presentations. Before beginning a lesson, the teacher must take the time to engage children's interest and prepare them for the lesson to come. Teachers can help children focus their attention during presentations by modeling calm, still posture, gaining eye contact, talking slowly, and using slow hand movements during lessons. To improve focus, the teacher must make eye contact, use a soft voice, and sometimes gently touch the child's shoulder. Saying the child's name or saying quietly, "Look," can also help children focus during the presentation.

The teacher in an inclusive Montessori classroom will have to structure the day to be able to work more closely with children with ADHD. While "normalized" children are self-directed and need much less guidance, children with ADHD may benefit from a structure in which they show their teacher every completed activity before putting it back on the shelf. In this way the teacher can discuss the work with them and see that they understand how to return the work to the shelf. The teacher and the child can then make a decision together about what work to do next.

As children learn these skills, the teacher can offer less guidance, fostering the child's development of independence. The teacher's goal is to help children move from this guided structure to the ability to make independent choices, focus on work, complete the work, and return it to the shelf.

Children with ADHD, especially those who are impulsive, benefit from the clear rules, privileges, and boundaries that are generally present in Montessori environments. These children may, however, need more practice learning the difference between appropriate and inappropriate behavior. Whenever behavior is inappropriate, the teacher must talk with the child individually about what was inappropriate, why it was inappropriate, and what the appropriate behavior is. The teacher must be consistent in doing this every time there is an inappropriate behavior.

An example would be helping a child understand that running in the classroom is inappropriate. The teacher first models walking slowly, then walks alongside the child, and finally instructs the child to walk from one side of the room to the other and back again. The teacher thanks the child for moving appropriately in the classroom. Then the child goes back to work. Repeating the walking practice several times is an option if the teacher sees this behavior again. Only if appropriate behavior is insisted upon will children with hyperactivity become aware of their behavior and learn how to control their bodies.

Intervening when inappropriate behavior occurs may be necessary, but demonstrating appropriate behavior at neutral times before or after the inappropriate behavior has been exhibited is always a good strategy. Role-playing activities such as how to walk across the classroom or how to tuck in a chair, walk around a work rug, or say "thank you" and "I'm sorry" can work very well for children with ADHD, and all children in a class benefit from these activities.

Children with ADHD must learn to control their impulses and learn to understand the reasons and emotions motivating their actions. There are many types of programs that can help children develop this awareness. See the Appendix for a list of MACAR resources related to children and behavior.

Children's sense of order develops because of the precise manner in which Montessori lessons are presented and the manner in which a Montessori prepared environment is organized. The carefully shown layout of each activity increases the child's ability to organize their work. The presentation of an activity shows children how to learn. Order and organization are included in the structure of the classroom, the presentations, and the daily schedule, all of which help children improve executive function.

As is evident in these suggestions, the teacher in an inclusive Montessori class must give more time to children with ADHD. This additional attention can be possible because, in a Montessori classroom, self-directed children function independently, choose their own work, and discover and correct any errors without adult help. They need less instruction, guidance, and support than children with ADHD.

If the teacher is giving a lesson and observes children who are not engaged in work, but not disturbing others, the teacher should continue presenting the lesson already in progress. The teacher can help the child who needs redirection after the lesson is finished. So long as children with ADHD do not interfere with other children's learning, their activity can be respected; at other times, children with more severe ADHD symptoms may require additional adult support to supervise their activities more closely. Though it is challenging, if the teacher is able to find the right balance, inclusion is possible.

The Montessori Silence Game and Children with ADHD

The Silence Game is an exercise in which children practice inhibition of movement. Dr. Montessori herself was surprised at the degree of self-control children were able to manifest and develop during this activity. During the Silence Game, children learn to keep their bodies still and be silent. For children with ADHD, this activity can be an enriching experience that fosters development of inhibition control.

In her book *Living, Creating, Sharing—A Montessori Life* (2016), Celma Perry describes the wonder of witnessing the Silence Game during her first visit to a Montessori school. She was awestruck as children sat in a circle in silence. One by one, the teacher whispered their names to call them to stand and wait in a line before going outside.

I could not hear any sound! ... Like magic each little one got up and very carefully stood by the teacher, turned towards the class, and happily waited for the next one to be called. (Perry, 2013, p. 60)

In the Silence Game, the teacher must prepare children for attention and focus. As the work period nears a close, the teacher dims the lights or rings a small bell, signaling that it is time to put away work and come together for a group activity. The teacher invites the children to sit. As the children gather, the teacher begins reading a story, singing songs, using finger plays, or another activity. When the entire group is present, a quiet discussion ensues about the work the children chose that morning.

- To prepare the children for the Silence Game, the teacher gains the children's eye contact, uses a soft voice, and discusses the challenge of making silence. The teacher gradually brings the class tension level down by talking quietly and slowly. The teacher asks for children to cross their legs, sit up very straight, and place their hands on their knees.
- The teacher then announces, "We will now play the Silence Game. I will place a candle in the center of the circle." (A sand timer may be used in place of a candle.)

The candle helps children maintain focus and inhibit movement during the game. When the teacher lights the candle, the Silence Game begins. At the beginning of the year, many classes make silence only for a second or two. By the end of the year, silence might reach 5 to 10 minutes or longer. Children experience deeper calm as silence is maintained for longer periods. Children with ADHD may need extra instruction. The procedure is much like a normal lesson. Language is introduced and children are given vocabulary to attach to their experience and perceptions.

- The teacher announces, "I am going to make silence."

Then, the teacher, in an overly-dramatic fashion, relaxes their head, shoulders, trunk and hands, closes their eyes, counts to five, then asks the children to describe those actions. A complete analysis and discussion is encouraged, and silence is postponed until the teacher asks the children to demonstrate what was modeled.

- The teacher requests, "Be silent with your head."

From there the teacher slowly repeats the imperatives, alternately indicating the different body parts:
- "Be silent with your shoulders."
- "Be silent with your body."
- "Be silent with your arms."
- The teacher continues with hands, legs, and feet. The teacher finally requests, "Be silent with your eyes" and the children close their eyes.
- The teacher makes this request last to be sure children have the opportunity to observe one another.

Additional phrases the teacher might speak during the game include:
- "I can make silence."
- "I speak to no one."
- "I am going to make silence."
- "If my whole body is still, I make silence."
- "I heard the silence we made."

The Silence Game helps all children, but it can be particularly helpful in developing gross motor control for children with hyperactivity. The Silence Game can also help children develop awareness and control of their body, auditory memory, auditory discrimination, and attention span. In addition, this activity contrasts sound and silence, as well as motor activation and inhibition. For some children the Silence Game is an extremely challenging task, but what it teaches them is invaluable.

Through direct instruction, the Montessori teacher can use the Silence Game to help children learn to calm their bodies and focus on a task. Some children with severe ADHD symptoms may need individual lessons. They may rarely be able to hold perfectly still, but they can improve their abilities. The teacher must guide those children to inhibition control, helping them learn to wait for their turn, to walk slowly, to talk in a quiet voice, and to control their body and behavior. These are critical skills.

The Silence Game may be practiced every day. This may be the first time many children with ADHD have experienced quiet or felt stillness. The Silence Game also helps children develop their executive functioning skill, which is especially important for children with attention deficits. With practice and help, children can enhance and use these skills during work periods.

Conclusion

If your classroom is chaotic, analyze your behavior to be sure you are a positive role model for your children. Are you calm and clear in your verbalization? Do you speak slowly to allow time for children to process your directions? Do you give encouragement through a smile or soft touch on the back? When you ask a child to modify a behavior, are you confident that you have the right and responsibility as the teacher to request what you are asking? Do you thoroughly understand learning differences and children with ADHD? Have you properly prepared the environment, presented the rules of the room, giving positive encouragement for appropriate behaviors and gentle, reasonable consequences for inappropriate behavior?

Some children have difficulty developing executive function (the ability to organize and prioritize information the brain is processing). Without this ability, children will have difficulty developing a cycle of work. Montessori teachers can help children with ADHD develop the ability to choose work, complete work, return it to the shelf, and find another interesting work, thereby developing the cycle of work. During every presentation, to help children stay focused, teachers must use very slow hand movements, slow and well-articulated speech, and eye contact.

Montessori teachers must give extra help so children with hyperactivity/impulsivity can learn to control their behavior and follow rules, all of which are based on respect for others and respect for their classroom environment. The

Montessori teacher must be a partner with these children, offering as much guidance as necessary to move each child toward the level of independence they can achieve.

With a nurturing, experienced, and well-trained Montessori teacher, children with ADHD are able to experience freedom and movement in the Montessori prepared environment. Finding the delicate balance that enables inclusion is possible for a capable, highly skilled, and resourceful Montessori teacher. By offering a welcoming environment, along with extra attention, kindness, and additional support, a Montessori teacher can offer children with ADHD a learning environment that will positively affect them for their entire lives.

"Another observation of supreme importance is that the child, when captivated by a piece of work, repeats the same series of movements time after time. ... It is true that in all these activities, the child may be said to be playing. But this kind of play is effortful, and it leads him to acquire the new powers which will be needed for his future."

(Montessori, 1949/1995, p. 180)

Chapter 8

Montessori Applied to Autism Spectrum Disorder

K. Michelle Lane-Barmapov

The Montessori curriculum has proven to be an effective system for teaching many children on the autism spectrum. This chapter will address early intervention using Montessori strategies combined with Applied Behavior Analysis therapy for children with autism. One of the goals of Applied Behavior Analysis therapy is also one of the goals of Montessori education—enhancing learning by enabling children to work independently.

Throughout my career, I have had the privilege of working with hundreds of children with autism and their families. I am a firm believer in Montessori early childhood education, the power of inclusion, and evidence-based treatment for children with autism. Every child with autism is unique. Some children with autism struggle to learn very basic skills. Children with more severe forms of autism may regress and lose abilities they have developed. Yet some children with autism may be gifted in certain areas.

In 2003, when I opened The Toronto Montessori School for Autism in Toronto, Canada, I created a blend of the Montessori curriculum and Applied Behavior Analysis (ABA) therapy for children with severe forms of autism. My school provided intervention for children who were unable to work with Montessori methods in the traditional manner. As an early childhood practitioner and school founder, I observed the benefits of my Montessori ABA therapy in the lives of countless children with autism.

ABA therapy for children with autism contrasts with Montessori education by using external reinforcement to motivate children to perform activities, because some children with autism may never develop intrinsic motivation to do these activities. Children with more severe forms of autism can benefit from one-on-one instruction and intervention with my Montessori ABA therapy, which can help them develop practical and crucial skills during early childhood. It can also help children with severe forms of autism master more skills, and hopefully retain more abilities throughout their lives.

Definition and Characteristics of Autism Spectrum Disorder (ASD)

Autism spectrum disorder (ASD) is a range of neurological disorders that affect communication skills, social skills, and sensory processing, as well as behavior and cognitive development (Anagnostou et al., 2014). Dr. Leo Kanner is credited with defining and creating the term *autism* in 1943 when he observed a group of children who had difficulty relating to others and to their environment (Long, Gurka & Blackman, 2011). The symptoms associated with an autism diagnosis must be present in early childhood, usually prior to the age of 3 (American Psychiatric Association [APA], 2013; Levy, Mandell, & Schultz, 2009). Severity of the disorder is based on the level of social communication skills and repetitive behavioral patterns (APA, 2013).

The diagnosis of autism has gone through many changes over the last few decades. In 2013, the fifth edition of the *Diagnostic and Statistical Manual of Mental Disorders* (DSM-5) combined previous subgroups (e.g., Asperger syndrome and childhood disintegrative disorder) under the heading **autism spectrum disorder** (APA, 2013).

Prior to 1990, intellectual delays were highly associated with the diagnosis (Long, Gurka & Blackman, 2011). Since 2000, intellectual delays within the diagnosis have decreased by almost half (Long, Gurka & Blackman, 2011). Within the last few years, children with autism have also been monitored for other disorders such as attention-deficit/hyperactivity disorder (ADHD) or anxiety (Anagnostou et al., 2014). Prior to the DSM-5, it was assumed that autism and ADHD could not co-occur. However, now they are no longer excluded from one another, and it is understood that autism and ADHD can co-occur (Mannion & Leader, 2014).

Working with Children with Autism

Many children with autism struggle to communicate and need help developing basic skills, such as pointing and joint attention (making eye contact). Joint attention happens naturally with "typically" developing infants who point and make eye contact to communicate their wants to their parents or other caregivers. This seemingly basic communication skill (i.e., ensuring another person is paying attention while pointing or gesturing to an object) can be challenging for children with autism to develop. Structured teaching and working with speech therapists can help children with autism develop this skill.

Some children with autism exhibit limited interest and can monopolize a conversation on a specific topic. They may have challenges evaluating social cues from peers who may not be as enthusiastic about that topic. Children with autism may also be unable to read facial expressions and may have other social communication challenges.

Additionally, children with autism often engage in repetitive self-stimulatory behavior called "stimming." The behavior itself is not harmful, but it can impede their development of other skills. To help children with autism engage in other activities and reach their full potential, an ABA approach can be useful.

Every scenario and child with autism is unique. For example, when we first began working together, Jack, a 13-year-old with autism, talked repeatedly about a trip he took to Reptile Park. He discussed the different types of reptiles and what they looked like, and could describe minute details of the various reptiles he had seen. It was wonderful that Jack was able to communicate his knowledge in great detail, but he was unable to discern social cues from the rest of the group indicating their disinterest in those very specific details. He benefited from the social skills techniques that we taught him.

When Aaron first came to The Toronto Montessori School for Autism, he resisted any human touch and would scream in any new environment. He was with us for 3 hours a day, and would scream for the entire length of his session. When I observe a child such as Aaron exhibiting challenging behaviors (i.e., screaming or biting), I hope that by offering appropriate supports that child can learn how to manage those behaviors. I was confident that Aaron's behavior was only temporary; fortunately we were able to find reinforcements and provide the extra support to help Aaron become comfortable in the new space. Aaron went on to learn how to use the Knobbed Cylinders on his own. I first needed to prompt Aaron by placing my hand over his hand and gently guiding him to put each cylinder in the corresponding hole. By using my blend of behavior therapy and the Montessori curriculum, he achieved success and developed new skills.

Lenz, another former student, spent half the day in the Montessori ABA therapy program and the other half of the day in a special class in the public school system for children with learning and behavioral challenges. When he was introduced to the Montessori World Puzzle Map, we found he became very engaged and learned to complete the puzzle quickly. Following his interest, we showed him the puzzle maps for each continent. He continued to find this work interesting and engaging.

Lenz was also very interested in the flags of the different countries. By using his interest in continents, countries, and flags, we were able to work on other skill areas (e.g., coloring the maps/flags and writing a few words about the countries in his journal book).

One day at snack time, Lenz was eating a cookie and he said, "Burkino Faso." The cookie actually looked like the shape of that country. For Lenz, we were able to find an area of interest that kept him engaged, and we were able to continue to build on his limited interest to help him learn other skills that benefited his overall development.

Early Indicators of Autism Spectrum Disorder (ASD)

Coordination

Children with autism show difficulties with coordination as early as 12 months (Anagnostou et al., 2014). These coordination difficulties include maintaining eye contact to communicate (Anagnostou et al., 2014) and delays in fine and gross motor skill development. Children with autism might not show imaginative play, might have difficulty with social communication/turn taking, and might interact with toys in a repetitive manner (Anagnostou et al., 2014).

Language
Children with autism may have varying receptive and expressive language abilities. Some have difficulties with language due to a lack of motor skill ability (Vistakova and Rihova, 2014). Early indicators include significant repetition of vocalizations (echolalia) or unusual tones in the voice when expressing words (Carson, Moosa, Theurer & Cardy, 2012). Pointing skills are not typically achieved, and regression of previously acquired language skills may occur. Augmentative methods of communication include the Bondy & Frost (1994) Picture Exchange Communication System (PECS), sign language, and electronic devices (Carson et al., 2012). These devices are typically used to assist children with communication skill development (Carson et al., 2012).

Attention
Joint attention occurs when eye contact is coordinated with social communication (Rao & Ashok, 2014). Joint attention appears to be a unique area of difficulty for children with autism (Rao & Ashok, 2014). In addition, some children have difficulty concentrating because the executive functions of their mind (the area of the brain that supports problem solving) are not well developed. Atypical executive functioning affects a large percentage of children with autism and leads to problems with focus as well as impulsive behaviors (May, Rinehart, Wilding & Cornish, 2013). Children with autism are also known for their repetitive and rigid behavior patterns that often affect their ability to sustain attention (May et al., 2013). Leyfer et al. (2006) found that a lack of attending ability, which is a symptom of ADHD, is present in about 50% of children with autism.

Perception
Children with autism may have difficulties perceiving another person's communication, including understanding facial emotions and physical cues,

and may lack the ability to look at the mouth of a person who is speaking (Johnels, Gillberg, Falck-Ytter & Miniscalco, 2014). Some individuals with autism have comparably more challenges with emotional perception in contrast to their cognitive abilities (Hudepohl, Robins, King & Henrich, 2015).

Brain Research

There are many misconceptions and myths around autism, and modern brain research provides us with critical information to understand how children with autism process information differently. Researchers are beginning to discover areas of the brain that affect children with autism (Thompson, 2013). By using functional magnetic resonance imaging (fMRI), Ozonoff et al. (2010) discovered that certain infants who look at images of human faces do not react to human eyes in the same manner as "typically" developing infants (Ozonoff et al., 2010). Their study indicated that infants who display difficulties with facial engagement at 6 months of age are often diagnosed with autism in early childhood (Ozonoff et al., 2010).

Many children with autism continue to show difficulties with emotional facial recognition as well as difficulties with facial motion detection throughout adulthood. Children on the mild end of the spectrum may develop more capable levels of emotional facial recognition (Harms, Martin & Wallace, 2010; Johnels et al., 2014; O'Brien, Spencer, Girges, Johnston & Hill, 2014).

The more information we have about the brain development of children with autism, the better we can support the needs of those children in various learning environments (e.g., at home or at school). From this knowledge, therapeutic strategies can be created and implemented.

Montessori Techniques Combined with Applied Behavior Analysis

The onset of autism happens in early childhood, and early intervention is highly beneficial. The Montessori early childhood program teaches concepts based in reality (such as dinosaurs) instead of concepts based on the imaginary (such as dragons). Montessori felt that young children could become confused when taught both concepts at an early stage of development (Montessori, 1909/2008).

Montessori also stressed teaching practical, daily living skills to young children. Activities such as rolling out a table mat or putting work back on the shelf are activities that can build skills for later in life. These activities are well suited to the needs of children with autism. Montessori education is exceptional when contrasted with many current play-based models designed for children with autism.

Montessori **Applied Behavior Analysis** (ABA) therapy is helpful for children on the more severe end of the autism spectrum who are unable to engage in traditional Montessori methods. These children need more support and are better served in a Montessori ABA program that offers effective therapeutic intervention (Lane, 2004/2008). Children who have milder levels of autism may require less support in order to benefit from learning within a Montessori environment.

ABA therapy can be used to help children with autism develop academic, verbal, social, and daily living skills. The therapy was developed by Ivar Lovaas (Virues-Ortega, Rodríguez & Yu, 2013; Lovaas, 1987). Lovaas based the therapy on Skinner's theory of operant conditioning (Lovaas, 1987). Lovaas is widely credited with creating the first method that can reduce, and at times eliminate, symptoms of autism (Lovaas, 1987). ABA has been identified as the most effective of all evidence-based treatments to date for children with autism (Reichow, 2012). However, some professionals in the autism field remain unconvinced that ABA is the best treatment for children with milder forms of autism (Tchaconas & Adesman, 2013).

One of the main differences between an Applied Behavior Analysis (ABA) model of teaching and the Montessori method is that the Montessori method is designed to encourage a child to do an activity through intrinsic motivation. If a child is not interested in doing an activity, teachers rarely coax, prompt or offer external reinforcement. Instead, children may come back to the lesson at a later date when they feel ready.

With ABA, hand-over-hand prompting and reinforcements are used to ensure that each child continues to acquire and practice skills they may otherwise never develop. Without extrinsic reinforcement, children with severe autism may never be able to perform the work independently.

Additionally, with Montessori methods, children are generally given the opportunity to practice with an activity for as long as they are interested; a child with autism, however, may not benefit from working at length with an activity. Without reinforcement some children may repetitively engage in one element of a task without learning to complete other steps of the task.

When Aaron first came to the school, he avoided human touch, and as mentioned previously, for the first week or so he screamed for the entire session. Our classroom was a prepared environment that ran like a clinic room with four children and four therapists working one on one in each class. When we found that Aaron enjoyed watching a short part of a video, we set up a television in the classroom. Anytime Aaron would stop screaming, we would immediately show him the specific part of the video he liked as reinforcement, thereby supporting his calmer behavior.

Over time we were able to pair the video with other reinforcements and we set up a teaching schedule. We used the Discrete Trial Teaching (DTT) model (see below) to track his progress doing Montessori activities. Initially, Aaron would not put the Knobbed Cylinders in the corresponding holes, but would hold them in his fingers as a self-stimulatory behavior ("stimming"). So we prompted him (gently, using hand-over-hand movements) to put the cylinder in the corresponding hole. Lastly, we gave him reinforcements every time he put the cylinder in the hole (regardless of the level of prompting). We continued this process with Aaron until he learned how to do the Knobbed Cylinders on his own. Most of the other activities also needed to be taught in this manner so that he could learn how to manipulate the materials appropriately.

Discrete Trial Teaching (DTT)

ABA therapy for children with autism often uses discrete trial teaching (DTT). When I created the Montessori ABA therapy program, I used a three-step DTT procedure (Skinner, 1969). I found that our students were able to generalize their learned skills at a faster pace, and we were better able to identify their specific challenges with DTT.

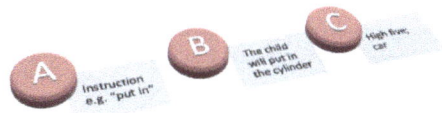

Figure 8.1 illustrates the three steps of a discrete trial with Montessori Knobbed Cylinders.

Three Steps of Discrete Trial Teaching with Montessori Knobbed Cylinders

    A. **Stimulus Descriptive S(d)**: The teacher says, "Put in."

    B. **Response Criteria**: Putting the cylinder in the appropriate hole.

    C. **Consequence (reinforcement)**: The child receives a hug, a high five, a toy car when the steps are completed.

With enough repetition, children can develop the skills to repeat the activity independently.

Stimulus Discriminative S(d)

In this case, the Stimulus Discriminative S(d) is the teacher's oral request, "Put in." The S(d) is the cue for the child to begin the activity and also helps the child learn language. The activity is removing, sequencing, and replacing the Knobbed Cylinders in the block. Simple language instructions are used to help the child become successful in understanding the request.

In my example with Aaron, communication and language were developed by using the simple instruction "put in" instead of "put in the knobbed cylinder." The latter would have been too many words for him to understand, and he would not have known what he was expected to do. Using the S(d) request "put in" helped Aaron understand what those words meant. The S(d) instructions help children learn what to do, and they are better able to respond to succinct language.

In my Montessori ABA program manual, I provide possible S(d) instructions for each lesson for the preschool (ages 3–6) program. For more information about these manuals, see the Appendix.

Response Criteria—Putting the cylinder in the appropriate hole

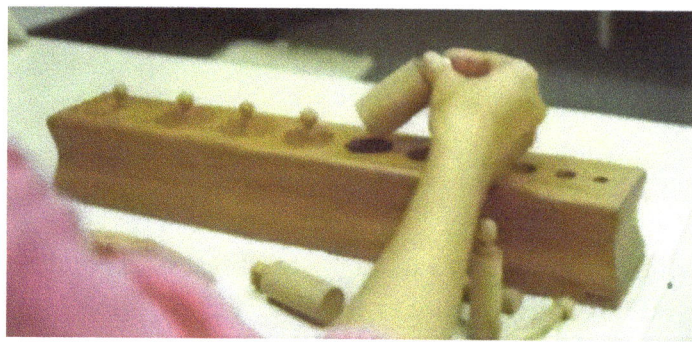

Figure 8.2 © Knobbed Cylinders Michelle Lane, 2001

When the child is receiving one-to-one instruction, or beginning to work with the materials independently, data collection is important. Observing and documenting the specific skills being tracked helps teachers, therapists, doctors, and parents understand what skills within the Montessori activity were acquired and what skills still need work.

Many skills are developing during the Knobbed Cylinder activity, including: taking the material to and from the shelf; rolling out the table mat; taking the cylinders out of the block; sequencing the cylinders from largest to smallest; and replacing them in the block. In order to determine the progress of the various skill acquisitions, they can be tracked separately. For example, if a child can sequence the cylinders from largest to smallest, the sequencing skill would be considered acquired and the response criteria for that skill is met. The teacher could continue to track the child's progress with replacing the cylinders in the appropriate holes and offer further instruction for that portion of activity.

Consequence (reinforcement)

The DTT ends with a consequence. In ABA we use tangibles so that the child finds the activity enjoyable (e.g., edible items or any item that the child can see or touch), as well as social reinforcements (e.g., high fives or hugs). It is important to choose the type of tangible reinforcement that can be easily removed. For example, some children will do well with reinforcements like toy cars and books, but may become upset when you take the book or car away. Reinforcements such as bubbles can be more helpful because once the bubbles pop you can move onto the next skill. You are not taking away the reinforcement, because the bubbles pop and go away. Similarly, social reinforcement such as a high five or a hug are helpful for children who no longer need tangible reinforcements.

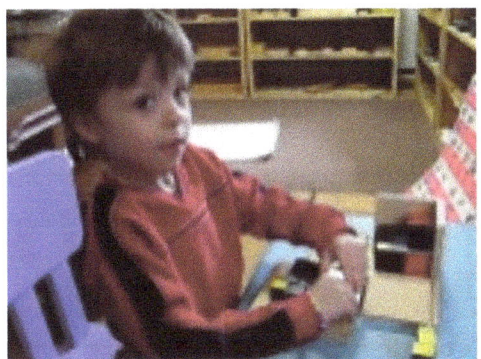

Figure 8.3 Photo courtesy of Michelle Lane-Barmapov. Used with permission.

The goal of ABA, which is also one of the goals in Montessori, is for the child to be able to do the activities independently. The child in the above photo (Figure 8.3) is working with the Trinomial Cube independently. He was receiving part-time Montessori ABA therapy in addition to other treatments. His parents shared with me that using this collaborative approach helped him improve in all areas of his development. Both the Montessori curriculum and ABA with DTT are beneficial for children who need intensive intervention. Blended together, they offer children with autism an incredible learning opportunity.

Montessori, Autism, and Inclusion

Sometimes, teachers are not sure how to support children with autism in their classrooms. Working in collaboration with consultants and other specialists may be necessary (e.g., behavior, speech, and occupational therapy). Nehring (2014) described this type of collaboration as Montessori scientific and medical pedagogy. My current research supports the benefits of professional collaboration (Lane-Barmapov, 2016).

At an inclusive Montessori school, Julie, a child with autism, spent hours working on a particular pouring activity. The teachers consulted with me because they were unsure whether or not to move Julie away from the pouring. She always chose this work and would exhibit negative behavior when they tried to direct her to another activity. I observed Julie and determined she was "stimming" (engaging in self-stimulatory behavior) off the water work and not reaching her full potential.

The teachers and I worked together to implement the Montessori ABA therapy approach to help Julie. Eventually Julie developed a routine, and she became accustomed to working with other Montessori activities, which not only helped her overall skill development, but also provided an opportunity for her to continue to be engaged in the Montessori method of education as she grew and developed with her peers. Ensuring Julie was engaging in other enriching Montessori activities also helped her develop her muscle movements and her problem-solving skills.

As a practitioner and a consultant to inclusive Montessori schools, I have observed the benefits of Montessori ABA therapy and am hopeful this technique can continue to help facilitate greater inclusion for children with autism in Montessori schools. Montessori ABA therapy is based on researched benefits, but is only one way to work with a child with autism in a Montessori environment.

Many strategies can facilitate inclusion in Montessori classrooms for children across a significant portion of the autism spectrum. When including a child with autism in a Montessori classroom, a Montessori teacher's instincts and ability to observe a child and make modifications based on observation are instrumental and of the utmost importance. In my research study, participants I interviewed often came up with their own adaptations for children with autism in their inclusive Montessori schools (Lane-Barmapov, 2016). Sometimes their own creative modifications were all that was needed to support children with autism in their classrooms.

Strategies such as visual schedules and relaxation techniques match up seamlessly with Montessori teaching methods. Groden, Cautela & Groden (1990) developed relaxation techniques for children with autism, which help to reduce stress and encourage self-control. Attwood (2007) pioneered methods for children with autism to teach friendship and conversation skills. All of these techniques can help support inclusion in the Montessori classroom for children on the milder end of the autism spectrum.

Visual Schedules

Visual schedules can be used to help children with autism organize daily activities and can also provide visual support to help reduce anxiety. Figure 8.4 shows pictures of activities that were cut out, laminated, and placed on separate sheets in a binder using Velcro (each curriculum page was labeled and color-coded). Every morning, the teacher and child choose which activities to work with by putting those pictures on the Velcro strips.

Figure 8.4 An example of a visual schedule in a binder. Each area of the curriculum is color-coded. © Lane-Barmapov 2012.

Some children with autism will need to have these pictures put in the correct order in which to do them to help reduce anxiety. Once each activity is completed, the child places the picture in the pocket of the binder labeled "All Done." On the left there is a place to put a picture of a reinforcement (such as a hug), but this child did not need an external reinforcement to do the work. The visual schedule worked as a support to manage his daily routine.

Transitions

When I consult to support children with autism at inclusive Montessori schools, I consistently notice that challenging behavior issues emerge during transition periods. When children go from a work period to outdoor play, for example, the noise level typically gets louder and the movements of children change. This can be a very challenging time for children with autism. Visual schedules and some type of warning (a 5- or 10-minute warning) are techniques I recommend that often have significant success.

Inclusive Communities

Figure 8.5 An older "typically" developing child at The Montessori Jewish Day School spontaneously helping a younger child on the spectrum. (Photo courtesy of Montessori Jewish Day School in Toronto, Canada.)

Within a Montessori mixed-aged classroom, children observe and help one another, and children with autism and "typically" developing children can work together. In the picture above, an older "typically" developing child at The Montessori Jewish Day School is spontaneously helping a younger child who is on the spectrum. Inclusive Montessori environments can be beneficial for children with autism who respond and relate to their peers in a unique manner.

I have collaborated with the staff of The Montessori Jewish Day School for over a decade to help foster an inclusive environment, not only for children with learning differences and varying exceptionalities, but also for "typically" developing children and families from a variety of backgrounds within their school community.

The Montessori Jewish Day School is an excellent model of inclusion. The school is able to support children ages 2 through 14 with integrated Montessori practice. Because classrooms function on the basis of social cohesion, children with learning differences and varying exceptionalities become a valued part of their community. They are intentionally included in social activities and events outside of school. The school community strives to include all children and help them feel good about themselves and their contribution to the community.

Today, as a parent, knowing that my children are learning to have compassion and empathy for others is important, and that, in part is why my family chose the Montessori Jewish Day School for our own children. I think everyone can benefit by learning to be comfortable in diverse and inclusive community environments. As an academic researcher, I see inclusion as an incredible opportunity within the Montessori community.

Inclusion benefits all children, not just those with differences and many Montessori schools are striving to be inclusive. During a research study I led focusing on how Montessori schools can support inclusion, one teacher described a talk she often has with her students at the beginning of the year. She asks the children if they can imagine our world with only one kind of flower. The children discuss how they like different types of flowers and colors. Once they have this discussion, the teacher leads the conversation by asking the children to think about the flowers as the individuals in the classroom. This discussion continues by asking the children if they would like a class where everyone wore the same kinds of clothes, had the same interests, etc. This leads to a discussion on inclusion (Lane-Barmapov, 2016, p. 35).

Conclusion

Every child with autism deserves intervention. Riley, a young child with whom I worked in a traditional ABA program before I developed the Montessori ABA program, was granted government funding for therapy very late and only had a few months before he aged out of the funded program at 6 years old. He was diagnosed on the severe end of the autism spectrum and did not show much developmental progress during the few months I worked with him. During our final meeting, the psychologist advised Riley's parents to consider putting him on the list for a group home as an adult. We need more options for children who age out of programs early on.

Sam was a child with whom I worked at the beginning of my career; he never received ABA therapy and was in diagnostic classes during all of his school years. He was also diagnosed with severe autism and had no communication skills. Now, as a grown man, he continues to have behavior outbursts. Because caring for an adult with autism is quite challenging, Sam currently goes to a care facility for adults on some weekends to give his parents respite.

When I work with a child who is diagnosed with severe autism, sometimes I think about Riley and Sam. Money for early childhood therapy is well spent, but unfortunately for Riley, Sam and many other children like them today, the resources are still not always available. The need for funding for early childhood education and therapy has never been greater. Many children continue to lack access to crucial therapy or quality early childhood programs.

Prior to founding The Toronto Montessori School for Autism, I worked in the field of autism for over a decade. When the school I loved and cherished closed because government funding vanished, I was heartbroken. But today I am still dedicated to helping children with autism by educating adults and consulting with inclusive schools. I have dedicated much of my life to serving children with autism, and I have also built on the skills I developed during my early childhood. My lifelong love of learning began when I was a child in a Montessori school.

I believe children can reveal their strengths in Montessori environments, and I have consulted with Montessori schools that serve children with autism who are showing exceptional abilities in specific areas, such as writing or math. Thanks to individualized learning, these children are able to accelerate in those subjects. The Montessori method of education can support children with a variety of exceptionalities, from children with autism to children who are academically gifted.

Early childhood education can lay a foundation for life. For children with autism, early childhood therapy can make the difference between a life in an institution and a life of thriving with minimal support.

Contrast of Typical Development and the Development of Children with Autism; Montessori Strategies that Enhance Learning for Children with Autism

Development of "Typical" Child	Development of a Child with Autism	Montessori Strategies that Enhance Learning for a Child with Autism
Cooperative Behaviors Usually has gained inhibition control by age 5 which enables children to cooperate with teachers and peers in a learning environment. Given encouragement, enjoys the acceptance of responsibility and independence. Follows a model of consideration of others	**Cooperative Behaviors** Cooperation requires a level of understanding of social skills. This is an area that is very challenging and is an inherent deficit within the disorder.	**Cooperative Behaviors** Although Montessori classrooms are split into three age groupings, the child with autism will need assistance learning how to engage with peers as well as teachers. The mixed aged groupings create an environment where other children can assist children with autism during their social skill lessons learning. Ways of working out conflict can be integrated in the Montessori curriculum (i.e. peace flower) as are lessons on self-awareness (i.e. naming emotions). These activities may need modifications to further support the child with autism.
Coordination: Gross Motor Walks, hops, runs, jumps, skips, throws, and catches ball by approximately age 5 if offered the opportunity to observe these movements.	**Coordination: Gross Motor** Repetitive movements and difficulty with imitation skills are contributing factors to the lack of ability to perform gross motor tasks. Some children have difficulty with coordination due to sensory dysfunction which impacts their reaction to sensory stimuli. Children with autism may have low muscle tone.	**Coordination: Gross Motor** The Montessori curriculum encourages movement. The sense training inherent within each activity (i.e. weight and repetition) helps to strengthen low muscle tone. Activities that encourage gross motor skills such as washing a chair, various ways to walk on a line (i.e. jumping, holding a bell) also encourage gross motor coordination. Most lessons will need adapted teaching methods rather than the typical Montessori presentations which are based on a child's ability to imitate the teacher and peers in the class.
Coordination: Fine Motor Cuts on a line, cuts out shapes, holds pencil, maintains line, and pressure, makes corners by age 5 if offered the opportunity to learn these movements.	**Coordination: Fine Motor** Children with autism have a range of fine motor capabilities. For many children, pointing skills are challenging. However, this appears to be due to the lack of joint attention which is inherent to autism. Fine motor manipulation may also be affected due to sensory dysfunction.	**Coordination: Fine Motor** There are many opportunities to develop fine motor coordination within the Montessori curriculum (i.e., Knobbed Cylinders, Metal Insets). Children with autism may need additional direction from the teacher or may need occupational therapy to help the child manage self-stimulatory behavior and experience greater benefit from these activities.

Development of "Typical" Child	Development of a Child with Autism	Montessori Strategies that Enhance Learning for a Child with Autism
Oral Language The average 5-year-old has a vocabulary of approximately 2,500 to 5,000 words and usage of this vocabulary or basic communication with appropriate sentence structure.	**Oral Language** This varies dramatically with the severity of autism. Many children with autism are nonverbal so they need augmentative communication tools to express themselves. Vocabulary can range from only one or two words to above the average typical development of oral language. Children who are considered high functioning often have the typical range of oral language but need to learn social nuances and cues.	**Oral Language** Prior to the DSM-5, a little less than half of children with autism were nonverbal. Having oral language may or may not be attainable but having the ability to communicate is important. The Montessori language curriculum is concrete and allows for language to develop through hands-on activities. For children who are nonverbal, adapting preliminary lessons allows the child to demonstrate their knowledge.
Written Language Matches, discriminates sensory information. Perceives patterns in shape, color, numbers.	**Written Language** This varies dramatically with the severity of autism. Some children do very well with written language while others have great difficulty in learning the symbols and sounds. There are many children who are very capable of learning patterns and relating these to patterns found in written language, however others find this extremely challenging.	**Written Language** Due to the hands-on nature of the Montessori curriculum, children with autism can demonstrate their knowledge of written language to the teacher. For children who are verbal, the phonetic-based approach helps Montessori children further learn to decode words. For a nonverbal child, using the Movable Alphabet or Sandpaper Letters can indicate if the child knows how to build words and if connections of words to images or objects are consistent.
Attention Inhibition control begins to develop at 2 to 3 years of age. Focuses on activity presentation and concentrates. Works with activities for periods of 10 minutes or longer.	**Attention** Attention-deficit/hyperactivity disorder (ADHD) may be co-occurring. Joint attention, (the ability to focus on facial expressions while communicating) may be impaired. Children with autism may hyper-focus while engaging in self stimulatory behavior and may be unable to focus on their surrounding environment and individuals within the environment.	**Attention** Children with autism may benefit from therapeutic intervention with the Montessori/applied behavior analysis (ABA) blend.

Development of "Typical" Child	Development of a Child with Autism	Montessori Strategies that Enhance Learning for a Child with Autism
Organization Order and sequence learned by imitation	**Organization** Imitation skills are typically challenging for children with autism. They have their own organization that often interferes with their ability to function within various environments. Changing the child's inherent idea of organization is challenging and often results in resistance.	**Organization** Although the Montessori environment is organized (i.e., each activity has a special place in the classroom, chronological order in which the activities are presented) the child with autism usually requires some type of intervention based (i.e., from visual schedules to intensive applied behavior analysis therapy) in order to learn how to navigate and choose work within the classroom.
Work Cycle Chooses one activity after another varying the challenge of choices.	**Work Cycle** Has a cycle but often it is not conducive to new learning and social opportunities. Once a work cycle is established it is difficult to change.	**Work Cycle** Having a consistent work cycle is usually very important for children with autism. Some will need minor support when they know what activities they can work on, while others will need to have the work chosen for them until they learn the skills required to make choices or to be comfortable with a new routine of work.
Work Choices Chooses variety of work, usually proceeding to more difficult concepts.	**Work Choices** Chooses activities that are part of their own routine. Often the work choices are not used in a similar way that a typical child would engage with the activities (i.e., lining up objects) and depending on the severity of autism, children may be consumed with self-stimulatory behavior that impedes their ability to choose other activities or work with other activities in the manner they were intended.	**Work Choices** Depending on the severity of autism, some children may be able to make choices in the work they have been shown. For many children, adaptations such as visual schedules and choice boards will have to accompany their daily routine to provide additional visual cues for choice support. For children with more severe autism, blending the Montessori curriculum with evidence-based methods of applied behavior analysis (ABA) are beneficial for the child to make progressions, and in this case, choice is typically guided by the therapist and/or teacher.
Work Habits Chooses work, uses procedure with purpose, replaces the work on the shelf.	**Work Habits** Tends to enjoy doing tasks that are part of the perceived routine and are repetitive in nature.	**Work Habits** Depending on the severity, work habits improve with intervention. All children are working at their own pace in the class and this provides the right atmosphere for the individual planning of the child with autism.

Development of "Typical" Child	Development of a Child with Autism	Montessori Strategies that Enhance Learning for a Child with Autism
Math Gains number to quantity concepts, math symbols, math concepts, and beginning computation by age 5.	**Math** Some children are able to work above and beyond "typical" children in this area while others struggle with learning the first ten digits (0-9).	**Math** Math provides the child with a concrete example of number and quantity. For the nonverbal child, matching the numbers to the number rods (one of the preliminary math lessons) is often presented at the same time in order for the teacher to determine if the child understands symbol and quantity. Activities such as numbers and counters can be a great jumping off point for visualization of how to count numbers as many children with autism are visual learners. The concrete abstraction of the Math curriculum gives the child additional support when forming complex numbers as well as doing mathematical equations which is unique to the Montessori method of education.

> "*The deviated child has no love for his environment because he feels it to contain too many difficulties.*"
>
> (Montessori, 1949/1995, p. 92)

Chapter 9

Montessori Applied to Varying Intellectual Abilities, from Gifted to Disabled

Joyce S. Pickering, with contributions from Sylvia O. Richardson

Most Montessori teachers have a deep knowledge of child development and developmental stages. Montessori teachers do not expect to be able to use one instructional plan with all children. With additional knowledge, Montessori teachers can better apply the Montessori method to the specific needs of all children.

In a Montessori classroom, children of varying abilities all receive individualized lessons and work at their own pace. All children, and especially those with varying exceptionalities, benefit from direct instruction using Montessori methods. For children with intellectual disabilities, this early childhood intervention can provide a lifetime support.

The Montessori method is based on the development of each child intellectually, physically, and emotionally. Children need not be engaged in the same lesson at the same time. The delivery of the hierarchical curriculum, which is presented from simple to complex and concrete to abstract, is individualized. The teacher keeps detailed notes of the progress of each child, and these records guide the presentation of lessons that are differentiated for each child at their level of development. In Montessori classrooms, children of varying mental, physical, and academic ability can be served at their level of understanding.

Intelligence and Processing

There is more to a child's innate abilities than an IQ score. There are two distinct abilities that affect learning. One is mental ability (IQ) and the other is perceptual ability (the ability to give meaning to sensory stimulus) which requires accurate processing. A child can have an IQ at average or above-average levels and have processing differences which affect their learning in language, math, or other areas. For this reason, there are children who are very intelligent, but have the specific learning difference, dyslexia, and struggle with reading and writing.

I have worked with children who have IQ scores in the superior ranges, but have language processing differences. Their reading/decoding is far below expectancy for age and IQ. Although they make many errors in their reading, they still have adequate comprehension.

There are children with low intellectual functioning who have poor comprehension skills, but can decode very well for their age. I have also worked with children who have below-average scores on an IQ assessment, but can decode well. The ability to decode in reading requires accurate processing of letters and sounds into words. It is a separate ability from what is measured on a test of intellectual functioning.

Intelligence Assessment

The most widely used IQ tests today are the Wechsler Adult Intelligence Scale (WAIS) and the Wechsler Intelligence Scale for Children (WISC). IQ tests are scaled using a standard deviation of 15 points. See Chapter 10, Figure 10.3, page 202, Normal Curve.

- Children with IQ scores of 85–115 are in the Normal range. Above 115 is Superior or Very Superior.
- With scores between 70–85, children are performing in the Low Normal range. Their learning proceeds at a slower rate than those in the average and above ranges. They can certainly learn to read, write, and spell, and do basic math. They will usually have difficulty with abstract reasoning, retaining, and applying information.

- In the range of 50–69, the intellectual disability (ID) is mild and not obvious in the early years. Many children with these scores can learn to read and do simple math to the 9–12-year-old level, and can be trained to do work and live independently.

- The IQ range of 35–49 is a moderate range of ID. In this range, intellectual delays are apparent in infancy. These individuals can learn health and safety rules and usually live with their family or in group homes as adults.

- Individuals with an IQ below 35 are in a severe range of ID and need assistance their entire life.

Definition of Gifted and Talented Children

The term "gifted and talented," refers to students, children, or youth who give evidence of high achievement capability in such areas as intellectual, creative, artistic, or leadership capacity, or in specific academic fields, and who need services or activities not ordinarily provided by the school in order to fully develop those capabilities. (No Child Left Behind Act of 2001, nagc.org)

Characteristics and Signs of Gifted Children

Gifted children often have a tendency to be perfectionist and idealistic. They may have heightened sensitivity to their own expectations and those of others. Some are mappers (sequential learners) and some are leapers (spatial learners). They may be so far ahead of their classmates that they know half the curriculum before the school year begins. Gifted children may also be problem solvers who think so abstractly and with such complexity that they may need help with concrete study and test-taking skills. Gifted children generally have unusual talent in one, or occasionally two, areas.

There are six areas where giftedness can occur:

- Creative Thinking
- Leadership
- General Intellectual Ability

- Psychomotor Ability
- Specific Academic Ability
- Visual/Performing Arts

Within these areas, gifted children usually have one or two subjects that they are best in and passionate about. Each gifted child has their own unique profile of strengths and weaknesses. Gifted children develop in their areas of talent earlier than "typically" developing children. Their motor coordination, for example, may develop along the typical milestones, while their language development may be rapid and their vocabulary may be extensive. Their processing of visual, auditory, and kinesthetic information may be accomplished at a rapid rate, helping them to understand situations and solve problems earlier than most children. Their attention may be typical for their age, but they may become quickly bored if not challenged. Development in their exceptional areas of talent is broader and deeper than the typical learner.

Montessori for the Gifted Child

With an individualized and differentiated program, the Montessori classroom offers gifted children the opportunity to self-direct and make choices about materials and subject matter to study. Unlike the traditional classroom, in which a gifted child must do the same lessons at the same time as their classmates, gifted children in a Montessori classroom can choose their work, work uninterrupted for extended periods of time, discover information in a creative way, and research areas of high interest. They can proceed through the curriculum at their own pace, working on activities that may be too challenging for other children their age.

Gifted children in a traditional classroom often say, "I'm bored." This is not a phrase that is heard in a well-run Montessori classroom in which the teacher is expected to give interesting and challenging lessons to all children, including those who are far advanced. No child is held back if they are ready for accelerated work.

Gifted and talented children are often perfectionists. In a Montessori classroom there is a philosophy that mistakes are not bad, but rather they are the way we learn. Many inventors experience hundreds of failures before a success. It is important to help gifted children learn patience and perseverance, or they may develop the habit of giving up on a task they cannot do easily and quickly.

Montessori multisensory materials make the abstract more concrete and are important for "typically" developing children. The educational materials in the early childhood classroom can be appropriate for older or younger children. Gifted children may grasp a concept in just one presentation of a lesson and may not need to practice with multisensory materials to master the concept being presented. They generally will not return to a lesson that they have grasped, unless the teacher shows them a new and higher concept using the same materials. They will move from multisensory materials to more abstraction and to paper and pencil tasks more rapidly than the "typical" child. However, if they know an answer to a problem in their head, they are often impatient if asked to show their work on paper.

A child who had attended a Montessori preschool until the age of 6 was heard to say, after transferring to a traditional school, "They won't let me finish my work." This is probably the hardest transition for a Montessori child who has rarely been interrupted during the extended work period in a Montessori classroom.

In summary, Montessori education provides gifted children with:

- a classroom in which the curriculum covers 3 years of study
- freedom to choose the work appropriate for the child's interest and level of ability
- procedures that allow children to proceed through the multi-year curriculum at their own pace, giving gifted children the opportunity to work at advanced levels in their areas(s) of advanced ability
- teachers trained to provide an individualized/differentiated program for each child
- a method that introduces new concepts at a concrete level and allows children to reach higher levels of abstraction at their rate of mastery

- encouragement for creativity and choice in creating projects to explore higher levels of understanding
- an emphasis on organization of work tasks in each lesson, enhancing executive function
- an emphasis on respect for everyone in the class, providing gifted children with a foundation in developing and maintaining social relationships with other children of varying abilities
- enhanced vocabulary development through the specific nomenclature used in each lesson
- teachers trained to introduce advanced concepts earlier than usual due to the use of multisensory manipulative materials (for example, the introduction of the decimal system in the early childhood classroom)

Intellectual Disabilities

Intellectual disabilities (ID) generally appear before adulthood and are characterized by significant impairment in cognitive functioning and challenges with two or more adaptive behaviors. For 25% of those with ID, the cause is genetic. IDs occur in 2–3% of the population. Approximately 75–90% of those are mildly affected.

Characteristics of ID include delays in language development, deficits in memory skills, difficulty with social rules, difficulty with problem solving, delays in adaptive behavior, and lack of social inhibitors. Some of the deficits are syndromic (associated with medical and behavioral signs and symptoms) and other deficits are non-syndromic (including intellectual deficits without other abnormalities).

Down syndrome (DS) is a genetic condition in which a person has 47 chromosomes instead of the usual 46. It was discovered by John Langdon Down. Although the cause is unknown, the chances of having a child with DS increase with the age of the mother. The population of individuals with DS in the U.S. is estimated at over 400,000, making it the most frequent ID. Other disabilities include velocariofacial syndrome, fetal alcohol syndrome, and genetic conditions. ID can occur because of issues during pregnancy, problems during birth, exposure to certain diseases (measles, meningitis), toxins (lead), malnutrition, or absence of a part of the brain called the arcuate fasciculus.

Language Training for Children with Intellectual Disabilities

In 1967, Dr. Sylvia Richardson wrote a paper detailing early intervention with Montessori techniques for children with intellectual disabilities. Dr. Richardson based her paper on her work at the University of Oklahoma Medical School. As Director of the Child Study Center there, she worked with Dr. June Shelton. Both were speech-language pathologists with Montessori early childhood training. Together they developed a program for the application of the Montessori method to children with intellectual disabilities. Excerpts from this paper are presented below.

> It is my firm conviction that:
> - early exposure to a variety of experiences in looking and listening is important in language development
> - perceptual and preverbal experiences are requisite in primary learning
> - motor movements are closely related to perceptual development
> - the development of motor patterns is related to the development of perceptual patterns
> - the orienting response (attention) is an important source of internal mediators
> - linguistic labels are mediating processes in learning, and
> - language development is part of and a result of primary learning.
>
> ...
>
> There are a number of Montessori education techniques that we have found useful in teaching intellectually disabled children, especially with regard to language development. These techniques are related to the research findings mentioned above.

...

In many children with language delay or disorders we are required to be of assistance or provide training in pre-linguistic skills, because of the perceptual-motor disorders exhibited by the children. Emphasis is on training in the motor bases of behavior (Kephart, 1960) such as posture, the development of laterality and directionality, and the development of body image; training in perceptual skills such as form perception, space discrimination, stereognosis, recognition of texture, size and structure; training in auditory perception (listening), in visual perception (looking), and in kinesthetic perception (muscular memory of movements, positions and postures). (c.f. Piaget and Hebb re: image primacy and primary learning.)

...

Language training for any child must begin at the beginning. We refer now to the theories of Piaget, Hunt, and Hebb as discussed earlier. In normal development, the baby must possess a psychic life antecedent to its life of motion. Through his senses he actively absorbs images of his environment for some time before he begins to express himself through motor activity. In order to orient himself in his world he must perceive the environment as a whole with interdependent parts. If he perceived only separates objects and not their relationships within the whole, he would be in chaotic confusion. He must also develop an inner orientation, which gives him a sense of the parts of his body, their movements and position. This inner orientation, or body-image, and the outer orientation that is concerned with relationships between the parts of the environment and the relation of the environment to himself, eventually result from looking, listening, touching and moving- all experimental roots or antecedents to language and speaking. The output will be a reflection of the way in which the organism has been able to integrate the sensory input.

Chapter 9

...

In order to assist the child in his task of orientation, his environment should be made pleasant, simple, and orderly in structure. The materials in our nursery are designed to attract his attention, to "educate the senses," and to allow manipulation by the child. Our goal is to assist him in his task of creating order in sensory input by presenting a carefully constructed sequence of experiences which proceeds slowly, (often painfully so for the teacher) from the concrete to the abstract.

...

Of importance, as the child is taught each activity, such as washing hands or polishing shoes, each step of the operation is presented in logical, orderly sequence—almost as one would program a computer. (c.f. Hebb on primary learning, and the Soviet stress on the conditioned response in the young child prior to the later control by the second signal system.) The child is trained to focus attention (orientation response) and to analyze each of his body movements as he repeats the sequence each time. Improvement of each step within an activity leads to a gradual decrease of clumsiness and extraneous activity. The method of presenting each step of these exercises to the child is based on the same type of premise proposed by Zaporozhets with regard to the need for receiving feedback en route in order to achieve complex voluntary behavior. The Montessori directress is trained to direct the child's attention to each external and proprioceptive cue. When she goes over each step of an exercise, such as washing the hands, verbalizing each action as it is performed, the child learns what to look at. He is being trained to use feedback from his own action and from the external situation.

It has also been noted that the more accurately an exercise can be taught in all its details, the more it seems to become a stimulus to an endless repetition (not perseveration but purposeful repetition) of the same exercise. Using this method with intellectually disabled children doing the exercises in Practical Life, one can demonstrate quite clearly that the functions of attention respond well to training. One can also observe over a period of time (which may be lengthy) the various responses to language described by Luria, from the primitive orienting response, through the impulsive type of response, to the selective, when the child simply obeys directions. Finally one observes the emergence of Luria's "pre-selective function" of language, where the child demonstrates appropriate response to self-instruction; he may even be heard telling himself what to do. Thus, simple exercises such as washing hands or polishing shoes can be presented as an integral part of language training when they are ordered to a definite end.

...

Many present-day educators in special education are presenting methods derived from Montessori, Seguin and even as far back as Comenius, often without realizing their source. Of all of these, Montessori formulated a system of lessons and coordinated training sequences, which originally were used successfully with intellectually disabled children. It is our own experience that early sensory-motor training, starting at the level of pre-verbal experience, is of major importance in the establishment of a language program for these children. Applications of these often overlooked basic approaches to education would greatly enhance the effectiveness of the work with intellectually disabled children.

Tribute to Dr. Sylvia Richardson

In 1967, when I called Sylvia out of the blue, I had never before contacted a complete stranger who was a professional recognized at the top of their field. I had read an article she wrote on learning disabilities. It was like manna from heaven to me. Sylvia's article helped me feel supported by science. Most of the people I spoke with told me that dyslexia did not exist.

Sylvia welcomed my call and invited me to have lunch with her. That lunch was the beginning of a lifelong friendship. She had a wonderful life with many strong and supportive friends. She lived for 94 years. She was a remarkable human being, and her humility and kindness were exceptional.

She was also known as an approachable doctor, and as we often walked the halls of conferences, we could not take two steps without someone thanking her for the help she had given them. She always stopped and talked and she always helped anyone who asked. She was truly a compassionate doctor.

"The Montessori Method, then, both for the pupil and the teacher is, in a word, observation."

(Orem, 1965, p. 79)

Chapter 10

Assessment: Observation, Screening, Evaluation

Joyce S. Pickering, with contributions from Laure Ames

Chapter 10 explains the reasons why an assessment might be needed, describes commonly used tests and test batteries, and offers information to help interpret results. This chapter also includes guidelines for observation to help teachers decide whether to recommend testing.

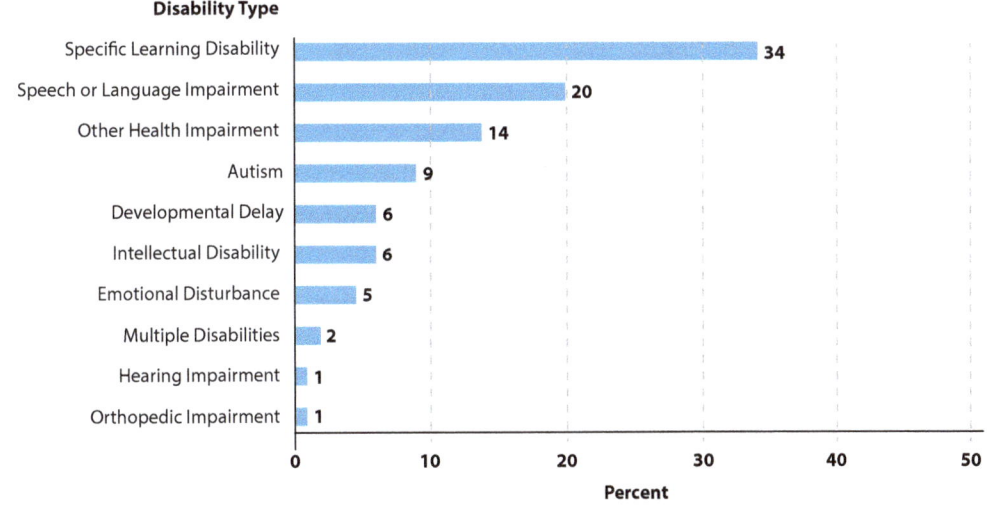

Figure 10.1 Prevalence of disabilities exhibited by children who are served under the Individual with Disabilities Education Act (IDEA) (Digest of Education, 2015).

Why Do We Assess?

Early diagnosis followed by therapeutic remediation, in partnership with strategic teaching, helps avoid the struggles that develop when children have learning differences and do not have access to services they need and deserve. To determine if they have a learning difference, children can be assessed as early as age 4. Parents of children with suspected learning differences should consider an assessment. Parents can request an evaluation through their public school system, whether they are attending a public or private school, or can have their child evaluated privately.

If a specific learning disability is diagnosed, parents can explain to their child that this has nothing to do with how "smart" they are, that it is a learning difference, and that there are different ways of teaching so they can learn. Parents should be very honest and tell their children it will not be easy, but with hard work and the specific learning methods they need, they will be able to achieve, and it will be worth the effort to learn to read and spell effectively and write expressively.

Informal observation by parents, teachers, and professionals, in conjunction with formal standardized measures, provide a good picture of a child's unique learning strengths and weaknesses. The goals of formal assessment should be to attain a profile of a child as a learner and to help plan an educational program for the child. All teachers can be more precise in their educational planning for a child if they know about the child's learning strengths and weaknesses.

Many parents and teachers do not want to assess a child because they see this process as "labeling," or believe the child will grow out of it. Unfortunately, some people perceive differences as negative. The true purpose of an evaluation does not end with a negative "label." In contrast to a label, a diagnosis is a description to give parents and professionals a way to communicate the child's needs. *Diagnosis is not the end of the process; it is the beginning.* From the diagnostic information gained through formal evaluation, an educational plan can be developed to help the child become more successful. Ideally, the only reason for an evaluation is to plan a beneficial educational program for the child.

It is difficult to help a struggling child without knowing, with some degree of precision, why they struggle. *If a child is struggling, we should want to know why.* Assessing the child's abilities is necessary. An evaluation gives the instructor a baseline from which to measure a child's progress. Subsequent testing, using the same tests as in the initial battery, provides a reliable indication of a child's progress. The information gained from repeated evaluations generates a profile for each individual child, so that lessons can be directed specifically toward the child's needs.

Guided observation (using a checklist), a screening battery, or formal evaluation can provide teachers with valuable information about a child's challenges. A comprehensive evaluation will provide a profile of an individual's abilities in perceptual (visual and auditory) processing, oral language, written language (reading, spelling, written expression), academic and adaptive skills, attention, and behavior. Over time in the classroom, the teacher can add informed observation to this profile of the child's performance. Using this profile, a specific plan can be made for a child's instruction and/or remediation. (For information about an assessment learning profile and a matching child profile educational plan, see the Appendix).

Observation in the Classroom is of Critical Importance

What should a teacher look for when considering whether to make a referral for an evaluation to determine if a child has a learning difference or some other condition impairing academic progress? To decide, a teacher must first observe classroom behavior. Below are guidelines for observations.

Observing Classroom Behavior:
- Does the child demonstrate age-appropriate self-control?
- Does the child have a cycle of work established? (The Montessori cycle of work indicates the ability to be self-directing in choosing work, engaging with the work, and completing and returning the work to the shelf before choosing another activity.)
- Is the child's activity level average, hyperactive, or hypoactive?

- Is the child easily distracted visually? Is the child easily distracted aurally?
- Does the child avoid certain types of work? What does the child avoid?
- Does the child need the teacher's guidance an average amount of time, rarely, or frequently?

Observing Classroom Performance:
- Does the child sequence appropriately?
- Are the child's gross motor skills coordinated?
- Are the child's fine motor skills coordinated?
- Is the child's perception within normal age limits? (For example: in Practical Life activities, does the child judge space accurately; in Sensorial and Math activities, does the child perceive pattern and gradation?)
- Is the child's oral language development within normal age limits (listening, vocabulary, verbal expression)?
- Does the child stutter or have articulation difficulties?
- Are the child's pre-writing or writing skills age-appropriate?
- Are the child's pre-reading or reading skills age-proficient?
- Is the child reading with fluency and understanding?
- What are the child's talents?

Observing Social Behavior:
- Does the child have many friends? Few friends?
- Are the friends older? Younger?
- Is the child immature in social situations?
- Does the child avoid social situations?
- Does the child display poor judgment in a group?

- Does the child overreact to most situations?
- Does the child have difficulty relating to adults? To peers?
- Does the child dislike being touched?
- Does the child have clowning behavior?
- Is there withdrawn (shy) behavior?
- Is there confrontational behavior?
- Is there manipulative behavior?
- Is there hostile/aggressive behavior?

Observing Motor Skills

- Is balance average for the child's age?
- Can the child do alternating movement (walking up stairs, skipping)?
- Does the child use his eye and hand together in coordination?
- Does the child have average coordination of gross motor skills (large muscles)?
- Does the child have fine motor coordination (hand)?
- Does the child show average perception of directionality?
- Are attempts at handwriting legible? Appropriately spaced?

The MATCH Teacher Checklist: Observation of Academic Performance in a Montessori Classroom is intended for the early childhood Montessori classroom. See the Appendix for more information. The Referral Form/Older Students is intended for children in the Montessori Elementary classroom (Figure 10.2). Ages are given for questions requiring specific knowledge of typical development.

If a teacher uses this list and checks a number of areas of concern, the teacher should talk with the parents about those areas. Depending on the age of the child, and the degree of concern, a consultation with school administrators and recommendation for a comprehensive evaluation may be needed.

REFERRAL FORM FOR _____

TEACHER: Smith   CHILD'S NAME: John
GRADE: 4   DOB: _____   SCHOOL: _____   DATE OF ENTRANCE: _____
LANGUAGE SPOKEN IN HOME: English
WHAT IS HIS/HER BEST SUBJECT? math   WHAT IS HIS/HER WORST SUBJECT? Reading

	YES	NO
CLASSROOM PERFORMANCE:		
1. Is easily distracted visually?	*	✓
2. Is easily distracted by noise?	*	✓
3. Over-reacts to most situations?	*	✓
4. Daydreams and has trouble attending?	*	✓
5. Is quiet and sluggish?	*	✓
6. Cannot follow directions. *at times*	✓ *	
7. Does not do well in math concepts and operations.	*	✓
8. Is not able to verbalize knowledge.	*	✓
9. Cannot express self on paper.	✓ *	
10. Handwriting is not legible.	*	
11. Cannot organize a paper.	*	
12. Is often absent.	*	✓
13. Poor organizational skills.	*	
14. Assignments not in on time.	*	
15. Does not request help when needed.	*	
SOCIAL BEHAVIOR	YES	NO
1. Has friends: Many		
Few	✓ *	
2. Friends are: Younger/Older	✓ *	
Peers		✓
3. Socializes with: Many		
Few	✓ *	
4. Is immature.	✓ *	
5. Appears to be trying, but success is limited.	✓ *	
6. Displays poor judgment in a group.	*	✓
7. Clowning behavior.	*	✓
8. Hostile/Aggressive behavior.	*	✓
9. Withdrawn (shy) behavior.	✓ *	
TEST BEHAVIOR	YES	NO
1. Seems to know material but cannot apply it when reviewed.	✓ *	
2. Has difficulty retaining material.	✓ *	
3. Knows it today but doesn't tomorrow.	✓ *	
OBSERVATIONS	YES	NO
1. Hearing loss.		✓
2. Wears glasses.		✓
3. Rubs eyes. *sometimes*	✓ *	
4. Difficulty saying certain words.	✓ *	
5. Frequently wants questions repeated.	✓ *	
6. Short attention span.	*	✓
7. Works with face close to book or paper. *sometimes*	✓ *	
8. Often forgets books, assignments, personal items, etc.	✓ *	
9. Difficulty with organization.	*	✓
PARENT CONTACTS	YES	NO
1. Have you met with the parents?	✓	
2. Are the parents positive?	✓	
3. Are the parents aware of difficulties in the classroom?	✓	
4. In your opinion, is there a supportive home environment?	✓	

* Yes answers indicate characteristics, which are often seen in students with learning differences.

© Joyce S. Pickering, M.A., LSH/CCC, 19

Figure 10.2 Referral Form for Older Students in a Montessori Elementary Classroom

Types of Evaluations

If any child is struggling, we should want to know why. There are several types of evaluations. These include:

1. A screening battery
2. A formal evaluation through a private practitioner
3. Various forms of evaluations done through the child's public school

A screening battery is discussed below. Professionals must look at the whole battery of tests when generating a diagnostic profile. One test does not a diagnosis make.

Screening Battery

To help our teachers at the Shelton School understand the learning differences their students have, an admission screening battery using select evaluation measures is administered to all incoming children. This battery of tests includes a wide range of measures. The purpose of the admissions screening is to determine the child's learning strengths and weaknesses so an educational plan can be determined. The screening battery consists of measures of mental ability, perceptual abilities, academic abilities, and questionnaires measuring attention, impulsivity, emotional difficulty, executive function, and behavior.

The screening battery of tests may include:

- The Slosson Intelligence Test for Children and Adults
- The Beery Visual-Motor Integration Test
- The Comprehensive Test of Phonological Processing—2nd Edition (CTOPP-2)
- The Gates Oral Subtests
- The WIAT Test for Early Reading Skills
- Oral Reading Fluency
- Spelling
- Math

A sample of writing of the alphabet and numerals is also included, as well as a parent and teacher questionnaire. A description of each of these measures can be found on the Shelton School website. See the Appendix. Other similar measures can be substituted for those suggested. The profile obtained from the screening is then used to plan the educational program for the child.

Select academic measures from the battery are re-administered in the spring to gauge progress over the school year. After many years of administering this battery, the Shelton School recognizes nine patterns seen in children with learning differences:

1. Pattern 1 indicates the characteristics of a specific reading disorder, or dyslexia, with weaknesses in reading decoding, spelling, and written expression.

2. Pattern 2 indicates the characteristics of a reading comprehension disorder. The child can decode well, but does not understand what is read.

3. Pattern 3 indicates the characteristics of ADHD (inattentive, hyperactive/impulsive, or combined presentation). In addition to difficulty with attention and executive functioning, children with ADHD are seen to have challenges with math and abstract meanings in reading comprehension.

4. Pattern 4 indicates the characteristics of a specific math disorder, or dyscalculia.

5. Pattern 5 indicates characteristics of a specific disorder in written expression (composition) and/or fine motor difficulty, or dysgraphia.

6. Pattern 6 indicates the characteristics of a communication disorder, with significant weaknesses in the oral language development (expressive, receptive, higher order, and social language) and/or speech (articulation, stuttering, etc.).

7. Pattern 7 indicates the characteristics of anxiety and mood disorders (including depression).

8. Pattern 8 indicates social challenges in interpersonal relationships.

9. Pattern 9 indicates the young child, 3 to 6 years of age, is at risk for learning disorders. Delays in coordination, speech-language, attention, and perception, the early signs of learning differences, are seen.

These patterns may occur individually or in combination (Pickering, J.S., 1993). When the child profile indicates difficulty in multiple areas, the learning difference is more complex.

When testing is done privately, the evaluator should use the criteria listed in the Diagnostic and Statistical Manual, 5th Edition to make diagnoses. Multiple types of measures may be used depending on the presenting concerns. If results do not meet full criteria for a diagnosis, specific areas of weakness can still be identified and appropriate intervention recommended.

What a Thorough Evaluation Includes

At the Shelton Evaluation Center, a comprehensive evaluation includes many of the measures listed below. This evaluation takes at least one full day of testing, followed by a reporting conference to explain results, and then a written report. This evaluation is done in greater depth than the Shelton Admissions Screening. A comprehensive evaluation should include the following measures:

- Background History and Family History
- Cognitive or Mental Ability
- Oral Language Ability
- Phonological Processing
- Letter-Sound Knowledge
- Automaticity/Fluency
- Word Recognition
- Decoding
- Reading Comprehension
- Spelling

- Written Expression
- Math
- Fine Motor Ability
- Working Memory
- Attention
- Executive Functioning
- Processing Speed
- Social/Emotional Ability

This psycho-educational battery of tests can identify cognitive delays, as well as language, learning, fine motor, and attention difficulties. It can also provide the basis for further testing for other exceptionalities, such as autism spectrum disorder or emotional disturbance. Additional specific tests may also be given to clarify any diagnoses.

Explanation of Tests

The following is a description of the specific measures and information gained from each test in a typical test battery given at the Shelton Evaluation Center. A battery of tests should be given by an experienced educational diagnostician, psychologist, or professional counselor and used to provide a profile of the child as a learner. This testing allows differential diagnoses by revealing the difficulties the child is experiencing.

History

Prior to an evaluation, the parents complete a questionnaire about the family's history of learning difficulties, attentional problems, and emotional problems, as well as the child's medical history. The child's history documents prenatal and birth information; early developmental milestones (cognitive, motor, social, and language); preschool and early education experiences; and the initial cause of concern that motivated the referral request. The evaluator interviews the parents after completion of this questionnaire on the day of testing.

Cognitive or Mental Ability Tests

Cognitive or mental ability (IQ) tests are used to assess various cognitive abilities. A weakness in a cognitive ability can underlie an academic difficulty. Overall low cognitive ability scores can indicate slower learning. Common cognitive ability tests include:

- Wechsler Intelligence Scales (WPPSI-IV, WISC-V, and WAIS-IV) (Wechsler, 1989; Wechsler, 2014; Wechsler, 2008)
- Stanford-Binet-V (Terman & Merrill, 1960)
- Kaufman Assessment Battery for Children (KABC) (Kaufman & Kaufman, 1983/2004)
- Woodcock Johnson Tests of Cognitive Abilities-IV (Schrank, Mather, & McGrew, 2014).

The Wechsler Intelligence Scale for Children—Fifth Edition (WISC-V) is a frequently given cognitive ability test. A full-scale IQ score is also obtained. These index scores are obtained by administering 10 subtests:

1. Block Design
2. Similarities
3. Matrix Reasoning
4. Digit Span
5. Coding
6. Vocabulary
7. Figure Weights
8. Visual Puzzles
9. Picture Span
10. Symbol Search

The WISC-V is administered verbally, usually taking about an hour. The patterns of performance both between and within the indexes indicate the child's cognitive strengths and weaknesses that impact learning. This comprehensive measure yields five index scores:

1. Verbal Comprehension (VCI)
2. Visual-Spatial (VSI)
3. Fluid Reasoning (FRI)
4. Working Memory (WMI)
5. Processing Speed (PSI)

The Slosson Intelligence Test for Children and Adults (Slosson, 2002) is shorter and can be given by a teacher or speech-language pathologist. It yields three index scores: Verbal, Performance, and Memory. The combined index scores yield a full-scale IQ score.

Perceptual Ability (Processing) — Visual, Auditory
These measures help determine whether visual and auditory processing are within normal limits and examine these early critical developmental areas underlying academic skills:

- The Beery-Buktenica Developmental Test of Visual-Motor Integration (Beery, Buktenica, & Beery, 2010) is a common test of visual perception, motor coordination, and visual-motor integration;
- The Comprehensive Test of Phonological Processing — 2nd Edition (CTOPP-2) (Wagner, Torgeson, Rashotte, & Pearson, 2013);
- The Test of Auditory Processing Skills — 3rd Edition (TAPS-3) (Martin & Brownell, 2005);
- The Phonological Awareness Test — 2nd Edition (PAT-2) (Robertson, 2007) are common measures of auditory perception.

Oral Language
Oral language ability underlies many academic skills. These commonly used tests of oral language ability measure language comprehension and production across the five language domains (i.e., phonology, morphology, syntax, semantics, and pragmatics):

- The Clinical Evaluation of Language Fundamentals—6th Edition (CELF-5) (Wiig, Semel, & Secord, 2013)
- The CELF-5 Metalinguistics (Wiig, Semel, & Secord, 2013)
- The Test of Problem Solving 3—Elementary (TOPS-3) (Bowers, Huisingh & LoGiudice, 2005)
- The Test of Problem Solving 2—Adolescent (TOPS-2) (Bowers, Huisingh & LoGiudice, 2007)
- The Comprehensive Assessment of Spoken Language—2nd Edition (CASL-2) (Carrow-Woolfolk, 1999)
- The Test of Language Development—4th Edition (TOLDP4/TOLDI4) (Newcomer & Hammill, 2008);
- The Preschool Language Scales—5th Edition (PLS-5) (Zimmerman, Steiner, & Pond, 2011)
- The Social Language Development Test (Elementary, Adolescent) (Bowers, Huisingh & LoGiudice, 2008)

Academic Ability

Pre-academic abilities in preschool children include knowledge of letters, sounds, and sound blending, and can be measured on the Gates-MacGinitie Oral Subtests (MacGinitie, MacGinitie, Maria, Dreyer & Hughes, 2000).

Informal assessment of writing letters and numbers can be done by asking the child to write as many letters and numbers as they know in order to determine the baseline of information that the child has attained. Some subtests of pre-academic skills are included in the broad measures of academic ability:

- The Wechsler Individual Achievement Test—3rd Edition (WIAT-III) (Wechsler, 2009)
- The Woodcock Johnson Test of Achievement—4th Edition (WJ-IV) (Schrank, Mather & McGrew, 2014)
- The Kaufman Test of Educational Achievement—3rd Edition (KTEA-3) (Kaufman & Kaufman, 2014).

Achievement tests measure reading, writing, and arithmetic. The assessment of each of these skills is divided into four components: basic skills, fluency, application, and comparison of reading and writing with oral skills (Tridas, 2007). It is important to go beyond the scores obtained in these measures and assess the types of errors made when diagnosing learning disabilities.

Additional measures of reading

During first grade and beyond, additional oral reading skills can be evaluated with:

- The Gray Oral Reading Test—5th Edition (GORT-V) (Wiederholt & Bryant, 2012). It yields scores for rate, accuracy, fluency, and comprehension with a total Oral Reading Index Score.

Additional measures of writing/spelling

Writing/spelling tests can be assessed with:

- The Test of Written Spelling (TWS-5) (Larsen, Hammill & Moats, 2013)
- The WIAT-III or Woodcock Johnson-IV

Written expression (composition) can be measured by:

- The WJ-IV
- The Kaufman Test of Educational Achievement, 3rd Edition (KTEA-III)
- The WIAT-III
- The Oral and Written Language Scales (OWLS-II) (Carrow-Woolfolk, 2012)

Additional measures of math

Math calculation, word problems, and fluency can be measured with:

- The WJ-IV

- The WIAT-III
- KeyMath—3rd Edition (KeyMath3) (Connolly, 2007)

Commonly used rating scales to measure behavior
- The Child Behavior Checklist (CBCL) (Achenbach, 1991)(includes parent and teacher forms)
- The Behavior Assessment System for Children—3rd Edition (BASC-3) (Reynolds & Kamphaus, 2015) (includes parent, teacher, and child self-report forms)

Specific scales that assess attention and/or emotional problems include:
- The Conners Comprehensive Behavior Rating Scales (Conners CBRS) (Conners, 2008)
- The Brown Attention-Deficit Disorder Scales (Brown, 2001)
- The Behavior Assessment System for Children—3rd Edition (BASC-3)
- The Behavior Rating Inventory of Executive Function—2nd Edition (BRIEF-2) (Gioia, Isquith, Guy & Kenworthy, 2000)

Continuous performance tests include:
- The Test of Variables of Attention (TOVA 8) (Greenberg, 1991–2015)
- Conners' Continuous Performance Test—3rd Edition (Conners CPT3) (Conners, 2014)
- The Quotient ADHD System (Teicher, M., 2002)

All these provide an objective, computer-generated assessment of a child's attention and impulsivity.

Autism Spectrum Disorder (ASD is a developmental disorder, not a learning disorder.)

Autism spectrum disorder measures may include:

- Autism Spectrum Rating Scale (ASRS) (Goldstein & Naglieri, 2009/2010)
- The Social Language Development Test
- The Autism Diagnostic Observation Schedule (ADOS) (Lord & Rutter, 2000)
- The Childhood Autism Rating Scale—2nd Edition (CARS-2) (Schopler & Van Bourgondien, 2010)
- The Autism Diagnostic Interview-Revised (ADI-R) (Rutter, LeCouteur & Lord, 2003)

Professionals who administer tests should make each child comfortable with both the setting and the tasks. Professionals must look at the whole battery of tests for the pattern of the learning difference when generating a diagnostic profile. Scores and the quality of performance should be used when making a diagnosis. Achievement of the child's best performance is the goal. IQ tests are not considered to be a total picture of the child's potential. Any test is "a snapshot in time" of the child's ability.

In public schools, children with learning differences are served in either general education (under the American with Disabilities Act or Section 504 of the Rehabilitation Act) or in special education (under the Individuals with Disabilities Education Act). Public schools usually have specific criteria that must be met before the school offers services to a child. For example, a child may demonstrate below-average reading and spelling, but not qualify for services unless they have a specific pattern of scores, regardless of the quality of the work or the significance of the struggle. Some public schools use progression through RTI (Response to Intervention) or Multi-tiered Systems of Support (MTSS) to determine the need for services. Parents can request an evaluation through their public school even if they are attending a private school.

Information Provided in Evaluation Reports

The tests mentioned above are used in comprehensive evaluations, and the results are described in a professional written report. A full evaluation report has a narrative and a summary data sheet of the performance on each test. To learn more about an evaluation report and data sheet, see the Appendix.

When administering a test, the examiner derives a raw score, which is the number correct out of the total possible. This raw score is interpreted using a statistical table, using the age and/or grade of the child. Test scores can be reported as standard scores, grade equivalents, percentiles, and/or stanines. The percentile and stanine are just two more ways of looking at scores. The percentile scale ranges from a low of 1 to a high of 99. The stanine range is from 1 to 9. The average standard score is 100, which represents the 50th percentile and 5th stanine. On any standardized test, the normal frequency distribution chart (Figure 10.3) has 68% of the population falling in the low average to high average range (85–115). The percentage falling above the mean is 15.86; the percentage falling below the mean is 15.86 (Slosson, 2002).

A teacher and/or parent receiving a comprehensive written report should be able to determine whether the child is performing at, below, or above the expected level for age and mental ability in each area measured.

Montessori Strategies for Children with Learning Differences

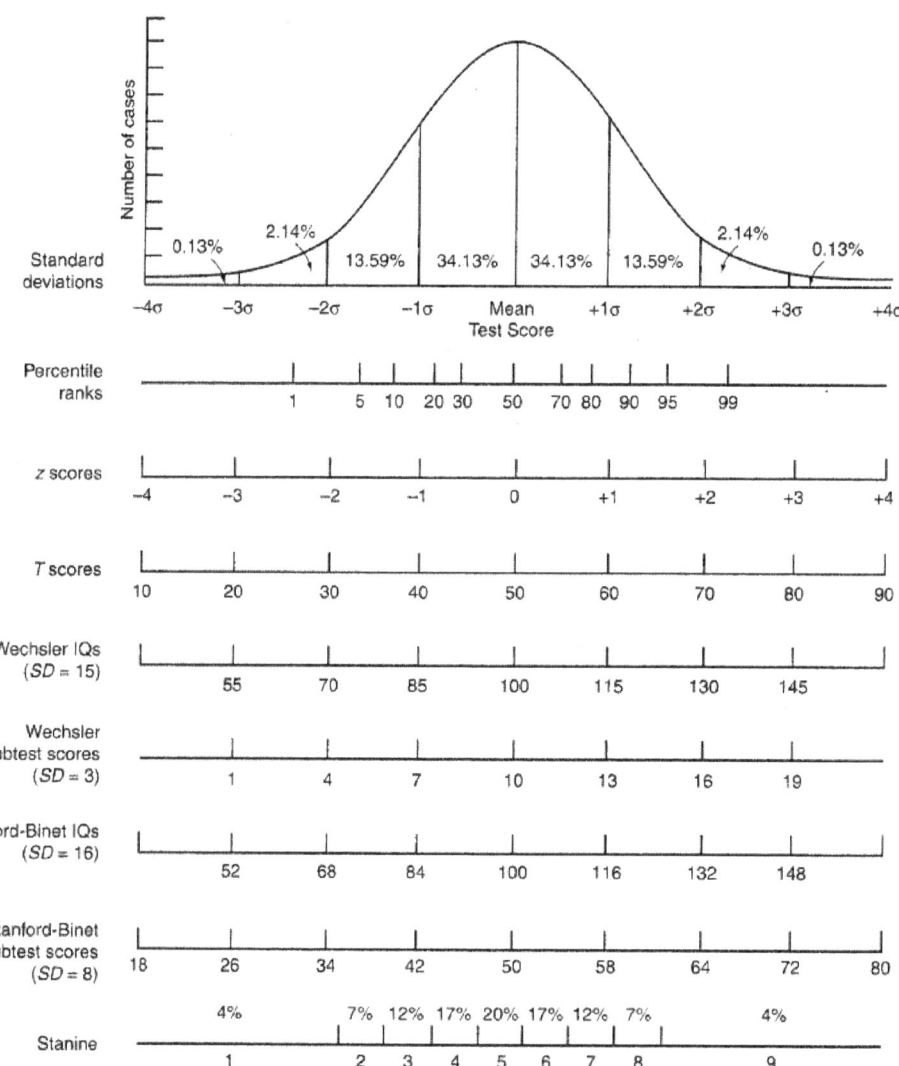

Figure 10.3 *Normal Curve*

When a Child Needs More Support

When a child needs more support than a school can provide, administrators should explore other services in the community that may be a better match for the needs of the child. If a school does not have the professional and medical resources (or parent cooperation) which a child needs in order to be safely included and benefit from the Montessori program, then the school must absolutely inform the parents of this situation, advocate on behalf of the child for the needed evaluations, medical specialists, therapy services, or other resources (including additional staff) needed to help the child, and recommend a more appropriate placement in a specialized and therapeutic educational setting.

Most Montessori teachers and administrators never want to "give up on a child;" however, they may be doing the child a disservice if they allow time to pass without the specific therapeutic services a child needs. For example, research indicates that if a child is not identified as dyslexic by the age of 8, and appropriate remediation implemented, over 75% have lifelong reading difficulty. A child may also need to be in a school that specializes in emotional disturbances or autism. They may need the highest level of training to help them optimize their growth and maturation. They may be able to return to the Montessori school after the appropriate placement has helped them.

The conversation with the parents regarding a recommendation for another school is never easy. It is made easier if the school has worked diligently with the parents to make the school work for the child, has clear documentation of the reasons the school is not the best placement, and helps the parents find the better placement for their child. The administrator must be very calm and supportive of the parent in these talks, realizing it is very emotional for the parents. The administrator must also be firm in the need for more specialized services to help the child.

Our goal as teachers and administrators in private or public schools is to help each child with their specific needs, to the best of our ability. Every difference cannot be remediated, but services provided can improve learning and the quality of life for each child. If the administrator and teacher have worked in partnership to try to optimize the Montessori program for the child and have shown their care for the child and the family, the parents may be disappointed their child needs another school or program, but they will have a positive feeling about the relationship they had with a caring and supportive school.

Conclusion

The importance of an evaluation cannot be overstated. The goal for every school should be that all children achieve at their highest level. Combining knowledge obtained from a child's learning profile with the teacher's observations to identify a child's challenges, allows the teacher to determine what each child needs. Careful observation combined with an appropriate evaluation and quality instruction provides the greatest chance of success for each child. It is our differences that make us stronger.

"The doer of a kindness reaps greater happiness than the receiver."

(Montessori, 1967/1995, p. 280)

Becoming Leaders:
About the Authors

Dr. Joyce S. Pickering

Throughout her career spanning five decades, Joyce S. Pickering, HumD, MA, CCC-SLP, CALT, QI has educated countless children and teachers. Her work has illustrated over and over again that early intervention through education is life-changing. She is a speech-language pathologist, Certified Academic Language Therapist, and a Licensed Dyslexia Therapist, and is credentialed by the American Montessori Society (AMS) in Early Childhood Montessori education. She has devoted her professional life to addressing the needs of students with language learning differences.

Currently, Joyce is Executive Director Emerita of the Shelton School and Evaluation Center in Dallas, TX, the world's largest private school for children with learning differences. In her role as Executive Director Emerita, she works with the Shelton Outreach and Teacher Training program, which she developed. She travels the world to present classes and keynote speeches about Montessori education and how to meet the needs of children with learning differences in a Montessori environment. She also worked for the development of a unique collaboration between the Shelton School, the University of Texas Southwestern Medical Center at Dallas, and the University of Texas at Dallas Center for Brain Health. The Shelton Outreach and Teacher Training department now answers more than 27,000 requests a year for information and resources.

Under Joyce's tenure as Executive Director (1990–2010), the Shelton School saw significant growth and development, including an expansion of the application of Montessori philosophy and practice, and, in 2009, the launching of the Shelton Montessori Teacher Education Center. This program now trains teachers in public and private schools in courses that are accredited by the Montessori Accreditation Council for Teacher Education (MACTE) and recognized by AMS at the Early Childhood, Elementary I, and Elementary II levels. The Outreach department also offers the Montessori Applied to Children At Risk (MACAR) training each year to help Montessorians with strategies for teaching children with varying exceptionalities.

Joyce has served on the Academic Language Therapy (ALTA) board and is presently its Vice President of Long Range Planning. She served as the Vice President for Academic Affairs on the International Dyslexia Association (IDA) board of directors. From 2010–2017, she was a member of the AMS board of directors, serving as president from 201–2017. She is currently an active member of several AMS committees. She is a founding member of the Alliance for Accreditation and the International Multisensory Structured Language Council (IMSLEC), which focus on the accreditation of multisensory structured language education training courses written for students with dyslexia. She has served on the IMSLEC board since 1995 and was president for 8 years.

Joyce has been honored by many institutions and organizations. She was the 2013 recipient of AMS's Living Legacy award, and in 2015, MACTE awarded her its Wisdom of the Elders award. She received the Margaret Rawson Lifetime Achievement Award from the International Dyslexia Association in 2010. Other awards include the IMSLEC Etoile DuBard Award of Excellence, the Altrusa International of Richardson Foundation, Inc.'s Outstanding Women of Today Award (for Education), and the Dallas Historical Society's Award for Excellence in Community Service (for Health/Sciences).

She is also an adjunct professor at Dallas Baptist University and a clinical assistant professor at the University of Texas Southwestern Medical Center.

Joyce is married to Dr. Robert Pickering, a former AMS president (1972–1974). Together they have 7 children, 13 grandchildren, and 3 great-grandchildren.

Dr. Laure Ames

Laure Ames, PhD, LPC-S, is Director of the Shelton Evaluation Center. She has a master's degree in counseling psychology and a doctorate in psychology from Southern Methodist University in Dallas, TX. She is a Licensed Psychological Associate and a Licensed Professional Counselor.

Laure has extensive clinical experience, having served on the staffs of the Dallas Child & Guidance Center, Terrell State Hospital, and Medical City Green Oaks Hospital. A personal commitment to understanding and helping learning-different children led her to join the staff at the Shelton School & Evaluation Center in 1993. While at the Shelton School, Dr. Ames coauthored the character education curriculum *Choices* and served as a primary investigator on the Center for Advanced ADHD Research, Treatment and Education (CAARTE) project in collaboration with The University of Texas Southwestern Medical School.

Laure has lectured extensively on assessing the young child, fostering self-esteem in learning-different children, the development of social competence in learning-different children, the implementation of the Choices social values curriculum, becoming an advocate, and the need for appropriate teacher preparation.

Laure is a past president of the Park Cities Learning Difference Association and is a member of the American Psychological Association, the International Dyslexia Association, and Children and Adults with Attention-Deficit/Hyperactivity Disorder.

Amy Kelton

Amy Kelton, MEd, CALT, LDT, QI, is Head of the Upper Elementary School at the Shelton School and Evaluation Center. She has worked with children with learning differences in Montessori schools for 23 years. She is a Qualified Instructor in Sequential English Education, and certified in the Association Method programs for the remediation of written language disorders, as well as in the advanced levels of Montessori Applied to Children At Risk (MACAR). She received her MACAR training directly from Dr. Joyce Pickering. Amy's credentials include a bachelor's of science degree in education, and a master's of education degree in educational leadership. She is a Certified Academic Language Therapist and a Licensed Dyslexia Therapist. She is AMS-credentialed (Elementary I). She has been a presenter at AMS conferences and International Dyslexia Association conferences, and she travels nationally and internationally to present courses in MACAR.

K. Michelle Lane-Barmapov

K. Michelle Lane-Barmapov, MHS founded the Lane Montessori School for Autism (previously known as the Toronto Montessori School for Autism) in Toronto, Canada. This not-for-profit school was the first in the world to combine Applied Behavior Analysis (ABA) with the Montessori curriculum.

In 2005, Michelle was bestowed The Premier's Award in recognition of her outstanding work in special education and Montessori. In the fall of 2010, Michelle left early childhood teaching to pursue a career as an academic. Michelle, who attended a Montessori school as a child, is currently a professor for the Faculty of Applied Health and Community Studies at Sheridan College, as well as a lecturer on the Montessori ABA blend that she designed.

Michelle is bilingual (French and English). Her educational background includes a BA in psychology and sociology, which she obtained at the age of 19. She was a social worker before becoming a Montessori teacher. She received a scholar's award for her post-graduate Montessori teacher-training at Sheridan College (2001). She has an American Montessori Society (AMS) Early Childhood credential. She is also a certified Elementary (6–9) Montessori teacher. In 2016, Michelle received a Master of Health Studies. Her thesis research, "Montessori and Autism: An Interpretive Description Study" can be found through the Athabasca University Digital Thesis Portal at http://hdl.handle.net/10791/211.

Michelle wrote the book *Autism: A Montessori Approach* in 2009, five program-tracking manuals for implementing the approach, and several published articles. Michelle is married to Oren Barmapov. They live in Toronto and share three children—Alliyah, Amos, and Jaguan.

Dr. Sylvia O. Richardson

Dr. Sylvia O. Richardson (1920–2014) held degrees in both education and medicine; she received a BA from Stanford University, an MA in Education of the Exceptional from Teachers College, Columbia University, and a MDCM (doctor of medicine and master of surgery) degree from the Faculty of Medicine, McGill University. She received her training in pediatrics from the Montreal Children's Hospital and the Boston Children's Medical Center. In 1984, Emerson College awarded her an honorable Language, Literacies, and Dyslexia degree (LLD). Sylvia held a Certificate of Clinical Competence in Speech-Language Pathology from the American Speech-Language-Hearing Association (ASHA) as well as Early Childhood credentials from both AMS and AMI.

In 1949, Sylvia established a Speech-Language clinic at Boston Children's Medical Center (the first in any children's hospital in the United States). She was associate director of the Learning Disabilities Clinic at the

University of Cincinnati's Cincinnati Center for Developmental Disabilities. She was president of ASHA from 1973–1974, chair of the Professional Advisory Board of the Learning Disabilities Association (LDA) for nine years, and president of the International Dyslexia Association (formerly the Orton Dyslexia Society) from 1984–1988. She was a founding member of the first AMS Board of Directors in 1964, and a public member of the International Multisensory Structured Language Education Council (IMSLEC) Board of Directors. She was a 30-year member of the National Joint Committee on Learning Disabilities, and its chair from 1997–1999. She was president of the Multidisciplinary Academy of Clinical Education, and founding president of the Florida Branch of the IDA.

Sylvia was a pediatrician, known for her work in evaluation and management of children with language-based disorders. She was a well-known speaker and consultant, both nationally and internationally. She contributed much to the literature of her field, with over 100 publications, and her consultant appointments were at state, national, and international levels. She received many honors, including 1964 Oklahoma Woman of the Year; the LDA Learning Disability Award and Pioneer Award; the Honors of the American Speech-Language-Hearing Association; the IDA's Samuel T. Orton Award, Margaret Rawson Lifetime Achievement Award, and Pioneer Award; the Distinguished Alumna Award from Teachers College, Columbia University; the Arrowsmith Award from the New England Network for Learning Disabilities; and the Luke Waites ALTA Award of Service, given to someone who has made a significant contribution to improve services received by dyslexic individuals.

Sylvia passed away on October 24, 2014, at the age of 94. She was married for 45 years to William R. Richardson, a pediatric surgeon. They had two sons and six grandchildren. For four decades, Sylvia was a friend and mentor to Dr. Joyce S. Pickering.

Additional Contributors

Community Contributors:
- Katie Massie
- Pauline Novak
- Christine Lowry
- Heather Malone
- Vivian Moore
- Hetal Sampat-Bihmani
- Andy Lulka

Parent Child Press Contributors:
- Jane Campbell
- Joe Campbell
- Jane Jacobs
- Ann Killeen

The Shelton School and Evaluation Center Contributors:
- Gulzar Babool
- Theresa Ball
- Pam Brockway
- John Hodges

Editorial Consultants: Carey Jones, Irene Baker

Diversity Consultant: April Milton

Book Designer: Shannon McMath

Special thanks to the American Montessori Society.

Special thanks to Regina Lulka and Montessori Jewish Day School for their contributions.

Special thanks to Loretta V. Boland and all MACAR July 2018 contributors.

Additional contributors may or may not endorse any or all of the viewpoints expressed herein. Parent Child Press and the authors are grateful to members of the community for their contributions, which helped create a more balanced work.

Dr. June Brooks Ford Shelton

June Brooks Ford Shelton, PhD (1920–2004) was born in Sapulpa, OK. In 1958, she received a BS in special education from the University of Oklahoma. As a young widow in her early 30s, she went back to school to try to learn why her son could not read. That led her to obtain a PhD in speech and hearing pathology in 1965, and begin a lifelong career of helping dyslexic children. From 1963–1965, she worked at the Child Study Center at the University of Oklahoma Medical Center. While there, she also received certification from both AMS and the Association Montessori Internationale (AMI). Later, in Dallas, TX, she was the director of the Day Study Unit of the Pediatric Neurology Division at Texas Scottish Rite Hospital for Children. She also served as director of the Language Disabilities Program at Texas Woman's University in Denton, TX. From 1970–1976, she was the executive director for Dean Memorial Learning Center in Dallas. Honors she received included Who's Who in the South and Southwest and Outstanding Teacher in Special Education.

In March 1976, June was approached by Dallas parents who wanted her to help their dyslexic children. Their persuasion, plus her broad knowledge and her passion to help bright children who learned differently, convinced June that the time was right to start her own school. The June Shelton School and Evaluation Center was officially incorporated in April 1976. The school year began with 48 students. As of 2019, with 232 employees and a student enrollment of 920, Shelton is the largest school in the world serving students with learning differences.

June passed away on July 24, 2004, at the age of 83. Her legacy continues through the many educators who were privileged to work under her direction.

Appendix I: Resources

General Resources

For information about the organization, Montessori Medical Partnership for Inclusion, visit: montessori4inclusion.org

For information about Multisensory Structured Language (MSL) remediation for children with dyslexia and other language learning differences, visit The International Multisensory Structured Language Education Council website at: imslec.org

For more information about dyslexia visit the International Dyslexia Association (IDA) website at: dyslexiaida.org

For more information about certification as a Certified Academic Language Therapist (CALT) or a Certified Academic Language Practitioner (CALP) visit the Academic Language Therapy Association website at: ALTARead.org

For more titles by Parent Child Press, visit: MontessoriServices.com

Montessori and Autism Resources

Visit: montessoriautism.com

MACAR Resources:

- Social skills/self-discipline development
- Oral language development
- Montessori Applied to Children At Risk (MACAR) curriculum manuals
- Sequential English Education (SEE) manuals
- The HOPE project
- MATCH Teacher Checklist
- Assessment learning profiles and matching child profile education plans examples
- Evaluation reports and data sheets examples
- Information and resources about training attention
- And more

Visit: Shelton.org/UsingMontessoriStrategies-Book

Appendix II: Developmental Charts

Typical Development - Developmental Chart

First Plane/Ages Birth – 6

Ages Birth - 3
- Developing fine motor skills (FMS) and gross motor skills (GMS)
- Developing language facility (vocabulary and verbal expression skills)
- Developing sustained attention and inhibition control
- Developing visual and auditory perceptual processing skills
- Sensitive Periods for the development of order, language, interest in small objects

Ages 3 - 6
- Continuing maturation of FMS/GMS
- Increasing language facility (vocabulary and verbal expression skills)
- Increasing ability for sustained attention/order
- Developing visual and auditory perceptual processing skills
- Prepared for higher cognitive functions of academics

Second Plane Ages 6 - 12
- Refining motor skills
- Refining the processing of language (verbal and written expression)
- Increasing ability for sustained attention and working memory
- Increasing processing speed and accuracy of verbal and non-verbal communication as well as written communication
- Academic progress smooth

Third Plane Ages 12 - 18
- Increasing well coordinated motor skills observed in handwriting/athletic skills
- Refining verbal and written expression
- Sustained attention, working memory, organization skills developed
- Increasing and refining processing speed and accuracy of verbal and written communication continues
- Academic progress smooth

Fourth Plane Ages 18 - 24
- Basic motor development complete
- Verbal and written expression achieves high level of communication skills
- Sustained attention, working memory and organizational skills mature
- Processing speed and accurate processing skills for verbal and written communication mature
- Prepared for post-secondary academics and career

©Joyce S. Pickering

Appendix II

Learning Differences - Developmental Chart

First Plane/Ages Birth – 6

Ages Birth-3
- Cognitive – average or above
- Adaptive – average or above
- Development of fine (FMS) and gross (GMS) motor skills may be delayed or disordered
- Speech-Language development delayed or disordered
- Development of sustained attention may not be attained by 3 years
- Visual and auditory perceptual processing skills inaccurate
- The foundation for learning and attention reveal an uneven development, which will affect all the following planes of development

Ages 3-6
- Cognitive – average or above
- Adaptive – average or above
- Development of FMS/GMS may be below average
- Speech-Language development below average in speech articulation and/or oral language communication (receptive and/or expressive)
- Sustained attention may not be developed typically/sensitive period for order delayed or remains disordered
- Auditory perceptual processing skills below average resulting in difficulty in progress in written language (reading, writing, spelling) and/or math
- Visual perception processing skills may be below average
- Progress is uneven, better in some subject areas than others, variable from day to day

Second Plane – Ages 6-12
- Cognitive – average or above
- Adaptive – affected by learning differences to varying degrees
- Motor coordination differences may be seen in overall body coordination skills, balance, rhythmic activities and/or handwriting
- Speech-Language weaknesses continue unless remediated
- Sustained attention may not be achieved in students with ADHD/difficulties with working memory and organization
- Visual and auditory perceptual processing skills in accuracy and speed continue to be a challenge, unless remediated
- Schoolwork continues to be erratic, better in some areas than others, variable from day to day

Third Plane – Ages 12-18
- Cognitive – average or above
- Adaptive – affected by learning differences to varying degrees
- All skills continue to present differences in academic progress depending on the individual combination of strengths and weaknesses, unless remediated

Fourth Plane – Ages 18-24
- Cognitive – average or above
- Adaptive – affected by learning differences to varying degrees
- All skills continue to present differences in academic progress depending on the individual combination of strengths and weaknesses, unless remediated

©Joyce S. Pickering

Communication Disorders – Developmental Chart

First Plane / Ages Birth – 6

Ages Birth - 3
- Cognitive – may be average or above, but not presenting this ability on verbal IQ tests
- Adaptive – below average to average
- Development of fine (FMS) and gross (GMS) motor skills may be average, delayed or disordered.
- Speech-Language development delayed or disordered
- Development of sustained attention may not be attained by 3 years
- Visual perceptual processing skills may be average. Auditory perceptual processing skills – below average for those with articulation problems.
- The foundation for learning and attention reveal an uneven development, which will affect all the following planes of development.

Ages 3 - 6
- Cognitive – may be average or above, but not presenting this ability on verbal IQ tests
- Adaptive – below average to average
- Development of FMS/GMS may be average to below average
- Speech development may be below average in speech articulation. Language perceptual processing skills below average in delayed or disordered language skills. Oral language communication (rceptive and/ or expressive) below average
- Sustained attention may not be developed typically/sensitive period for order delayed or remains disordered.
- Visual and auditory perceptual processing skills may be below average resulting in difficulty in progress in written language (reading, writing, spelling) and/or math
- Progress may be uneven, better in some subject areas than others, may be variable from day to day.

Second Plane Ages 6 - 12
- Cognitive – may be average or above, but not presenting this ability on verbal IQ tests
- Adaptive – below average to average
- Motor coordination differences may be seen in overall body coordination skills, balance, rhythmic activities and/ or handwriting
- Speech-Language weaknesses continue unless remediated
- Sustained attention may not be achieved in students with ADHD/difficulties with working memory and organization
- Visual and auditory perceptual processing skills in accuracy and speed may continue to be a challenge, unless remediated
- Schoolwork continues to be erratic; better in some areas than others, may be variable from day to day.

Third Plane Ages 12 - 18
- Cognitive – may be average or above, but not presenting this ability on verbal IQ tests
- Adaptive – below average to average
- All skills continue to present differences in academic progress depending on the individual combination of strengths and weaknesses, unless remediated.

Fourth Plane Ages 18 - 24
- Cognitive – may be average or above, but not presenting this ability on verbal IQ tests
- Adaptive – below average to average
- All skills continue to present differences in academic progress depending on the individual combination of strengths and weaknesses, unless remediated.

©Joyce S. Pickering

Appendix II

Autism Spectrum Disorder (ASD) - Developmental Chart

First Plane/Ages Birth – 6

Ages Birth-3
- Cognitive – average to below average
- Adaptive – below average
- Development of fine (FMS) and gross (GMS) motor skills may be delayed or disordered
- Speech-Language development delayed or disordered
- Development of sustained attention may not be attained by 3 years
- Visual and auditory perceptual processing skills may be inaccurate
- The foundation for learning and attention reveal an uneven development, which will affect all the following planes of development

Ages 3-6
- Cognitive – average to below average
- Adaptive – below average, improved with treatment
- Development of FMS/GMS may be below average
- Speech-Language development below average in speech articulation and/or oral language communication (receptive and/or expressive)
- Sustained attention may not often be developed typically/sensitive period for order delayed or remains disordered
- Visual and auditory perceptual processing skills below average in specific areas resulting in difficulty in progress in written language (reading, writing, spelling) and/or math
- Progress is uneven, better in some subject areas than others, variable from day to day

Second Plane – Ages 6-12
- Cognitive – average to below average
- Adaptive – below average, improved with treatment
- Motor coordination differences may be seen in overall body coordination skills, balance, rhythmic activities and/or handwriting
- Speech-Language weaknesses continue unless remediated
- Sustained attention may not be achieved in children with ADHD/difficulties with working memory and organization
- Visual and auditory perceptual processing skills in accuracy and speed may continue to be a challenge, unless remediated
- Schoolwork continues to be erratic, better in some areas than others, variable from day to day

Third Plane – Ages 12-18
- Cognitive – average to below average
- Adaptive – below average, improved with treatment
- Children continue to present differences in academic and work skills, depending on the individual combination of strengths and weaknesses, unless treated

Fourth Plane – Ages 18-24
- Cognitive – average to below average
- Adaptive – below average, improved with treatment
- Children continue to present differences in academic and work skills, depending on the individual combination of strengths and weaknesses, unless treated

©Joyce S. Pickering

Intellectual Disabilities (ID) - Developmental Chart

First Plane/Ages Birth – 6

Ages Birth-3
- Cognitive – below average
- Adaptive – below average
- Development of fine (FMS) and gross (GMS) motor skills may be delayed or disordered
- Speech-Language development delayed or disordered
- Development of sustained attention may not be attained by 3 years
- Visual and auditory perceptual processing skills often inaccurate
- The foundation for learning and attention reveal an uneven development, which will affect all the following planes of development

Ages 3-6
- Cognitive – below average
- Adaptive – below average
- Development of FMS/GMS may be below average
- Speech-Language development below average in speech articulation and or oral language communication (receptive and/ or expressive)
- Sustained attention may not be developed typically/sensitive period for order delayed or remains disordered
- Visual and auditory perceptual processing skills may be below average resulting in difficulty in progress in written language (reading, writing, spelling) and/or math
- Progress in pre-academic/academic skills is below average

Second Plane – Ages 6-12
- Cognitive – below average
- Adaptive – below average
- Motor coordination differences may be seen in overall body coordination skills, balance, rhythmic activities and/ or handwriting
- Speech-Language weaknesses continue unless remediated
- Sustained attention may not be achieved in students with ADHD/difficulties with working memory and organization
- Visual and auditory perceptual processing skills in accuracy and speed may continue to be a challenge, unless remediated
- School work continues to be below average

Third Plane – Ages 12-18
- Cognitive – below average
- Adaptive – below average
- All skills continue to present differences in academic progress with below average performance noted across subjects, significant difficulty with abstraction

Fourth Plane – Ages 18-24
- Cognitive – below average
- Adaptive – below average
- All skills continue to present differences in academic progress. Depending on the level of ID, the student may be able to be educated in basic reading, writing, spelling, and math or trained in life skills and specific work skills

©Joyce S. Pickering

References

Achenbach, T. M. (1991). *Manual for child behavior checklist/ 4–18 and 1991 Profile*. (CBCL) Burlington, VT: Department of Psychiatry, University of Vermont.

American Speech-Language-Hearing Association (Ad Hoc Committee on Service Delivery in the Schools). (1993). *Definitions of communication disorders and variations*. https://www.asha.org/policy/RP1993-00208/

American Speech-Language-Hearing Association. (2015, August 29). *Learning two languages*. http://www.asha.org/public/speech/development/BilingualChildren

American Speech-Language-Hearing Association. (2018). *Language-based learning disabilities (reading, spelling, writing)*. http://www.asha.org/public/speech/disorders/LBLD.htm

American Psychiatric Association. (1968). *Diagnostic and statistical manual of mental disorders, 2nd ed.* (DSM-II). Arlington, VA: American Psychiatric Association.

American Psychiatric Association. (1980). *Diagnostic and statistical manual of mental disorders, 3rd ed.* (DSM-III), Arlington, VA: American Psychiatric Association.

American Psychiatric Association. (2013). *Diagnostic and statistical manual of mental disorders, 5th ed.* (DSM-5). Arlington, VA: American Psychiatric Association.

Anagnostou, E., Zwaigenbaum, L., Szatmari, P., Fombonne, E., Fernandez, B. A., Woodbury-Smith, M., & Scherer, S. W. (2014). Autism spectrum disorder: Advances in evidence-based practice. *CMAJ: Canadian Medical Association Journal*, *186*(7), 509–519. doi:10.1503/cmaj.121756

Association Montessori Internationale. (2017). *Biography of Dr. Maria Montessori.* https://montessori-ami.org/resource-library/facts/biography-dr-maria-montessori

Attwood, T. (2007). *The complete guide to Asperger's syndrome.* London: Jessica Kingsley Publishers.

Barkley, R. A. (2017, November). *Presentation.* Presentation at the International Dyslexia Association's Reading, Literacy, and Learning Conference, Atlanta, GA.

Beck, L. E. (1993). *Infants, children and adolescents.* Boston, MA: Allyn and Bacon.

Beery, K., Buktenica, N., & Beery, N. (2010). *Beery-Buktenica developmental test of visual-motor integration, 6th ed.* (Beery VMI). San Antonio, TX: Pearson.

Berlyne, D. E. (1963). Soviet research on intellectual processes in children. *Monographs of the Society for Research in Child Development, 28*(2), 165–183.

Birsh, J. R. (2011). *Multisensory teaching of basic language skills, 3rd ed.* Baltimore, MD: Brookes Publishing.

Bondy, A. S., & Frost, L. A. (1994). The picture exchange communication system. *Focus on Autistic Behavior, 9*(3), 1.

Bounds, G. (2010, October 5). How handwriting trains the brain. *The Wall Street Journal,* https://www.wsj.com/articles/SB10001424052748704631504575531932754922518

Bowers, L., Huisingh, R. & LoGiudice, C. (2005). *Test of problem solving 3* (TOPS3 Elementary). Austin, TX: PRO-ED.

Bowers, L., Huisingh, R. & LoGiudice, C. (2007). *Test of problem solving 2* (TOPS2 Adolescent). Austin, TX: PRO-ED.

Bowers, L., Huisingh, R. & LoGiudice, C. (2008). *Social language development test.* Austin, TX: PRO-ED.

Brackett, M. A., & Caruso, D. R. (2005–2009). *Emotional literacy for educators.* New Haven, CT: Emotionally Intelligent Schools, LLC.

Brown. T. E. (2000). *Attention deficit disorders and comorbidities in children, adolescents, and adults.* Arlington, VA: American Psychiatric Publishing, Inc.

Brown, T. E. (2001). *Brown attention-deficit disorder scales* (Brown ADD Scales). San Antonio, TX: Pearson.

Brown, T. E. (2005). *Attention-deficit disorder: The unfocused mind in children and adults.* New Haven, CT: Yale University Press, p. 22.

Brown, T. E. (2018). *Brown executive function/attention scales.* London, U.K.: Pearson.

Brutten, M., Richardson, S., & Mangel, C. (1973). *Something's wrong with my child.* New York, NY: Harcourt Brace Jovanovich.

Carrow-Woolfolk, E. (1999). *Comprehensive assessment of spoken language* (CASL). San Antonio, TX: Pearson.

Carrow-Woolfolk, E. (2012). *Oral and written language scales, 2nd ed.* (OWLS-II). Austin, TX: PRO-ED.

Carson, L., Moosa, T., Theurer, J., & Cardy, J. (2012). The collateral effects of PECS training on speech development in children with autism. *Canadian Journal of Speech-Language Pathology & Audiology, 36*(3), 182–195.

Center for Disease Control and Prevention. (2017, May). *Attention deficit hyperactivity disorder (ADHD).* https://www.cdc.gov/ncbddd/adhd/data.html

Christensen, C. M. (2011). *Disrupting class: How disruptive innovation will change the way the world learns.* New York, NY: McGraw-Hill.

Colli-Grisoni, A. (1957). *Montessori: 1907–1957.* Amsterdam: Association Montessori Internationale, p. 3.

Connolly, A. J. (2007). *KeyMath-3 diagnostic assessment.* San Antonio, TX: Pearson.

Conners, C. K. (2008). *Conners comprehensive behavior rating scales* (Conners CBRS). San Antonio, TX: Pearson.

Conners, C. K. (2014). *Conners continuous performance test, 3rd ed.* (Conners CPT3). San Antonio, TX: Pearson.

Corman, C. L., & Greenberg, L. (1997). *All you wanted to know about attention deficits but didn't know whom to ask.* Los Alamitos, CA: The TOVA Company (formerly Universal Attentional Disorders, Inc.).

Critchley, M. (1947/1964/1984). *Developmental dyslexia* (Limited ed.). London: William Heineman Medical Books.

Dattke, J. (2014). A Montessori model for inclusion. *NAMTA Journal, 39*(3), 106–119.

Denckla, M. B. (1996). A theory and model of executive function: a neuropsychological perspective. In G. R. Lyon and N. A. Krasegor (Eds.), *Attention, memory, and executive function* (pp. 263–278). Baltimore, MD: Brookes Publishing.

DeFries, J. C., & Alarcon, M. (1996). Genetics of specific reading disability. *Mental Retardation and Developmental Disabilities Research Reviews, 2,* 39–47.

Dennis W., & Dennis, M. G. (1940). The effect of cradling practice upon the onset of walking in Hopi children. *Journal of Genetic Psychology, 56,* 77–86.

Dennis, W. (1960). Causes of retardation among institutional children. *Journal of Genetic Psychology, 96,* 47–59.

Diamond, A. (2012). Activities and programs that improve children's executive functions. *Current Directions in Psychological Science, 21*(5), 335–341. doi:10.1177/0963721412453722

Dorer, M. J. (2016). *The deep well of time: The transformative power of storytelling in the classroom.* Santa Rosa, CA: Parent Child Press/Montessori Services.

Eden, G. (2003, Spring). The role of brain imaging in dyslexia research. *Perspectives,* 14–16. Baltimore, MD: International Dyslexia Association.

Francis, D. J., Shaywitz, S. E., Stuebing, K. K., Shaywitz, B. A., & Fletcher, J. M. (1996). Developmental lag versus deficit models of reading disability: A longitudinal, individual growth curves analysis. *Journal of Educational Psychology, 86*(1), 3–17.

Gardner, R. (1968). A psychologist looks at Montessori. In J. L. Frost (Eds.), *Early childhood education rediscovered.* New York, NY: Holt, Rinehart and Winston, p. 78.

Garrison, J. (2014, July 25). Cursive writing standards in the works for Tennessee schools. *The Tennessean,* https://www.tennessean.com/story/news/education/2014/07/25/cursive-writing-standards-works-tennessee-schools/13175611/

Gandhi, M. (1953). *Towards new education.* Ahmedabad, India: Navajivan Publishing House, p. 33.

Gilger, J. W. (2003, Spring). Genes and dyslexia. *Perspectives,* 6–8. Baltimore, MD: International Dyslexia Association.

Gillingham, A., & Stillman, B. (1960). *Remedial training for children with specific disability in reading, spelling and penmanship.* Cambridge, MA: Educators Publishing Service, p. 40.

Gioia, G., Isquith, P., Guy, S., & Kenworthy, L. (2000). *Behavior rating inventory of executive functioning (BRIEF).* Torrance, CA: Western Psychological Services.

Goldstein, S., & Naglieri, J. A. (2009/2010). *Autism spectrum rating scales (ASRS).* North Tonawanda, NY: Multi-Health Systems, Inc.

Gordon, C. (Winter 2005). Searching for the first public Montessori program in the U.S. *Public School Montessorian, 17*(2), 24–25.

Gray, C. (1992). *How to write social stories.* Jenison, MI: Jenison Public Schools.

Greenberg, L. *Test of variables of attention (TOVA 8, 1991–2015).* Los Alamitos, CA: The TOVA Company.

Groden, J., Cautela, J., & Groden, G. (1989). *Relaxation techniques for people with special needs: Breaking the barriers* [Video file]. Providence, RI: Groden Center.

Harms, M. B., Martin, A., & Wallace, G. L. (2010). Facial emotion recognition in autism spectrum disorders: A review of behavioral and neuroimaging studies. *Neuropsychology Review, 20*(3), 290–322. doi:10.1007/s11065-010-9138-6

Hallowell, M. E. (1995). *Driven to distraction.* New York, NY: Simon & Schuster, p. 262.

Hallowell. M. E. (2009). *Answers to distraction.* New York, NY: Anchor/Knopf Doubleday.

Hebb, D. O. (1947). The effects of early experience on problem-solving at maturity. *American Psychologist, 2*, 306–307.

Hebb, D. O. (1949). *The organization of behavior.* New York, NY: Wiley.

Hotz, R. (2016, April 5). The power of handwriting. *The Wall Street Journal*, D1–D2.

Hudepohl, M., Robins, D., King, T., & Henrich, C. (2015). The role of emotion perception in adaptive functioning of people with autism spectrum disorders. *Autism*, 19(1), 107–112. doi:10.1177/1362361313512725

Hughes, C., & Pickering, J. S. (2014). *The health and optimism provided with exercise (hope) study.* Dallas, TX: Shelton School.

Hunt, J. M. (1961). *Intelligence and experience.* New York, NY: The Ronald Press Company, p. 122.

Hunt, N., & Marshall, K. (2005). *Exceptional children and youth, 5th ed.* Boston, MA: Cengage.

International Multisensory Structured Language Education Council (IMSLEC), www.imslec.org

International Dyslexia Association (2002, November 12). *Definition of dyslexia.* https://dyslexiaida.org/definition-of-dyslexia/

Itard, J. M. G. (1801). *De l'education d'un homme sauvage*. Paris, France: Goujon, l'an X.

Johnels, J. A., Gillberg, C., Falck-Ytter, T., & Miniscalco, C. (2014). Face-viewing patterns in young children with autism spectrum disorders: Speaking up for the role of language comprehension. *Journal of Speech, Language & Hearing Research*, 57(6), 2246–2252. doi:10.1044/2014_JSLHR-L-13-0268

Kaufman, A. S., & Kaufman, N. L. (1983/2004). *Kaufman assessment battery for children–II* (KABC-II). San Antonio, TX: Pearson.

Kaufman, A. S., & Kaufman, N, L. (2014). *Kaufman test of educational achievement comprehensive form, 3rd ed.* (KTEA-3). San Antonio, TX: Pearson.

Kephart, N. C. (1960). *The slow learner in the classroom*. Columbus, OH: Merrill.

Krasa, N., & Shunkwiler, S. (2009). *Number sense and number nonsense*. Baltimore, MD: Brookes Publishing.

Lally, K., & Price, D. M. (1998, January 4). Learning how we read. *The Palm Beach Post*, 6A, p. 1. (Lally article used for National Institutes of Health (1998) quote.

Lane, K. (2004/2008). *Autism: A Montessori approach program tracking manual and curriculum guide for children with autism and other communication disorders*, Toronto: MLMAS [2008 Manual converted to 5 separate manuals based on curriculum area]

Lane, K. (2009a). A Montessori approach to autism. *NAMTA Journal*, 34(2), 64–72.

Lane, K. (2009b). *Autism: A Montessori approach*. Toronto, Canada: MLMAS.

Lane-Barmapov, M. (2014, September 18). *Montessori & autism* [Webcast]. *American Montessori Society*, https://amshq.org/Events/Webinars/Webcasts

Lane-Barmapov, K. M. (2016). *Montessori and autism: An interpretive description study* [master's thesis]. Retrieved from Athabasca University Dissertations and Theses database, http://hdl.handle.net/10791/211

Larsen, S. C., Hammill, D. D., & Moats, L. (2013). *Test of written spelling, 5th ed.* (TWS-5). Austin, TX: PRO-ED.

Levy, S. E., Mandell, D. S., & Schultz, R. T. (2009). Seminar: Autism. *The Lancet, 374,* 1627–1638. doi:10.1016/S0140-6736(09)61376-3

Leyfer, O. T., Folstein, S. E., Bacalman, S., Davis, N. O., Dinh, E., & Morgan, J. (2006). Comorbid psychiatric disorders in children with autism: Interview development and rates of disorders. *Journal of Autism and Developmental Disorders, 36*(7), 849–861. doi:10.1007/s10803-006-0123-0.

Lillard, A. S. (2005). *Montessori: The science behind the genius.* New York, NY: Oxford University Press.

Lillard, A. S. (2017). *Montessori: The science behind the genius, 3rd ed.* New York, NY: Oxford University Press.

Lillard, P. P. (1972). *Montessori: A modern approach.* New York, NY: Schocken Books, pp. 143–144.

Long, C., Gurka, M., & Blackman, J. (2011). Cognitive skills of young children with and without autism spectrum disorder using the BSID-III. *Autism Research & Treatment, 2011* (759289), 1–7. doi:10.1155/2011/759289.

Lord, C., & Rutter, M. (2000). *Autism diagnostic observation schedule* (ADOS). Torrance, CA: Western Psychological Services.

Lovaas, O. I. (1987). Behavioral treatment and normal educational and intellectual functioning in young autistic children. *Journal of Consulting and Clinical Psychology, 55*(1), 3–9.

Luborsky, B. (2014). Occupational therapy and Montessori—kindred spirits: Moving toward a scientific and medical pedagogy. *NAMTA Journal, 39*(3), 208–248.

Luria, A. R. (1957/1960). *Experimental analysis of the development of voluntary action in children.* Paper read to XV International Congress of Psychology, Montreal, Canada.

Luria, A. R. (1959). The directive function of speech in development and dissolution. *Word*, 15, 341–352 and 453–464.

MacGinitie, W. H, MacGinitie, R. K., Maria, K., Dreyer, L. G., & Hughes, K. E. (2000). *Gates-MacGinitie reading tests, 4th ed.* (GMRT). Boston, MA: Houghton Mifflin Harcourt.

Mannion, A., & Leader, G. (2014). Review: Attention-deficit/hyperactivity disorder (AD/HD) in autism spectrum disorder. *Research in Autism Spectrum Disorders, 8*, 432–439. doi:10.1016/j.rasd.2013.12.021

Martin, N., & Brownell, R. (2005). *Test of auditory processing, 3rd ed.* (TAP-3). Novato, CA: Academic Therapy Publications.

May, T., Rinehart, N., Wilding, J., & Cornish, K. (2013). The role of attention in the academic attainment of children with autism spectrum disorder. *Journal of Autism & Developmental Disorders, 43*(9), 2147–2158. doi:10.1007/s10803-013-1766-2

Montessori, M. (1909/2008). *The Montessori method.* La Vergne, TN: BN Publishing.

Montessori, M. (1912/1997). *The discovery of the child.* Oxford, England: Clio Press.

Montessori, M. (1912/1988). *The Montessori method* (A. E. George, Trans.). New York, NY: Frederick Stokes.

Montessori, M. (1913). *Pedagogical anthropology* (F. T. Cooper, Trans.). New York, NY: Frederick A. Stokes.

Montessori, M. (1914/1966). *Dr. Montessori's own handbook.* Cambridge, MA: Robert Bentley.

Montessori, M. (1936/2006). *The secret of childhood.* Chennai, India: Orient Longman Private Limited.

Montessori, M. (1938/1939). *The four planes of education* (M. Montessori, Ed.). Amsterdam, Netherlands: Association Montessori Internationale. http://www.montessori-namta.org/Books-by-Montessori/The-Four-Planes-of-Education

Montessori, M. (1948/1986). *To educate the human potential.* Madras, India: Kalakshetra.

Montessori, M. (1949/1995). *The absorbent mind.* New York, NY: Henry Holt and Company.

Montessori, M. (1966). *The secret of childhood.* New York, NY: Ballantine Books, p. 42.

Montessori, M. (1971). *The four planes of education.* Amsterdam, Netherlands: Association Montessori Internationale.

Myers, D., (2003, November). *Psychoactive medications used for children and adolescents* handout.

National Institute of Child Health and Human Development. (2016). *Learning disabilities.* https://www.nichd.nih.gov/health/topics/learningdisabilities

Nagc.org. *A brief history of gifted and talented education.* Retrieved from http://www.nagc.org/resources-publications/resources/gifted-education-us/brief-history-gifted-and-talented-education

Ncld. *The state of learning disabilities: Understanding the 1 in 5.* (n.d.). Retrieved from https://www.ncld.org/the-state-of-learning-disabilities-understanding-the-1-in-5

Nidcd.nih.gov. *Statistics on voice, speech, and language.* (2016, December 12). Retrieved from https://www.nidcd.nih.gov/health/statistics/statistics-voice-speech-and-language

Nehring, C. (2014). Implementing inclusion theory into practice. *NAMTA Journal, 39*(3), 38–63.

Newcomer, P. L., & Hammill, D. D. (2008). *Test of language development, 4th ed.* (TOLDP4 and TOLDI4). Torrance, CA: Western Psychological Services.

No Child Left Behind Act of 2001, P.L. 107–110, 20 U.S.C. (Title IX, Part A, Definition 22), §7801, 22. National Association of Gifted Children website, www.nagc.org)

O'Brien, J., Spencer, J., Girges, C., Johnston, A., & Hill, H. (2014). Impaired perception of facial motion in autism spectrum disorder. *Plos ONE*, *9*(7), 1–6. doi:10.1371/journal.pone.0102173

Orem, R. C. (1965). *A Montessori handbook: Dr. Montessori's own handbook.* New York, NY: G.P. Putnam's & Sons, p. 79.

Orton, S. T. (1937). *Reading, writing and speech problems in children.* New York, NY: W. W. Norton and Co., Inc.

Ou, S., & Reynolds, A. J. (2014). *Preschool education and school completion.* Montreal, Quebec, Canada: Encyclopedia of Early Childhood Development. http://www.child-encyclopedia.com/school-success/according-experts/preschool-education-and-school-completion, p. 1.

Ozonoff, S., Iosif, A., Baguio, F., Cook, I. C., Hill, M. M., Hutman, T., …Young, G. S. (2010). New research: A prospective study of the emergence of early behavioral signs of autism. *Journal of the American Academy of Child & Adolescent Psychiatry*, *49* (3), 256–266.e2. doi:10.1016/j.jaac.2009.11.009

Perry, C. (2016). *Living, creating, sharing—a Montessori life.* Santa Rosa, CA: Parent Child Press.

Phillips, J. (2013). To write, or not to write: The benefits of teaching cursive in Montessori. *Montessori Leadership 15* (2), 6–8.

Piaget, J. (1936/1952). *The origins of intelligence in children* (M. Cook, Trans.). New York, NY: International Universities Press.

Piaget, J. (1945/1951). *Play, dreams, and imitation in childhood.* (C. Gattegno and F. M. Hodgson, Trans.). Originally published as *La formation du symbole chez l'enfant*, 1945. New York, NY: Norton.

Piaget, J. (1963/1966). *The psychology of intelligence.* Totawa, NJ: Littlefield, Adams, p. 132.

Piaget, J. (1970). *The science of education and the psychology of the child.* New York, NY: Grossman.

Pick, H. (1963). Some Soviet research on learning and perception in children. *Monographs of the Society for Research in Child Development, 28*(2):187–189.

Pickering, J. S. (1971). *Early childhood center research project report.* ESEA Title IV.

Pickering, J. S. (1976). *Montessori applied to children at risk administrator's 1 manual.* Saō Paulo, Brazil: Escola Graduada de Saō Paulo.

Pickering, J. S. (1976). *Montessori applied to children at risk oral language development curriculum.* Saō Paulo, Brazil: Escola Graduada de Saō Paulo.

Pickering, J. S. (1976). *Montessori applied to children at risk practical life manual.* Saō Paulo, Brazil: Escola Graduada de Saō Paulo.

Pickering, J. S. (1976). *Montessori applied to children at risk sensorial manual.* Saō Paulo, Brazil: Escola Graduada de Saō Paulo.

Pickering, J. S. (1983). *Sequential English education* (SEE). Saō Paulo, Brazil: Escola Graduada de Saō Paulo.

Pickering, J. S. (1983). *Sequential English education* (SEE), *book 1, handwriting.* Saō Paulo, Brazil: Escola Graduada de Saō Paulo.

Pickering, J. S. (1992). Successful applications of Montessori method with children at risk for learning differences. *Annals of Dyslexia, 42*(1), 90–109.

Pickering, J. S. (1993). *Assessment to instruction.* Dallas, TX: Shelton School.

Pickering, J. S., & Ames, L. (1993). *Choices.* Dallas, TX: Shelton School.

Pickering, J. S. (1995). Montessori education and sequential English education. In *Clinical Studies of the International Multisensory Structured Language Education for Students with Dyslexia and Related Disorders* (McIntyre, C., & Pickering, J., Eds.). Poughkeepsie, NY: HAMCO Corporation, pp. 111–113.

Pickering, J. S. (2009). *Empowering students for self-discipline by direct teaching*. Dallas, TX: Shelton School.

Pickering, J. S. (2012). Montessori applied to children at risk. *Montessori Life*, Vol. 24. New York, NY: American Montessori Society.

Pickering, J., & P. Novak (2015, March 6). *MACAR Workshop Track Session 1: Planes of development of children with learning difference* [PDF document]. http://www.shelton.org/uploaded/documents/conf_presentations/AMS_2015/1_AMS_2015_Planes_of_Development.pdf

Pickering, R. G. (1978). *Current assessment for Montessori in the perspective of modern day educational philosophy*. Dissertation, Saõ Paulo, Brazil, p. 144.

PR Newswire. (2013, July 11). HandHold adaptive and Carol Gray, creator of social stories, announce new handheld autism technology. *PR Newswire US*.

Press-Register Editorial Board (2012, July 13). *In defense of cursive*. http://blog.al.com/press-register-commentary

Ratey, J. J. (2008). *SPARK: The revolutionary new science of exercise and the brain*. New York, NY: Little Brown and Company.

Rao, V. S., & Ashok, M. (2014). Joint attention routines in intervention for children with autism spectrum disorders. *Journal of Indian Association for Child & Adolescent Mental Health*, *10*(4), 292–298.

Reichow, B. (2012). Overview of meta-analyses on early intensive behavioral intervention for young children with autism spectrum disorders. *Journal of Autism & Developmental Disorders*, *42*(4), 512–520. doi:10.1007/s10803-011-1218-9

Reynolds, C. R., & Kamphaus, R. W. (2015). *Behavior assessment system for children, 3rd ed.* (BASC-3). San Antonio, TX: Pearson.

Richardson, S. O. (1965). Language disorders in children. *Topics in Language Disorders*. American Speech-Language-Hearing Association.

Richardson, S. O. (1965). A pediatrician looks at Montessori for neurologically impaired children. *The American Montessori Bulletin, 4*(4).

Richardson, S. O. (1967). Language training for mentally retarded children. In *Language and mental retardation* (Schiefelbusch, R. L., Copeland, R. H., & Smith J.C., Eds.). New York, NY: Rinehart and Winston.

Richardson, S. O. (1984). *CLAP—Coordination, language, attention and perception.* Lecture presented at Orton Dyslexia Society-Florida Conference, Orlando.

Robertson, C. (2007). *The phonological awareness test–2* (PAT2). Austin, TX: PRO-ED.

Ross, R. S., & Ross, M. G. (1982) *Relating and interacting: An introduction to interpersonal communication.* Englewood Cliffs, NJ: Prentice-Hall, Inc.

Rutter, M., LeCouteur, A., & Lord, C. (2003). *Autism diagnostic interview, revised* (ADI-R). Torrance, CA: Western Psychological Services.

Schopler, E., & Van Bourgondien, M. E. (2010). *Childhood autism rating scale, 2nd ed.* (CARS-2). Torrance, CA: Western Psychological Services.

Schrank, F. A., Mather, N., & McGrew, K. S. (2014). *Woodcock–Johnson IV tests of achievement.* Itasca, IL: Riverside.

Schrank, F. A., Mather, N., & McGrew, K. S. (2014). *Woodcock–Johnson IV tests of cognitive abilities examiner's manual, standard and extended batteries.* Itasca, IL: Riverside.

Seguin, E. (1864/1907). *Idiocy and its treatment by the physiological method.* New York, NY: Teacher's College Columbia University, p. 133.

Shaywitz, S. (2003). *Overcoming dyslexia: A new and complete science-based program for reading problems at any level.* New York, NY: Alfred A. Knopf.

Shedd, C. L. (1967). Some characteristics of a specific perceptual motor disability—dyslexia. *Journal of the Medical Association of State of Alabama, 37,* 152, 56.

Shedd, C. L. (1968). Ptolemy rides again or dyslexia doesn't exist? *Journal of the Medical Association of State of Alabama.*

Shedd, C. L. (1968). *Testing: A pre-clinical evaluation for learning disabilities.* Prepared by the Reading Disability Center and Clinic of the Medical College of Alabama and the Perceptual Development Center, Natchez, MS, pp. 4, 5, 485.

Sherman, G., & Cowen C. D. (2003, Spring). Neuroanatomy of dyslexia through the lens of cerebrodiversity. *Perspectives,* 9–13.

Silver, L. B. (1993). *Advice to parents on attention-deficient hyperactive disorder.* Arlington, VA: American Psychiatric Publishing, Inc.

Skinner, B. F. (1969). *Contingencies of reinforcement: A theoretical analysis.* New York, NY: Appleton-Century-Crofts.

Skinner, B. F. (1974/1976). *About behaviorism.* New York, NY: Vintage Books/Random House, Inc.

Slosson R. L., revised by Nicholson, C. L., & Hibpshman, T. L. (2002). *Slosson intelligence test, revised* (SIT-R3), East Aurora, NY: Slosson Educational Publications.

Smith, S. L. (2002, May/June). What do parents of children with learning disabilities, ADHD, and related disorders deal with? *Pediatric Nursing.*

Standing, E. M. (1984). *Maria Montessori: Her life and work.* New York, NY: Plume, p. 38.

Subcommittee on Attention-Deficit/Hyperactivity Disorder Steering Committee on Quality Improvement Management. (2011). ADHD: clinical practice guideline for the diagnosis, evaluation, and treatment of attention-deficit/hyperactivity disorder in children and adolescents. *Pediatrics, 128,* 1–16.

Tannock, R. & Schachar, R. (1996). Executive dysfunction as an underlying mechanism of behavior and language problems in attention deficit hyperactivity disorder. In N. C. J. H. Beitchman, M. M. Konstantareas, & R. Tonnock (Eds.), *Language learning and behavior disorders: Developmental, biological, and clinical perspectives.* Cambridge, England: Cambridge University Press, pp. 128–155.

Tchaconas, A., & Adesman, A. (2013). Autism spectrum disorders: A pediatric overview and update. *Current Opinion in Pediatrics*, *25*(1), 130–144. doi:10.1097/MOP.0b013e32835c2b70

Teicher, M. (2002). *Quotient attention deficit hyperactivity disorder* (Quotient ADHD). Belmont, MA: McLean Hospital.

Terman, L. M., & Merrill, M.A. (1960). *Stanford-Binet intelligence scale: Manual for the third revision form L-M, with revised IQ tables by Samuel R. Pinneau.* Boston, MA: Houghton Mifflin Harcourt.

Thompson, T. (2013). Autism research and services for young children: History, progress and challenges. *Journal of Applied Research in Intellectual Disabilities, 26*(2), 81–107. doi: 10.1111/jar.12021

Tridas, E. Q. (Ed.) (2007). *From ABC to ADHD: What every parent should know about dyslexia.* Baltimore, MD: The International Dyslexia Association.

Virues-Ortega, J., Rodríguez, V., & Yu, C. T. (2013). Prediction of treatment outcomes and longitudinal analysis in children with autism undergoing intensive behavioral intervention. *International Journal of Clinical Health & Psychology, 13*(2), 91–100.

Yale Center for Dyslexia and Creativity. Dyslexia FAQ. 2018. Retrieved from http://dyslexia.yale.edu/dyslexia/dyslexia-faq

Vitásková, K., & ihová, A. (2014). Oral motor praxis in individuals with autism spectrum disorders in the context of modern speech and language therapy. *Social Welfare Interdisciplinary Approach, 4*(2), 110–120.

Vygotsky, L. S. (1939). Thought and speech. *Psychiatry, 2*, 29–52.

Wagner, R. K., Torgeson, J. K., Rashotte, C. A. & Pearson, N. A. (2013). *Comprehensive test of phonological processing, 2nd ed.* (CTOPP-2). Austin, TX: PRO-ED.

Waites, L. (1990). *Specific dyslexia and other developmental problems in children: A synopsis.* Dallas, TX: Texas Scottish Rite Hospital.

Webmd.com. ADD and ADHD (Attention Deficit Hyperactivity Disorder) Health Center. Retrieved from https://www.webmd.com/add-adhd/default.htm

Wechsler, D. (1989). *Wechsler preschool and primary scale of intelligence-revised* (WPSSI-R). San Antonio, TX: The Psychological Corp./Pearson.

Wechsler, D. (2008). *Wechsler adult intelligence scale, 4th ed.* (WAIS-IV). San Antonio, TX: Pearson.

Wechsler, D. (2009). *Wechsler individual achievement test, 3rd ed.* (WIAT-III). San Antonio, TX: Pearson.

Wechsler, D. (2014). *Wechsler intelligence scale for children, 5th ed.* (WISC-V). Bloomington, MN: Pearson.

Whitescarver, K., & Cossentino, J. (2008, December). Montessori and the mainstream: A century of reform on the margins. *Teachers College Record, 110* (12), 2571–2600.

Wiederholt, J. L., & Bryant, R. B. (2012). *Gray oral reading tests, 5th ed.* (GORT-V). Austin, TX: PRO-ED.

Wiig, E. H., Semel, E., & Secord, W. A. (2013). *Clinical evaluation of language fundamentals, 5th ed.* (CELF-5). San Antonio, TX: Pearson.

Wiig, E. H., Semel, E., & Secord, W. A. (2014). *Clinical evaluation of language fundamentals, 5th ed., metalinguistics* (CELF-5 Metalinguistics). San Antonio, TX: Pearson.

Wofford, C. (2015, March 21). Rediscover the lost art of writing. *The Dallas Morning News*, Viewpoints/Local Voices, p. 25A.

Zaporozhets, A., & Elkonin, D. (Eds.) (1971). *The psychology of preschool children* (J. Shybut & S. Simon, Trans.) Cambridge, MA: MIT Press, pp. 231–242.

Zimmerman, I. L., Steiner, V. & Pond, R. E. (2011). *Preschool language scales, 5th ed.* (PLS-5). San Antonio, TX: Pearson.

In Praise of *Montessori Strategies for Children with Learning Differences*

"After leaving my Montessori roots for many years, Joyce's words have convinced me that I need a set of Metal Insets for my special education classroom! To regular education teachers and special educators alike, this book is a great introduction to the Montessori method. Joyce Pickering's extensive knowledge and expertise will be useful to both seasoned Montessori and special educators."

Heather Malone- Preschool Intervention Specialist

"Joyce Pickering's extensive scholarly expertise in both Montessori education and learning differences captures the community of cooperation and compassion that Dr. Montessori brought to existence over a century ago—and *Montessori Strategies for Children with Learning Differences* will be significantly valuable for the following centuries. This book will definitely be your go-to resource for children with learning differences."

Hetal Sampat- Early Childhood Montessori Educator

"Montessori guides are trained to observe how children learn and adapt lessons to children's needs. Incorporating techniques designed to assist children with learning differences into the Montessori curriculum, and giving children with learning differences a secure and trusting relationship and one-on-one lessons with these techniques can be a crucial early intervention for children with learning differences."

Vivian Moore- Montessori Educator and Child Development Instructor

"Joyce and her colleagues have worked for years to implement the Montessori method to help children with learning differences find success in school, and to get rid of the stigma of being labeled or diagnosed with a learning disability. It is important to remember that these differences make us unique and diverse. When early childhood educators understand these differences, they can foster a culture of compassion and understanding. *Montessori Strategies for Children with Learning Differences* is a welcome addition to any teacher's collection where there is often a lack of resources about children with learning differences."

Bethany Ziegler- Early Childhood and Infant/Toddler Montessori Teacher

www.ingramcontent.com/pod-product-compliance
Ingram Content Group UK Ltd.
Pitfield, Milton Keynes, MK11 3LW, UK
UKHW050419240426
12048UKWH00015B/716